Immigration
and Social Policy
in Britain

CATHERINE JONES

TAVISTOCK

PUBLICATIONS

First published in 1977
by Tavistock Publications Limited
11 New Fetter Lane London EC4P 4EE
Photoset by Red Lion Setters,
Holborn, London
Printed in Great Britain at the
University Printing House, Cambridge
First published in paperback in 1980
ISBN 0 422 74680 0
© Catherine Jones 1977

British Library Cataloguing in Publication Data
Jones, Catherine
Immigration and social policy in Britain.
1. Great Britain – Emigration and immigration –
History
I. Title
325.41   JV7624
ISBN 0-422-74680-0

To my mother and father

Contents

Acknowledgements

This book has been quite a long time in the making. I do not think it would have materialized at all without the help, encouragement, and guidance I have received from friends, colleagues, and organizations at various stages.

My thanks are due in the first place to the Social Science Research Council, for agreeing to sponsor an enquiry into 'The Response of the Statutory Social Services to New Commonwealth Immigration'. The information the survey provided (which formed the basis for chapters seven and eight) was indispensable for the design of this book and, without the SSRC's help, it could not have been completed.

In turn, the successful completion of the Survey was due, first of all, to the cooperation, patience, and forbearance of a wide range of social service representatives who were prepared, not merely to respond in a nominal sense by detailing someone to complete the questionnaire, but actively to put themselves out and, in many cases, volunteer to be interviewed — notwithstanding their own crowded timetables. The Survey operation as such, however, owed much to the thoroughness with which my research associate, Rosamund Chorley, sifted through and organized the initial questionnaire returns, timetabled the eventual interview schedule (in itself a major feat), and herself conducted many of the interviews.

Brian and Barbara Rodgers of Goostrey, Cheshire (former members of the Social Administration Department at Manchester University), Professor Garth Plowman of the London School of Economics,

Dr Steven Lukes of Balliol College, Oxford, and Professor S.E. Finer of All Souls College, Oxford, each had the patience and generosity to read (and in some cases re-read) the manuscript at various stages of its preparation and to offer valuable criticisms and suggestions.

The Nuffield Foundation kindly awarded me a grant towards the cost of having the final manuscript typed in preparation for publication. For the typing of the manuscript itself, however, I am indebted to Mrs Judith Scammels of Worsley, Manchester, whose speed, accuracy, and above all good sense can scarcely be overstated.

I have been very fortunate, therefore, in all the help I have received. The interpretations presented and the conclusions arrived at in this study are, nevertheless, mine and my responsibility. One can only help a writer so far, after all. After that he is on his own.

Catherine Jones
November 1976

PART I

The argument

1

Introduction:
immigration and social policy

Mass immigration to this country furnishes not merely a commentary
upon, but in many ways a test of, prevailing statutory social policy.
Such at least is the proposition underlying this study. It is one that I
hope to demonstrate and develop by comparing three instances of
mass immigration, each coinciding with a different phase of British
social policy development. Thus we shall be examining the years of
Irish immigration, c. 1800-61; the years of East European Jewish
immigration, c. 1870-1911; and the years of New Commonwealth
immigration, c. 1950-71.[1] Before proceeding to the case-studies
themselves, however, I shall first explain my approach in greater detail
and then, in the following chapter, set the scene for the rest of the
book by discussing British social policy development over the whole
period in question.

The idea of looking at the relationship between immigration and
statutory social policy in the context of social policy development, was
one that arose out of an initial duality of research (and teaching)
interests: New Commonwealth immigration and its impact upon
present-day social policy, on the one hand, and nineteenth/early
twentieth century social policy in Britain, on the other. What had
seemed at the start to be two quite separate fields of interest, however,
came gradually to appear more closely connected. In particular, the
study of present-day immigration and its social policy implications
seemed to demand some historical perspective.

New Commonwealth immigration, to judge from the evidence

available, was of three-fold significance for contemporary statutory social policy. To begin with, the mere presence of such newcomers in this country helped to show up some of the shortcomings — as well as some of the strengths — of Welfare State social services provision. Yet such a presence seemed, in the second place, to furnish not merely a passive commentary upon but an active test of the problem-solving capabilities of social service agencies faced by sometimes novel, sometimes controversial, and often greatly increased demands upon their facilities. Set against this, however, there was a third tendency apparent: for the social services themselves to feature as bones of contention in the host-immigrant context and for them thus to constitute a problem-exacerbating as well as a problem-solving resource.

However the significance attributable to New Commonwealth immigration in these respects did not seem peculiar to New Commonwealth immigration *per se*. Evidence relating to earlier periods of social policy development in Britain seemed to suggest that first the Irish and subsequently the East European Jews, for instance, had been of comparable import as newcomers. They too, in other words, had seemed to show up the current scope and ethos of the social policy prevailing in their day. They too had apparently tested the problem-solving capacities of existing social services. And they too had helped expose social policy as a focus for host-immigrant resentments.

None of this, of course, implied any necessarily deliberate intention on the part of the immigrants themselves. All of this, however, seemed to point to there being common factors linking these and possible other immigration experiences — irrespective of the precise characteristics of the various immigrants themselves, of the precise condition of the British society into which they came, and of the precise layout of the social services they each encountered.

The point seemed one worth further exploration. So far as early Irish and East European Jewish immigration was concerned, this meant the collection of mostly secondary source material — since the breadth of subject-matter encompassed made first-hand research in both these areas an unrealistic proposition for one whose primary objective was, after all, to provide a fresh commentary upon, rather than a major addition to, the groundline evidence.

Inevitably, however, secondary source material was to prove in many respects less than complete and often less than appropriate for my purposes. It was at this stage and for these reasons that I decided finally against any attempt to include further instances of immigration (other than the three already referred to) in this study.[2] It was at this stage also that it proved necessary to carry out limited first-hand research in the field of New Commonwealth immigration.[3]

Nevertheless, the evidence accumulated did seem to support the notion of there being a consistent interrelationship between certain forms of immigration and ongoing British social policy. Moreover there seemed three broad reasons for this pattern.

To begin with, early Irish, East European Jewish, and New Commonwealth immigration could all loosely be described as instances of mass economic immigration to this country. In other words, they all involved large numbers of people; and they all involved a movement of people from less prosperous or less promising circumstances into what was evidently considered to be a more prosperous or more promising environment. This is not to say, of course, that there were not additional — sometimes powerful — motives present on each occasion. Nevertheless the numbers involved, and the characteristics of the immigrants in each case, would seem to support the idea of there being at least an underlying economic rationale for coming to Britain.

Upon arrival, such newcomers were bound almost by definition to constitute a relatively deprived, vulnerable and conspicuous group, in comparison with the bulk of the native population. As such they were likely, not merely to fall more than usually within the ambit of any existing social services (or projected social policy), but to be noticed more than usually whenever they did so. Mass economic immigration to Britain, in other words, was likely at the very least to furnish some sort of commentary upon the scope and ethos of contemporary social policy.

In the second place, Britain was nothing if not an ambivalent host society throughout this period; since the very qualities which served recurrently to attract — or even necessitate — mass immigration were also among those qualities which made such immigration difficult to come to terms with, whenever it occurred.

The capacity of a society both to attract and to accommodate large scale economic immigration would seem to depend, on the one hand, upon its ability to afford such newcomers apparent opportunitites for advancement and, on the other, upon its ability to adjust to the prospect of these opportunities being fully taken up. But herein lay the rub. The ideal, from the potential immigrant's point of view, might have been a loose-knit, uncomplicated, easy-going social structure chock-a-block, nevertheless, with economic opportunity. Such an ideal was epitomized, in the minds of nineteenth-century migrants at least, by the image of the New World as a half-empty, expanding, exploratory economy. But it was hardly applicable to Britain — either in the nineteenth or the twentieth century. Britain's attractiveness over this period was the product of industrial and post-industrial development, rather than one of untapped virgin potential.

This was scarcely a trivial point. Industrial development might both attract and benefit from an influx of additional (cheap) labour from time to time. Nevertheless the same industrial development engendered social and political repercussions — the effects of which were to render this an increasingly complex and self-conscious society: less and less accessible, in a way, to large-scale, allegedly 'less civilized',[4] immigration. The country's international self-image — whether as workshop of the world, as moral/political pace-setter among nations, or as latter-day mother country of a onetime empire — amounted in this respect to an extension of the same ambivalence.

In the third place, the development of statutory social policy was not merely part and parcel of the repercussions referred to above; it served if anything to draw attention to, and provide an additional focus for, any debate over mass immigration.

Thus, to take the first half of this statement: industrialization and post industrial development entailed such a dislocation of social conditions as to give a sizeable proportion of the population active grounds for unease — if not for outright frustration or despair. At the same time, changes in the balance of the economy led to changes in the distribution of acknowledged power and influence within British society. Money talked — and eventually labour talked — just as the possession of land had talked earlier. Some of those who felt themselves to be most familiar with — if not most threatened by — the social consequences of industrialization were thus successively in a position, not merely to voice their opinions, but to expect to be listened to. This, after the experience of industrialization had tended, arguably, to favour a belief not merely in the alterability of social as well as economic conditions, but in the desirability, perhaps, of such alteration. These considerations help, at least, to account for the development and subsequent expansion of statutory social policy.

Yet the significance of this social policy, so far as mass immigration was concerned, was bound to be double-edged. On the one hand, needy immigrants might be expected materially to benefit from services designed, at the very least, to cater in some way for the weakest and most vulnerable sections of the population. On the other hand, however, the mere existence of any statutory social policy implied some degree of unease or dissatisfaction with the existing or 'natural' state of society, on the part of those whose opinions mattered. Furthermore, it implied some determination, however narrowly or broadly based, to engineer or maintain a more suitable alternative.

This then was hardly the relaxed, open-ended, easy-going environment of which any immigrant might have dreamed. A mass influx of impoverished outsiders was, in turn, almost the last thing so ambitious and self-conscious a society could want — for all that the extra manpower might be useful. The very appropriateness of existing social services to meet what were presumed to be immigrant requirements could, in such circumstances, become a focus for resentment in itself. Hence, I would suggest, the tendency of mass immigration to show up prevailing social policy not merely as a problem-solving but also as a problem-exacerbating resource.

These therefore seemed the common factors — applicable to each of the case-studies under review and broadly explanatory of the parallels between them. It is against this background that we shall look for the more specific points of contrast and comparison between each immigration-social policy encounter.

We will begin by looking in more detail at the manner in which social policy has developed in Britain. This discussion will, I hope, set the scene for the case-study presentation in two ways. To begin with, it should throw light on the nature of the social policy prevailing at the time of each period of immigration — and hence should provide a framework within which the impact of particular newcomers upon particular social policies and social services may the more readily be assessed. At a more general level, however, the discussion of social policy development should furnish some commentary upon the development of the host society itself — given that I shall be trying to account for social policy in terms of its being a response to social, economic, and political conditions and ideas. Following this discussion, therefore, we may be better placed to comment on Britain as a host society *vis à vis* successive groups of immigrants.

Each of the case-studies will open with commentary on the

characteristics of the immigrants, the apparent reasons for their coming, and the manner in which they were received by contemporary public opinion. This will lead, naturally enough, into the principal area for debate: namely the significance of the immigration for contemporary social policy. Here we shall be concentrating essentially on the extent to which, and the ways in which, the presence of the newcomers seemed to expose social policy, stretch its problem-solving capabilities and reveal its problem-exacerbating potential.

The main lines of presentation, therefore, will be much the same from one case-study to the next. Nevertheless, in terms of length and degree of complexity, these will be three very different exercises. Social policy tends to become thicker on the ground from one period to the next, as does the quantity of source material available on both the social policy and the immigrants in question. For these reasons alone one can expect the Irish to be the shortest and simplest, and the New Commonwealth to be the most ambitious, of the three case-studies. The fact that the New Commonwealth discussion draws upon first as well as second-hand material, constitutes a further, qualitative, difference between this and the earlier two exercises. Differences such as these, however, do not prevent the drawing of valid comparisons between the separate case-study material. It is on the basis of such comparisons that we will arrive eventually, I hope, at a framework of analysis sufficiently comprehensive as to account, not merely for the similarities, but for the contrasts and gradations between these three immigration-social policy encounters.

2

Social policy development
in the host society

This is a wide-ranging subject on which to attempt a summary discussion. In effect, the choice lies between trying primarily to describe developments and trying primarily to explain them — since one cannot seriously attempt both within the space available. I have chosen to concentrate upon analysis at the expense of detailed description; partly because it is the factors underlying social policy development that seem most central to the present discussion, and partly because the presentation of case-studies later in this book should go some way to make up for factual shortcomings. Nevertheless this does, at this stage, mean an account that assumes some knowledge on the reader's part — although not so much, I hope, as to be meaningless without it.

Looked at from this distance, the development of statutory social policy from the early nineteenth to the mid-twentieth century would seem to fall into three broad periods, or phases. This is not to suggest that precise chronological boundaries might be drawn separating the close of one period abruptly from the commencement of the next. I suggest merely that one may, with hindsight, detect such contrasts of style, scope, and objectives between social policy in the middle years of the nineteenth century, social policy in the years surrounding the turn of the century, and social policy in the middle years of the twentieth century, as to regard these periods as fundamentally distinct from one another in this respect.[1]

It is around these distinctions that I shall structure this discussion.

(i) *Take-off*

Statutory social policy begins to acquire prominence in Britain from the first half of the nineteenth century. The 1834 *Poor Law Amendment Act* and the 1848 *Public Health Act*, to say nothing of factory legislation and education grants, are landmarks almost too familiar for repetition here. Yet, not-withstanding the documentation available, one is still bound to question why it was that collective interference should from this time have begun to accumulate.

Social policy arises, virtually by definition, out of a dissatisfaction with the contemporary state of society — or with social conditions as they currently exist. Yet such a truism does not take us very far. Within any given social establishment it is still necessary to ask who is dissatisfied, why are they dissatisfied, to whom does their dissatisfaction matter, what do they or others think should be done about it, and what, in practice, may be expected by way of any engineered response. Social policy is in other words the product of a particular social, economic and political order — not simply a reflex reaction to any given degree of severity or unevenness in social conditions.

To state this is, once again, to state the obvious. Nevertheless the fact that statutory social policy appeared to take off in Britain only after her industrial revolution, seems to have prompted many commentators to view early policy development as a response by national leaders to the 'intrinsic' horrors of industrial living and working conditions, as experienced by growing masses of the population. 'The first industrial nation' (Mathias 1969), by now allegedly the workshop of the world, was battling to knock the worst out of an industrial revolution whose consequences it was at last beginning to appreciate. Thereafter, once statutory intervention had got under way, it was presumably a case of self-generated growth in governmental action.

Superficially there is much to sustain this synopsis. Certainly the rigours of early factory regimes, along with the wretchedness of urban living conditions, for a mushrooming wage-labour force dependent utterly upon the dictates of a trade cycle, have been amply documented. In the case of both factory and public health legislation, moreover, the targets for reform can be identified exclusively as the consequences of rapid industrialization and its urban accompaniments. Statutory services once on the ground, furthermore, did tend to show up areas for additional or intensified government action.

Even so, this is hardly a sufficient explanation for the emergence and proliferation of statutory social policy in Britain. While the lot of the labouring classes was undoubtedly a hard one in the nineteenth century, it is by no means proven that the majority were actually worse off than their counterparts of a century before.[2] Nor indeed was this the first time that dissatisfaction had been expressed either by them, about them, or on their behalf. Again, while this was an age of marked social policy development, not every such piece of policy seems to have been geared consciously to cope with the aftermath of industrialization. The *New Poor Law*, for instance, was arguably still setting its sights on the problem of the rural destitute rather than on those of the urban unemployed (Rose 1972 : 12).

So, if one assumes a causal relationship to exist between the experience of industrialization and the subsequent development of social policy in Britain, it is to the effects of industrialization upon the social, economic, and political order in general — rather than upon the extremes of living conditions in particular — that attention must be directed.

Dissatisfaction over social conditions was being expressed in many quarters in the first decades of the nineteenth century. The poor, be they unemployed labourers, uneasy craftsmen, or simply soldiers returning from the wars, were protesting at their lot, while the propertied classes were protesting at the waste and the worry of it all (Webb and Webb 1929). Not every protest carried the same import or the same weight politically. The Agricultural Labourers' Revolt of 1830 was at once a last, hopeless fling for them and a signal for others to demand counter-action. But the protests of ratepayers over the mounting expenses of the old poor laws were met eventually by a *Poor Law Amendment Act*. Those who made and paid the money called the tune.

In itself this was hardly a novel state of affairs — except that those recognized as the money-makers and money-payers of 1830 represented a rather different social gathering from their pre-industrial equivalents. However exaggerated the label, the industrial revolution had intervened and begun to make its impact. To say that the nineteenth and early twentieth centuries witnessed the emergence of manufacturing and subsequently of labour-force interests as factors to be reckoned with in a society hitherto governed essentially by the dictates of land and trade, can be no more than a primitive simplification. Yet it contains enough truth, perhaps, to service this discussion.

From 1832 manufacturing interests were in effect assured of representation, as £10 householders, in the House of Commons. This 'enfranchisement of the middle classes' has accordingly been cited, very often, to explain both the harshness of the *New Poor Law*, on the one hand, and the repeal of the *Corn Laws*, on the other. Yet to explain all in terms of current parliamentary representation is effectively to skirt the point. Manufacturing interests gained representation, belatedly, because they were recognized at last as commanding a vital national resource.

It is against this backcloth that one can view the successive efforts of the Chartists to secure a niche in the governmental process as premature and hence doomed to meet the failure they experienced (Briggs 1959 : 299). Labour and labour-force skills may have been a vital resource in an industrializing society, but they were not convincingly recognized as such until somewhat later. The 1867 and 1884 *Reform Acts* were proof, perhaps, of such eventual recognition. It was not until the present century that the logic of franchise extension resulted in the emphasis being placed upon manhood suffrage rather than upon the representation of perceived vital national resources. Everyone was by this time, perhaps, accounted part of the national resource.

To demonstrate that there were changes in the accountability of government, however, does not of itself explain the development of statutory social policy. We have still to consider what it was about manufacturing and other, subsequent 'interests' that encouraged a growth in government intervention.

Business interests in the early nineteenth century were, to some extent, on the horns of a dilemma. They wished to be left alone to pursue their affairs. Yet, in so far as they were expected to contribute towards the costs of government, they wished for some say in the activites of government and desired that government to be as effective and efficient as possible.

Three related sets of consequences followed from this stance — none of which was readily compatible with the wish to be left alone. In the first place, pressure for efficiency in central and local government helped to render the latter both more capable and more credible as agents of intervention in domestic affairs. In the second place, rationalization of existing governmental activity tended, by its very thoroughness, to admit the validity of some public intervention in society. Further applications of the principle, once acknowledged, were hard to resist. In the third place, pressure for efficiency could actually promote an enlargement of the government's role in any sphere of involvement once established. To be effective it was necessary to be thorough, and ideas as to what thoroughness entailed tended to grow rather than diminish with experience.

To take the first point: domestic government in the early nineteenth century was undoubtedly corrupt and inefficient by latterday standards; yet it had arguably been appropriate for the sort of tasks traditionally expected of it. So long as the main business of government was conceived of as relating to international affairs, and its domestic role consisted largely of keeping the peace and raising necessary revenue, then a gathering of protege 'civil servants' and local unpaid dignitaries may well have seemed sufficient. Yet fundamental social and economic upheaval at once subjected the system to strains it could not possible cope with and brought into prominence those social groupings bound to question its validity.

The administration of the old poor laws forms an obvious case example. The poor laws were traditionally regarded as an adjunct, more or less, of keeping the peace. The duty of relieving and controlling its poor was firmly a parish responsibility under the eye, watchful or otherwise, of the local JP. Yet such a localized, lay system could hardly be expected to cope either with too much poverty in any one parish, or with too much movement of the poor from one parish to another. Both such difficulties seem to have been experienced, with mounting momentum, from the latter eighteenth century onwards — partly as a side-effect of the Napoleonic Wars, partly as a result of some restructuring in agriculture, but also as a result of the movement of growing numbers of landless labourers into the expanding industrial towns, where jobs were not invariably to be had for the asking. Against this backcloth it is scarcely surprising to read of an increase in estimated total poor law costs from some £2 millions in 1784 to £4 millions in 1803 to a mammoth nearly £8 millions in 1818 (Webb and Webb 1929: 1-2; Redlich and Hirst 1958: 108). It is hardly surprising either that the ratepayers of the period, backed by the theorists of the day,[3] — should have been calling out for reform.

The target for reform was ostensibly simple: to cut the costs. Nevertheless some regard for preserving a rationale in public activity, some fear of the possible riotous consequences if the poor laws were abolished altogether, and some conviction — among a growing proportion of ratepayers — that obsolete and corrupt administration was in large measure responsible for any excesses, made poor law reform a question of administrative overhaul rather than a matter of merely axing relief.

The solution arrived at was novel in two respects. In the first place the impracticality of the parish as a viable administrative unit was, at last, formally acknowledged. The units had to be larger if they were to be effective and efficient. Parishes were to be grouped into Unions for the purposes of administering the *New Poor Law*. In the second place and more significantly, the new administration was to exist theoretically outside of the traditional local government structure. JPs and parish vestries notwithstanding, the new Unions were to elect their own Boards of Guardians who, in turn, would appoint their own paid officials and implement policy subject only to the supervision of a central government commission.[4]

The idea of by-passing traditional local government, by relying upon specialized bodies to deal with specific areas of public business, was not really a new one. Several items of responsibility — such as road maintenance, street lighting and cleansing, the provision of water supplies, as well as the matter of poor relief — had assumed greater urgency from the eighteenth century but were manifestly too big, too specialized, or too expensive for the average parish to cope with, particularly in the fastest-growing urban industrial centres. The Turnpike Trusts and Improvement Commissions of the latter eighteenth century were in a sense the licensed, occasional, forerunners of the *New Poor Law* administration of 1834 (Webb and Webb 1963: 148-51 *et seq.*). Yet the latter represented a statutory innovation and was an attempt, moreover, not simply to provide an *ad hoc* solution to the problems of poor relief from one locality to another, but to establish a nationwide specialist system, under central direction.

It was to prove a significant innovation. In a sense, it was a sugar-coated pill. Notwithstanding the popular resentments aroused, the *New Poor Law* did succeed for a time in reducing the costs of poor relief (Webb and Webb 1929: 114-15). In addition it allowed ratepayers, particularly ratepayers in the new industrial towns, more say in the administration of their money than had usually been the case under a land-oriented system of JPs and parish vestries. Yet it established a precedent for nationalized, *ad hoc* interference which was there to be copied wherever other, more controversial, causes were taken up — such as public health or popular education. By the last quarter of the century, indeed, so numerous and confusing had become these separate systems of administration that the reform of local government itself had at last to be embarked on. In effect, the existing *ad hoc* systems, apart from the poor law and (briefly) education, were combined into one, via a network of county and district councils ostensibly designed to function as standardized, elective, multi-purpose local authorities: ready-made outlets, in other words, for any furture advances in government activity (Smellie 1968: Ch. 4). JPs and parish vestries were by now little more than an anachronism.[5]

One other strand of development had meanwhile been taking place. Once again it could be traced back to the effects of middle class, urban pressure for efficiency and some say in their own affairs, yet this time in rather a different way. The reform of municipal corporations legislated for in 1835 was limited, of course, in its immediate application.[6] Nevertheless it attempted to establish some sort of prototype — of elective, responsible, multi-purpose city government — for chartered municipalities whose styles of management had hitherto often been eccentric to say the least. The lure of such a format, along with the undoubted powers and prestige of municipal status, henceforth seemed irresistible to many sizeable manufacturing centres not previously incorporated.[7]

Their enthusiasm was understandable. Not only was a municipal corporation set apart from the dictates of county government; it was in a position to anticipate or withstand some of the rigours of centralized 'ad hocery' as well. Liverpool was not the only city to anticipate, and hence evade, the contents of the 1848 *Public Health Act*, for instance, by securing advance, comprehensive legislation of its own (Smellie 1968 : 32). Even where they did not get in first, moreover, municipal corporations (as convenient outlets, if nothing more, for central government) stood to see their powers gradually accumulate, as the scope of national legislation mounted up (Smellie 1968 : 32-3; Redlich and Hirst 1970 : 137-38). In this case, pressure for efficiency and independence, within a context of expanding social policy ideas, would seem to have given rise to a multi-purpose local machinery whose validity was subsequently upheld as the rationale for post-reform county boroughs.

So much for the development of statutory executive potential. We must turn now to consider the second theme referred to above: namely that the philosophy drawn upon to justify an initial rationalization of domestic governmental activity suggested, in fact, a positive role for government which, once admitted, was capable of extension.

There were many theories in circulation at the start of the nineteenth century to explain why the granting, or excessive granting, of poor relief was not merely expensive, but was actually detrimental to the proper workings of the social and economic order (Briggs 1959 : 299). The philosophy which justified an overhaul of the poor laws, however, had to go somewhat further than this — given that political opinion, on balance, was not in favour of abolishing the poor laws altogether (for reasons of humanity, perhaps, as well as public safety). Some sort of philosophy was essential: since if action was to be efficient it had to be deliberate and evince some overriding plan, or rationale. Hence the timeliness and appeal of Jeremy Bentham's cogent views in this respect and the ease with which Chadwick, notwithstanding his limited personal position, was able to render them operational (Finer 1952).

The poor should be relieved, so ran the argument, only once they had proved their incapacity to help themselves. In the case of the able-bodied (and therefore ostensibly employable) poor, together with their families, this could be effected simply by ensuring that the situation of those on relief 'shall not be made really or apparently so eligible as the situation of the independent labourer of the lowest class' (*Poor Law Report* 1834 : 228). Less eligibility, guaranteed by means of the workhouse test, would thus ensure that all those who could possibly secure employment would do so rather than apply for relief since, as Bentham had pointed out, rational individuals could be relied upon to opt for the lesser evil when faced with the choice. In place of a previous variety in parochial method and approach, the present system was intended for uniform, rational application by every union in the country.

There was much to recommend it. Such a *New Poor Law* promised not merely to cut the costs of poor relief but actively to promote the interests of society by ensuring that as many as possible of those who could work were driven to do so. However misguided or ill-informed the views of the 1832-34 Commission may now be adjudged, in respect of either the characteristics of the poor or the dimensions of poverty in this period, their recommendations were significant in that they postulated a positive, necessary (albeit an 'automatic') (see Rodgers 1969 : 35) role for government in the running of society. Such a notion may have gone clean against the predilections of an expanding, business community, yet in this case there was at least the promise of less expense than before, and a greater say than before, over the administration of a long-established provision.

The principle of necessary intervention, however, did not have to stay within the limits of traditional governmental activity. Once acknowledged, it might be invoked wherever factors vital to the nation's well being were seen to be at risk and therefore in need of some direction or support. For all its *laissez-faire* protestations, the society of the *New Poor Law* could not regard itself as altogether a self-regulating entity. Accordingly, as concepts of what might be vital to the nation's well being tended to broaden, so the potential scope for necessary intervention tended to increase.

That concepts of what was vital to the internal good functioning of society did tend to broaden, seems evident enough. From assuming, in the 1820s and 1830s, that all might be well so long as the labour-force was industrious, informed opinion came gradually to regard a sufficiently healthy, a sufficiently skilled, and a sufficiently well-motivated populace as being also essential. Concepts of what might be 'sufficient' in these respects continued to enlarge in the present century, until a post-war Welfare State proclaimed the right of every citizen to individual equality of opportunity, not merely as a prerequisite for national efficiency, but as a target for social justice.

Clearly the adjustment was to be profound: both in the breadth and in the quality of conventional social thinking. From an appreciation that there might be certain vital factors at risk in society's make-up, the emphasis was to shift to a consideration of the type of society most to be desired — with the implication that this could or should be arranged by statutory intervention. By which time of course a rather different assortment of opinion leaders were to be pronouncing, on the basis of a very different social order from that of the early nineteenth century, and on the basis of an already impressive accumulation of statutory intervention in domestic affairs.

Yet, while I have suggested that a precedent for necessary government intervention might thereafter be invoked wherever ideas seemed to require it, to assert that the development of statutory action simply followed from 'advances' in social thinking would be not only facile, but actively misleading. Apart from anything else, it begs a very obvious question. We need to try, in other words, to unravel why collective wisdom 'advanced' in the fashion that it did.[8]

In part it appears to have been a self-generating process: action,

once embarked on, generated ideas for futher action. A third consequence, I suggested, of middle-class pressure for efficiency in
government was that any government action was designed to be
deliberate and effective. In so far as it strove to be effective, and
therefore thorough, it was bound to uncover fresh areas for necessary
action: 'necessary' if only in the sense that it seemed to impinge upon
the effectiveness of the original provision. Having once embarked on
deliberate intervention, in other words, it was difficult either to stand
still or draw back — given that the initial action stood no chance of
being conclusive, even if so intended.

The classic illustration of this process is to be found in the history of
the poor law after 1834. For all its rational pretensions, the *New Poor
Law* was doomed to fail in its attempt to solve the problem of
pauperism. The dimensions and characteristics of poverty were not at all
as had been anticipated. Yet it was, if anything, the very size and
intractability of the problems encountered by the poor law
administration (together with the quality of its administrators), which
drew attention to new areas for action both within and alongside the
poor law itself. Hence the view of social policy development that sees
the public health movement as essentially an offshoot of poor law
expertise, and that sees twentieth-century health, social security, and
welfare services as essentially the products of nineteenth-century poor
law exploration. By this analysis the poor law stands as the parent, more
or less, of most subsequent social policy.

Yet the phenomenon of experience prompting further or more
elaborate action was not confined to the working of the poor laws as
such. A comparable process can be seen in operation within any trial
area of social policy. Popular education, for instance, affords a good
example of the logic of mounting intervention. In 1833 the government
of the day instituted a novel grant in aid of popular education, as
provided by the rival 'National' and 'British' voluntary societies.[9]
Once public money was being spent, however, it was natural to want,
first, to inspect what was being done with the money and, later, to
introduce some form of quality control of the schools on which the
money was being spent. Hence the timeliness of Kay Shuttleworth's
teacher-training scheme and later, in response to a rapid increase in
education expenditure by the government, the Revised Code of
1862.[10] Eventually of course the drive to be effective as well as
efficient helped bring government to the point of declaring itself
responsible for 'filling in the gaps' in elementary provision:[11]   if

education was so important, then it was important that every child have access to it. Once embroiled in the direct provision of elementary education, needless to say, the requirements for secondary, or higher elementary, popular provision began to make themselves felt (see Lowndes 1937 : 52-4 *et seq.*). Involvement would seem, in this case, to have bred further involvement in so far as public money was involved an in so far as statutory interest and expertise in the subject of education began to build up.

Nevertheless, the notion of self-generated development, and of a concomittent expansion in public ideas as to the proper role of statutory intervention, scarcely provides a sufficient explanation of the changes in conventional thinking. It does not explain, for instance, why intervention started and it takes little account of developments taking place outside the current statutory machine. Above all it does not tell us why ideas, which might have been the product of statutory experience, proved politically acceptable when they did. The process might have been cumulative, in other words, but the interaction involved was hardly confined to the internal workings of the statutory machine.

The acceptability of new ideas to the operative public can at first and in part be attributed to the same sort of sectional self-interest as helped support the overhaul of the poor laws: a desire, on the part of the business community, for greater economic and social efficiency, such as might be promoted, conceivably, by measures of statutory intervention. Those convinced of the need for further activity, were not slow to appeal to this factor. The ups and downs of public health reform, however, showed that self-interest could point in several directions. Chadwick was at some pains to demonstrate the relationship between public ill-health and high poor relief expenditure, and to show how money spent on sanitary improvements would mean a long term saving for both ratepayers and employers (Chadwick 1842). Nevertheless public health reform spelt immediate expense, along with unprecedented interference by central government in local and professional affairs. It was only the (equally immediate) fear of cholera perhaps — that non-respector of persons — which rendered public health reform a political possibility. Even so, the eventual Act was muted. Once Chadwick's embryonic Board of Health had failed to stem the ravages of the 1849 cholera epidemic, the collapse of the Board and the personal downfall of Chadwick, would seem to have been inevitable (see Finer 1952 for full account). Nevertheless the idea

of public health management survived — a tribute, perhaps to the
convictions of those towns and those professionals already involved in
implementing the suggestions of 1848; but an indication also of some
heightened long-term perspective on the part of the money-paying
community.

Self-interest is of course a factor capable of being read in to very
many situations. Certainly a developing, politically effective, interest
in popular education is capable of this interpretation. As early as 1858
William Cowper MP was haranguing the National Association for the
Promotion of Social Science on the shortcomings of English popular
education — as compared to the far superior, statutory, arrangements
prevailing in Prussia, for instance.[12] An educated work force was
presumably just as vital as a healthy one, if the workshop of the world
was to retain its pre-eminence. The influential public was being
exhorted to enlarge its horizons — for its own sake.

Yet to interpret all developments in mid-nineteenth century social
thinking in terms of the expanding self-awareness and irreducable
self-interest of a growing, competitive, industrial economy, would be
to offer only half an answer, if that. Informed or enlightened
self-interest may have been a sentiment to which reformers were
prompt to appeal, in various guises. But self-interest did not become
informed or enlightened of its own accord, nor simply as a
consequence of the logic of intervention self-interestedly embarked
upon. The problem of initiatives in social reform remains unaccounted
for.

It is at this point, of course, that we are on the most difficult
ground. The contribution of individuals, and groups of individuals, to
the formation of ideas is far more easily described than accounted for.
Nevertheless the nineteenth century has been labelled, with some
justice, as an age of great names in social reform. Great names or no,
one can hardly make real sense of development of social thinking
without taking the individual and the voluntary contribution into
account.

Hitherto in this discussion I have emphasized the consequences of
middle class pressure for efficiency and effectiveness in so far as it
affected the scope and style of government. Yet such pressure was
hardly a sufficient force for social reform in itself. If anything it seems
to have been a tool for committed groups and individuals to make use
of or derive inspiration from. The precise layout of the *New Poor Law*,
for instance, was a good deal more ambitious, not to say idiosyncratic,

than the demands of ratepayers for a cut-back in expense need have required. Yet, thanks partly to a careful, advance publicity campaign, it was found to satisfy them on essentials. Again it was not simply the logic of the *New Poor Law*, so much as the investigations of individuals within its employ, which demonstrated a connection between poverty and ill-health and sparked off a public health campaign.

It was not so easy, of course, to make public health reform seem to fall in with the predilections of public opinion, even with the help of the Health of Towns Associations (Finer 1952 : 237-39). Even less amenable were causes such as popular education or factory reform, where the necessity or efficiency appeal was so much more remote. The ten hours campaign had to be a long one (Fraser 1973 : 22-6), while that for state education — thanks to divisions amid the ranks of its own protagonists — was destined to be longer still.[13]

Not every initiative came from within the ranks of government service or even from parliament. Nevertheless the apparent preoccupation of social reformers of all colours with the political and governmental machine was understandable. After the parliamentary reforms of 1832 and the poor law landmark of 1834 it was both something they had access to and something they could not afford to ignore. Effective reformers, campaigners, activists, or investigators were drawn almost by definition from those same, enfranchised, influential classes as made up operation public opinion. Whatever their hopes of statutory action (or statutory restraint, as in the case of many education partisans), they were bound to be mindful of the voting public.

The public were, accordingly, bombarded with evidence, revelation, and recommendation relating to social conditions. It came in many forms. Chadwick's famous Sanitary Report (1842) set a precedent for horrific detail which many were anxious to emulate in subsequent exposés. The frequency and thoroughness of parliamentary commissions of enquiry rendered this deservedly the age of blue books as well as of great names. The social novelists of the period were writing heart-rending weekly episodes for the literary magazines. All in all, the public proved remarkably resilient — devouring the detail, apparently, without swallowing the message. Nevertheless some shift in public expectations of government can be attributed to this source, as well as to the conditioning influences of statutory services already on the ground.

There remains the problem of the motivation behind these

initiatives. Individual motivation, however, is much more difficult to generalize about than is the collective response to it. No one explanation will suffice to account for the activities of what were a very motley band of reformers. At one extreme there was the blanket humanitarianism of Lord Shaftesbury, reminiscent, perhaps, of the gentlemanly philanthropy of an earlier age, although he was hardly without his following in this one. Somewhat narrower in their focus were the moral and religious campaigners, anxious to promote a thrifty, hard-working, God-fearing, law-abiding population. Rather more the man of his time, seemingly, was Chadwick the archetypal, efficient administrator: rather too much, perhaps, of what the other new men were looking for. Different from him were the scientific investigators, notably the medical men in pursuit of epidemiological data, or the social scientists exchanging evidence through the National Association. Different again were the political radicals, such as Hulme or Hobhouse, campaigning for the rights and welfare of the respectable, as yet unenfranchised, working classes.

Clearly, to try to type-cast and compartmentalize motivation in this way, represents no more than a crude approximation to the truth. Humanitarian sentiments were by no means confined to the obvious good men battling against evil conditions, any more than was a desire for effective government confined to civil servants or a sense of social injustice the sole property of the radicals. What is clear, however, is that pressure for social reform was no single, consistent force, but rather an amalgam of widely differing motivations.

The net import of this discussion is to suggest a particular image of British society in the mid-nineteenth century — roughly from the 1830s to the 1860s. The impact of industrialization was beginning to make itself felt, not simply in the life-styles and living conditions of a growing proportion of the population, but also in the increasing economic (and hence political) importance of business interests in the fortunes of the nation. Political rationalization, in the light of this, led in turn to some restructuring of government which, being pressed to show efficiency and effectiveness, became gradually more credible and more capable as a potential intervener in domestic affairs. Both the process and its effects were made use of by an assortment of social reformers or reforming groups; each having access to the political machine and each anxious, from various motives, either to battle with or control some of the perceived social consequences of industrialization: consequences that impinged more directly upon the lives of the working classes than on those of the voting, ratepaying public. This public had to be rendered more enlightened, if only in the guise of its own self-interest.

(ii) *Transition*

So much for what might be termed the period of take-off in British statutory social policy. We have next to consider what was, arguably, a fundamentally different stage of development both in society and in social policy: namely the period stretching roughly from the 1870s until the outbreak of the First World War. The labelling is of course artificial. Most aspects of society's affairs continued without dramatic upheaval and, in many respects, the period witnessed the continuation of processes preivously begun and already remarked upon in this discussion. Government efficiency, for instance, and government intervention in domestic affairs continued to accumulate still, for a time, on an *ad hoc* basis until the overhaul of local government was more or less rendered inevitable. Individual reformers or voluntary groupings were, if anything, even more conspicuous in their political manoeuvrings and in their interactions with statutory machinery, on behalf of sections of the masses and their welfare. The influential public, no less conscious of its self-interest than before, had to contend with even more evidence aimed at its social enlightenment.

There was, however, one important difference: from 1867 every male householder (and £10 lodger) in the boroughs and, from 1884, every male householder in the counties received the right to vote. A redistribution of seats in 1885, according due parliamentary preponderance at last to urban representation, set the seal on this process. The voting public had in other words been enlarged and re-aligned to represent appropriately what might be termed the urban working classes. In view of their numerical preponderance it was a very different audience to which government, thereafter, had in principle to address itself.[14]

Not surprisingly there are conflicting interpretations as to why such electoral reform materialized when it did. Apart from those content to imply merely that, once capital had been enfranchised, it was only logical that labour should come next, the rival theories fall really into two camps. On the one hand there are those who hold that the franchise was extended simply on account of a growing realization, on the part of the propertied classes, of the importance of the quality and the motivation of labour to the future prospects of the economy and of the nation.[15] Such a view would accord well enough with the development of an informed and sophisticated self-interest such as I have attempted to imply.

On the other hand there are those who reckon that the vote was granted more out of fear than out of sophisticated self-interest (Briggs 1959 : 494-97). The working classes were coming to feel themselves important and, in the last resort, essential: if they were not appeased with the vote, therefore, there might be untold, even revolutionary, consequences. This sort of interpretation rests on an appreciation of the growing self-awareness and self-organization evident by this time of at least the skilled, and newly skilled, working classes — whether one were to measure this in terms of friendly society and model union membership, co-operative trading ventures, or mechanics institutes support. Self-help and self-propaganda have hitherto been ignored in this discussion, if only because these were not, by definition, in a position directly to influence earlier statutory social policy, except via the utterances of radical politicians or the loyalties of non-conformist businessmen. Balked of the vote in 1832, the artisan classes were no more successful in their attempts to get in on the political arena under the banner of Chartism. 1867 was perhaps no more than a belated, timorous recognition of a force no longer to be put off.

Yet whether one espouses the former 'consensus' interpretation or the latter 'conflict' interpretation of the extension of the franchise, the notion of informed self-interest behind the move still obtains. Whether the working classes were regarded in themselves as a vital component of society which must needs, therefore, be drawn into its considerations — or whether they were seen merely as a potentially disruptive element to be appeased at all costs — majority opinion did not grant the vote out of sheer, disinterested altruism.[16] A similar observation can be made concerning the content of social policy legislated for in the period following 1867: whether it was designed to buy off the working classes or to build up the working classes, it was nevertheless portrayed primarily as being in the national interest.

In many respects this can be termed a transitional period. The working classes had, roughly speaking, been granted political representation. Their vote became important therefore (especially once it became a secret vote);[17] yet they did not straightaway infiltrate the corridors either of parliament or of the civil service themselves. Unlike the middle classes enfranchised before them, they lacked the means, both financial and otherwise, to do so readily.[18] Others, however, were prompt to speak for them. The latter nineteenth century was illumined by the outpourings of 'socialist' groupings speaking on behalf of, rather than as, the working classes. Neither Hyndman's Social Democratic Federation of 1884 nor the Fabian Society founded in the same year, could be described as truly working class in anything save the import of their proposals (see Hobsbawn 1964 : Ch. 14). It was not until 1900 that a Labour Representation Committee was formed, with trades union backing, and thereafter that the first Labour representatives began to trickle in to parliament in their own right, as members of a separate political party.[19]

There was no sudden change, in other words, in the class composition of the potential policy-makers and policy-debaters after 1867, any more than there was any sudden change in the style of executive government. What was apparent, however, was some shift in the focus and an increase in the quantity of social policy, both considered and legislated for. There are three main ways of interpreting this phenomenon — all of which have some evidence to sustain them. In the first place one can argue that this was really the outcome of intrinsic, ongoing development on the part of statutory intervention already embarked upon. In the second place one can see this as essentially a response to an additional, numerically decisive, voting public. In the third place it can stand as the outward proof of a growing appreciation — on whatever grounds — of the importance of the populace to the nation's well-being.

In themselves these themes are not mutually exclusive. Indeed they prove, for the most part, to be complementary. One might even suggest that, had there not been three such factors all pointing in the same direction, it is doubtful whether social policy on behalf of the working classes could have assumed such prominence in this period.

The first theme requires no extended elaboration here. Mention has already been made of the long term spin-off effects of comprehensive poor law responsibilities and of the logic of increasing educational commitment, once any sort of commitment had been acted upon. One might speak also of the logic of public health advance until its culmination, in 1875, or of the logic of accumulating factory, mine and workshop regulation. Any service, once initiated, tends to develop its own brand of expertise and its own intimate awareness, both of the limitations of its powers and the possibilities for their useful extension.

Were this approach adhered to in its entirety, one would have to do little more than try to explain how statutory action commenced — not why it developed thereafter.

The second approach, however, is rather more problematic. The notion of a response to a wider voting public, could mean either that this public was to be cajoled or that this public was to be conditioned. On the whole it seems to have meant both. Robert Lowe's famous remark about the need to educate 'our masters' — or rather that 'I suppose it will be absolutely necessary to educate our masters' (*Oxford Dictionary of Quotations:* 572) — could be read either way. The gentleman himself, however, seems in no doubt of what he meant. Writing in the same year (1867) on 'Primary and Classical Education', he observed:-

> 'The lower classes ought to be educated to discharge the duties cast upon them. They should also be educated that they may appreciate and defer to a higher cultivation when they meet it, and the higher classes ought to be educated in a very different manner, in order that they may exhibit to the lower classes that higher education to which, if it were shown to them, they would bow down and defer.'
> (Lowe 1867)

The masses were in other words to be gentled and trained for useful activity: not a novel idea in nineteenth-century educational thinking, but one which may have seemed especially apposite after 1867. Yet, notwithstanding the scorn expressed by H.G. Wells (1934) and others over the minimal schooling provided for in 1870, elementary education functioned also as guaranteed outlet, thereafter, for working-class aspirations. To the extent that the Revised Code was slowly whittled away and to the extent that 'higher elementary' provision was attempted, the possibility of such aspirations was not wholly ignored. By 1904, Sir Robert Morant, Permanent Secretary to a fairly recent Board of Education, was writing of the purpose of the public elementary school as being: 'to form and strengthen the character and develop the intelligence of the children entrusted to it, and to make the best use of the school years available' (*Code for Public Elementary Schools,* 1904: Introduction).

Education was not the only area of social policy to manifest some ambivalence, or ambiguity, of purpose in this period. No matter how 'popular' the target, it was never simply a straight response to presumed popular inclination. The affairs of the populace, after all, were still being managed by those who felt themselves, rightly or wrongly, to know best. Accordingly, while working-class welfare topics might have figured more prominently in the legislative debates and enactments of the period, some element of paternalism, or moral-social direction, was never far away.

Thus, while aspects of the poor law were frequently under discussion, it was the deserving categories of pauper — the young, the sick, the old and eventually the 'genuinely unemployed' — who stood to benefit from any relaxation in the system; not the hard core, able-bodied poor for whom, indeed, the test workhouse was a temporary answer (Webb and Webb 1929 : 377-95). Once the possibility of old age pensions came under debate, concern was expressed as to the effect such a provision might have upon the disposition to save among the working classes.[20] The Royal Commission on the Housing of the Working Classes was perturbed as much by the moral and social risks of slum living as it was by the physical hardships engendered (HM Government 1885 : 14-16 *et. seq.*). All in all, the Charity Organisation Society was not alone in its belief that the poorer classes needed watching, albeit for their own good. The idea of indiscriminate social welfare, unaccompanied by any personalized supervision, still seemed wild dangerous nonsense to very many people.

With hindsight, these may seem like the sentiments of an ageing century and of a dying era. Certainly, by 1905, both major political parties were highly conscious not only of the importance to them of a working-class vote but also of the disturbing potential of a Labour Party, now formally in the parliamentary arena. The Conservatives set up a Royal Commission to investigate the workings of the Poor Law, as part of a last, desperate, pre-electoral effort to win confidence. The Liberals embarked thereafter on a wide-ranging, unprecedented sequence of social policy legislation. The climate, seemingly, had changed. School meals, a school health service, a children act, old age pensions, labour exchanges, a 'people's budget' prior to statutory unemployment and health insurance: altogether they smacked of a novel, welfare orientation, if not of an incipient 'welfare state'.[21]

Some patriarchal thinking was in evidence nonetheless.[22] Much though non-contributory pensions or national health insurance might smack of impersonal provision 'as of right', there were at least minimal moral safeguards. Non-contributory pensions, for instance, were intended for respectable old people — not for those who had

prison, nor for those who had previously been in the
ng poor relief unless, by any chance, they had also
ntribute for at least ten years to the funds of a friendly
rt 1966 : 222; Gosden 1974 : 281). It was only a residual
erhaps, and one designed as much to ease friendly society
anx. as to promote upright citizenship. Yet it evidently had to be
built in. Similarly, in the parliamentary debates preceding national
health insurance one can trace an anxiety as to the possible, deleterious
moral consequences of state-subsidized, compulsory insurance which
was only barely appeased by the knowledge that the friendly societies,
along with the industrial insurance companies, would be invited to
become the agents of this system. Friendly societies epitomized to
many, all that was most admirable in working-class self-help so, if the
system served to boost their image and their business, then there was
at least something to recommend it.[23]

Interestingly enough, the opponents of such statutory daring
included not only members of the Charity Organisation Society, as
one might expect, but their obvious, Fabian opponents. Neither the
Majority nor the Minority Poor Law Reports of 1909 had been in
favour of compulsory, state insurance (HM Government 1909). The
Minority Report, for all its zeal in recommending the break-up of the
Poor Law was not prepared, in the last resort, to chance undermining
the individual's will to help himself by favouring compulsory
insurance. Nor indeed were any of their far-reaching welfare proposals
devoid of some residual element designed to ensure the effective
co-operation and honest endeavour of individual citizens.[24] The
intellectual socialists, in other words, were no more disposed than were
the rest of the comfortable classes to trust to the common man's
independent reponse.

Other items in the Liberal government's social legislation
programme are even less amenable to a straightforward vote-catching
interpretation. True, school meals and a rudimentary school health
service would mean an easing of many burdens. Yet they rated also as
an invasion of parental rights and responsibilities such as many
commentators were not slow to point out and such as the working
classes had not noticeably been asking for (Gilbert 1966 : 112 *et seq.*).
Much the same could be said of the 1908 *Children Act* together with all
the piecemeal legislation leading up to it. It is at this point, perhaps,
that we should consider the implications of there being an interest in
the population, as opposed to merely the electorate.

There were two contributory factors here. In the first place, the build-up of social policy, together with an associated, growing public interest in social conditions, helped in itself to render political opinion more and more conscious of the state of the nation. In the second place, pressure of national interests and national fortunes made the state of the nation seem ever more vital to future well being and even future survival.

The first point can be illustrated readily enough. Elementary education, after 1870, was a conspicuous source of information. Notwithstanding previous voluntary efforts, the intake of virtually all children into the nation's schools soon after 1870, seems to have provided something of a shock. 'They were a wild lot' remarked one observer (Lowndes 1937 : 16). More particularly, they were often an ill-clothed or ill-nourished lot — hardly in a condition to benefit from even rudimentary instruction. Teachers and school boards were not slow to protest. Notwithstanding the efforts of voluntary bodies scattered over the country to tackle the problems, demands for statutory schoool meals and school health service provision were beginning to mount up even before the shock of Boer War recruitment fitness figures (Lowndes 1937 : 226-7).

Education records, moreover, or more exactly the records of school board visitors in London, furnished Charles Booth with a practical starting point for what was intended to be an objective, factual, assessment of the nature and extent of poverty in this city. While in a sense Booth's efforts were part of a long Victorian tradition of social exploration and 'exposure', his determination to get to the facts and to let the facts, in the end, speak for themselves, rendered his study of *The Life and Labour of the People in London* (1889-1903), not only a time-consuming and expensive undertaking, but one whose findings were very difficult to dismiss. Notwithstanding the heyday of Victorian materialism, apparently, no less than 30 per cent of London's population could be described, at the end of the century, as living in poverty and this, for the most part, through no obvious fault of their own. The long-cherished notion of poverty as being no more than the outward visible sign of an inward spiritual deficiency, was effectively discredited at last.

The point was driven home by the efforts of Seebohm Rowntree, a self-confessed disciple of Booth who, in studying the more practicable population of York, was able not only to refine his methods of approach and analysis but also to render his evidence that much more pointed. 'Poverty' was precisely defined in terms of necessary items of expenditure. In particular, the nutritional requirements for physical efficiency were specified and the consequences of inadequacy in diet were spelt out. Once again, roughly 30 per cent of a city's population were found to be living in conditions of poverty, whether 'primary' or 'secondary',[25] and the incidence of physical deficiency was one of the messages proclaimed.

The evidence revealed in *Poverty: A Study of Town Life*, was timely. Simultaneously, it seemed, the country's efforts to recruit manpower for the Boer War were encountering parallel facts. In 1904 an Inter-departmental Committee on Physical Deterioration (HM Government 1904) both confirmed the physical inadequacy of no less than one third of would-be Boer War recruits and recommended, for instance, a future statutory provision of school medical inspection and school meals for needy children, such as was very soon enacted.

While a growing awareness of foreign industrial and imperial competition could foster a mounting national interest in the quality of its populace, war, it seemed, was the decisive agent. That long-cherished reservations about the wisdom, let alone the moral rectitude, of the state's seeking to intervene between parent and child should be overborn only after the humiliations of South Africa, seems more than coincidence. True, the *Children Act* had been preceded by decades of piecemeal child protection legislation, an acknowledgement of the work of voluntary child rescue endeavours as much as of Poor Law potential, yet the 'Children's Charter' of 1908 was something more than the sum of its precedents. The state acknowledged a formal, composite, interest in the well being of its future generation (see Heywood 1965 : 108 *et seq.;* McMillan 1911). If it sought also to cater for the elderly (through old age pensions) and for its current work force (through national health and unemployment insurance), this was perhaps no more than an extension of the same, belated, demographic interest.

All in all, the development of social policy from the latter nineteenth century up to the outbreak of the First World War seems to be a case of activity on behalf of, rather than by, the working classes. It was on their behalf, moreover, not out of any sudden, exaggerated sense of moral responsibility but because the logic and evidence of ongoing social intervention, the composition of the voting public and the national interest all seemed to point in the same direction.

(iii) *Transformation*

Much the same could be said, perhaps, about social policy development in years following the First World War on up to the 1940s. Yet, once again, the overall style and scope of social policy deliberation seems to have differed so markedly from anything which had gone before as to render 'the emergence of the welfare state' a distinctive period in British experience. Notions of social reconstruction and ideals of universal rights and responsibilities with regard to social well being were hardly snatched out of the air in the 1940s. Attempts to understand how and why they materialized when they did tend to rest upon three lines of approach, comparable to those brought out in the previous discussion. In the first place one can look at events in terms of the in-built pressures for extension and rationalization emanating from what was, by 1914, already a wide-spread collection of statutory social services. In the second place one can view this period as a coming of age, via the growing importance of the Labour Party, of the working classes in a policy-making, rather than merely in a voting, capacity. In the third place one can acknowledge the extent to which two world wars, interspersed with a world depression, both extended and refined an appreciation of what was necessary to the national interest.

So far as the extension or refinement of existing social services was concerned, the years between the two world wars functioned very much as a period for the preparation, and incubation, of new ideas. The shortcomings of pre-war initiatives were not slow to make themselves felt. As early as 1921 the Dawson Report (HM Government 120) came out in favour of a future health service — as opposed to the system of worker health insurance which, however generously laid out, was bound both to limit the health services offered and to exclude the non-insured population from its facilities. The state — rather than the professions, the philanthropists, or the Approved Societies — should control the disposition of health services and the population at large should have access to them, as and when required. In view of the economic situation, of course, no immediate change was expected; yet subsequent discussion throughout the twenties and thirties was to concentrate, more or less exclusively, not on whether but on how some sort of national health service was eventually to be drawn up.

The subject of education seemed to provoke a comparable inter-war dissatisfaction and a comparable inter-war debate over how to rationalize and 'complete' an existing, statutory system. Elementary provision coupled with a secondary, scholarship, possibility seemed by now little more than a temporary expedient. The Hadow Reports of 1926 and 1931 (HM Government 1926, 1931), respectively, urged secondary education for all — albeit of a varying content — and a restructuring of initial, 'primary' instruction so as to prepare children systematically for such a universal second stage. Once again it was a case of no immediate statutory action on such proposals but rather of their further elaboration through a series of informed discussions and reports throughout the 1930s.

Yet the most prominent example of re-thinking centred, not unnaturally, upon provisions for the unemployed. No sooner had the 1911 insurance framework been extended, after the First World War, to cover most of the working classes and to include dependent's allowances in the cash benefits provided for, than the system as a whole was subjected to the impossible, unprecedented, strains of a prolonged depression (Gilbert 1970 : 56 *et seq.*). Long term, large-scale unemployment was not an insurable risk. After a series of temporary shifts to provide uncovenanted or transitional benefits, then transitional payments, for those whose contribution rights had either run out or never accumulated (Gilbert 1970 : 89-97, 175-76), unemployment assistance was at last separated both from the trappings of insurance and from the local limitations of the Poor Law (by now re-named public assistance) (Gilbert 1970 : 178). Once the Unemployment Assistance Board was in operation, there was further discussion not simply over the respective potential of national insurance and national assistance but also over whether it was right to single out the unemployed as a category and relieve them, alone of the destitute, from dependence on local public assistance. It was not long before the Assistance Board was deprived of its 'Unemployment' prefix in acknowledgement of its broadening scope.[26]

Against this background of re-evaluation, based on an experience of the limitations and inherent shortcomings of existing social policy, it was scarcely surprising, perhaps, that Sir William Beveridge should have been commissioned in 1941 to examine the existing schemes of social insurance in operation and to submit proposals for their rationalization and improvement. Nor was it surprising that a *National Insurance Act* and a *National Assistance Act* should subsequently have materialized, along with a government commitment to full employment, an education act, and an act to set up a National Health Service. Once the period of depression was over, in other words, the fruits of experience and reflection were to make themselves felt.

The receptivity of governments and parliaments to such ideas, however, can be viewed in a different light. It was, arguably, not simply the logic of experience but also a change in the composition of the legislative authority that enabled the coming of the Welfare State. In 1900 the Labour Representation Committee had managed to return two members to parliament. By the end of 1910 Labour representation had risen to some forty-two MPs while, by 1924, an unprecedented — albeit minority — Labour Government could count on no less than 151 parliamentary votes. In 1929 Labour emerged as the largest single parliamentary party and in 1945 it won the post-war election. By such a token the working classes were, presumably, increasingly assured of having their interests taken into account.

Labour party emergence was not wholly the same thing, of course, as effective working-class representation. Not all the working classes were ever convinced into voting for the Labour party and not all elected representatives of the Labour party could even remotely be described as working class (Blondel 1963 ; McKenzie and Silver 1968). It is at this point, and in this century, perhaps, that a simple class or 'interest' interpretation of the machinations of government becomes least appropriate. The nomenclature of political groupings bears only a rough, instrumental relationship to the distribution of distinctive, or superficially distinctive, sectional interests. Neither the staying power of the deferential voter nor the infinite variety of the modern, self-designated, middle classes fit neatly into a political portrayal, which consists essentially of a mounting confrontation between Conservative and Labour political parties. Nevertheless, the fact that the two principal parties now included one party which was ostensibly committed to representing working class interests would seem to account for at least some popularization of social policy.

A closer look at the evidence, however, suggests a change of heart more fundamental than that implied by a mere shift in party political groupings. War, as I suggested earlier, could be decisive in shaping ideas as to what was requisite for national success. Two world wars, separated by a world depression, certainly left their mark. Titmuss's thesis that the more a war effort has to involve and depend upon the co-operation of the mass of the population, the greater the implications for statutory, universal, social policy, becomes virtually a self-evident truth when applied to British experience in the twentieth century (Titmuss 1958 : Ch. 4). So also does the Peacock and Wiseman (1961) contention: that the public's expectation of what it must support in terms of government expenditure becomes drastically and permanently enlarged as a result of wartime emergency experience. Social policies which were effected and accepted and paid for in wartime, could be and were expected also in peacetime, afterwards.

The argument requires no very elaborate exposition. Zeppelin raids notwithstanding, the First World War depended rather more upon the morale of the men in the trenches, and those employed in the war effort at home, than it did upon the well-being of the general population. The numbers of men required for the trenches were sufficiently great, however, as to render their subsequent 'out of work' donation (including dependent's allowances) decisive precedent for unemployment insurance benefits (Gilbert 1970 : 56 *et seq*.); just as the 'homes for heroes' commitment helped to initiate a break-through in housing policy — by virtue of the reliance, for the first time, upon local authority initiatives backed by government subsidies in this sphere (Cullingworth 1966 : 16-17). The men from the trenches, when joined with their families at home, amounted to a conclusive electoral factor: the more so since the 1918 Representation of the People Act had given the vote not simply to all men over twenty-one but also to all women over thirty. Paupers and older women were at last enfranchised as much, in the latter case, because of their wartime exploits as nurses, lorry-drivers, munition workers, and farm labourers, as because of the earlier efforts of the Suffragettes.[27]

For the rest, the interwar period was distinguished for pointing the connection, more clearly than ever before, between national well-being and popular satisfaction. Prolonged, mass unemployment spelt disaster on both counts. Once John Maynard Keynes had held out to government the possibility of controlling levels of unemployment by controlling the level of domestic, job-creating, expenditure, the way was open for postwar, full employment undertakings. Domestic government could at last be expected to be the manager of the national estate.

Added to all this were the experiences of the Second World War. This, as Titmuss has pointed out, meant above all a community involvement (Titmuss 1950 : 507 *et seq*.). Neither wartime efforts nor wartime hardships could, this time, be confined merely to an operational section of the population. The outcome was seen to depend as much on community morale as on the operational strength of the fighting services themselves. In this respect, the Blitz, or rather the expectation of a Blitz, was decisive. Given the likelihood of German bombers, a wartime government was bound to be concerned, not simply with the fitness of its fighting recruits (as in 1899) or even with the morale of the war workers (as in 1914), but with the state of confidence and commitment of the general population. Two sets of consequences followed from this. In the first place, wartime government was driven to take on responsibility for popular welfare on a scale never hitherto attempted. Once accepted, such responsibility was not easily to be shed in the years following the war. In the second place, the need to keep up community morale during the war encouraged the making of promises to the populace over what would be done to reform and improve British society, once the war had been won.

The first point requires only sample illustration. It was the expectation of early bombing raids (with an estimated likely casualty rate of some seventy-two victims per ton of bombs dropped) (Titmuss 1950 : 14), which prompted the early formation of an emergency medical service. The nationalization of hospital functions and streamlining of interlocking medical facilities thus involved was destined not for long to be restricted to the treatment of blitz casualties alone (Titmuss 1950 : 466-68). By the close of the war, indeed, so instrumental and publicly revealing had been this experience, that the future provision of a nationalized, salaried, hospital service accessible to the general population, had become a virtual certainty.

Of comparable significance were the welfare responsibilities increasingly shouldered by government partly to shore up evacuation arrangements and partly to cope with the disruptions and human misery brought about by bomb damage. Once again, as with the operation of the EMS, this proved an educational experience. Evacuation, in so far as it operated according to plan, exposed not simply the extent of physical and emotional deprivation among the population transported, but also the dearth of reception facilities and social service capacity in the receiving areas. A massive programme of subsidized hostel, canteen, and nursery provision had to be embarked upon (Titmuss 1950 : Ch. 11, 373-4). Such provisions, along with the services offered to homeless families displaced in the major cities would traditionally have fallen within the ambit of the poor law. Yet 'welfare' could no longer be regarded as something which only the destitute could require, since war was no respecter of persons. Welfare divorced from any stigma of poor relief was, again, a habit not easily to be shelved with the close of the war.

Such experiences added weight, of course, to notions of what might be required in the way of postwar social reconstruction. As early as 1941 the Minister of Health was promising that the Britain of the future would possess a national hospital service, much on the lines of the EMS (Titmuss 1950 : 504). More importantly, social reconstruction meant a utilization, not simply of wartime experience, but of the extended social policy discussion which had taken place in the preceding interwar years. Britain after the war was not to be the same sort of place as the Britain of the Great Depression. Given this sort of undertaking, then both the ideas and the experiences were there to be drawn upon.

Thus it was that when Beveridge was commissioned to head an interdepartmental committee of inquiry into social insurance he produced, not a plan for administrative rationalization, so much as a personalized blueprint for a new, socially responsible, society. Arguing that social insurance could not satisfactorily be dealt with in isolation from other aspects of social policy, he named his 'five giants on the road of social reconstruction', of which Want was only one (HM Government 1942 : 6, par. 2). The time was ripe, he proclaimed, for thoroughgoing rather than piecemeal social reform and, judging by the record sales of his Report, the public agreed with him. One could not begin to insure a population against risk of loss or interruption of earnings, he argued, unless at the same time they were to be freed from the major hazards of disease, ignorance, idleness and squalor. Nor could one trust all to insurance without some form of safety-net national assistance to cater for the *un*common, *un*insurable risk.

The response to such initiatives was not long in coming. Before even the war was ended, the Butler Education Act was on the statute book proclaiming free secondary, as well as primary, education as of right — according to the 'age aptitude and ability' of every child. The return of peacetime government witnessed a wealth of social legislation embodying, more or less, the breadth of Beveridge's proposals but also drawing, in each case, upon experience and ideas accumulated within each area of social policy both before and during the war. It was, as the great man himself had hoped, a 'British revolution': as much a development from the past as a cumulative departure from it (HM Government 1942 : 17, par. 31). How far the creation of such a Welfare State could be described as a 'Labour' or working-class achievement, by virtue of the fact that it was a postwar Labour government which was responsible for enacting most of the legislation, would seem a somewhat artificial matter for debate.

The fact that Welfare State legislation was enacted within such a relatively short space of time and, for the most part, by a single postwar government according, more or less, to the grand design suggested in the Beveridge report endowed it, perhaps, with an air of unity and consistency of purpose more apparent than real. Notwithstanding the separate, developmental background to each piece of legislation in each sphere of social policy, the label Welfare State — applied after the event[28] — implied some sort of overall, cohesive effort. Yet the principles variously embodied in such an effort were, to say the least, not necessarily complementary.

Thus, while national insurance rested upon notions of strict, contractual equality, with everyone paying the same and everyone entitled to the same (according to his family commitments) irrespective of financial or occupational position, education and health services were geared rather to equality of access — and to treatment as of right, according to requirements. This was a right to equal, tax-supported, opportunity, in other words, as opposed to strict equality of treatment. That there were two different sorts of equality being legislated for does not seem fully to have been appreciated at the time. True, one could argue that without the equlity of opportunity provided for by health, education, and employment services, for instance, equality of treatment via national insurance would be a nonsense. The first, so Beveridge might have argued, were prerequisites for the practicability and the justice of the second. Yet the efficacy of the combination hinged first upon a belief in the fundamental social equality of individual citizens and, second, upon a belief in the alterability or removability of what had hitherto been major, societal obstructions to such equality.

The 1940s were austere times for Britain: times when equal shares for all out of scarce resources, after an all-out war-effort, seemed no more than appropriate and just. They were optimistic times also: when to legislate for equal opportunity — or an equal chance to take one's chance — seemed ostensibly to be the same thing as to legislate for a new social order. New towns, for instance, were expected to epitomize a new, classless, society (Ratcliffe 1974 : 43). Individual achievement would, henceforth, be none other than the measure of individual potential.

Several developments took place to undermine such confidence. To begin with so called affluence, coupled with inflation, arrived. By the mid-1950s, the majority of the electorate was no longer so apparently convinced of either the wisdom or the justice of equal treatment in what was manifestly an increasingly unequal situation. Equal contributions spelt hardship for the poor. Equal benefits spelt irrelevance for the better-off (George 1968 : 36, 51-2 *et seq.*). Obsolete, apparently, were notions as to the pooling of scarce national resources between members of a population who felt they had more in common than they had to divide them. In so far as an affluent society was not an equal society (Titmuss 1962), such trappings of the Welfare State could appear outmoded, if not actually prejudicial to the national interest.

That this had not become a more equal society (if only in terms of individual freedom to manoeuvre) was of course something of a disappointment — if not almost a betrayal of wartime hopes. Equality of opportunity, it seemed, required rather more than the simple provision of a free, competitive, educational system or a free, comprehensive, health service to bring it about. Evidence of social disadvantage in the education system and of social discrepancies in the benefits derived from the health service began to mount up (Brown 1969). Once attention began to be focussed on the subtleties of social handicap resulting from deprived domestic or community environments, the question became essentially one of how far back ought the state — or could the state — practicably go in an effort to achieve something approaching individual equality of opportunity. War-time and post-war promises of individually tailored treatment in a few key respects by means of mammoth statutory provisions were exposed as having been naive — if not actively misleading.

In social policy terms therefore, the 1950s and 1960s were in many respects a period of reckoning: a period of coming to terms with the provisions and commitments of a Welfare State legislated for amid the somewhat ambiguous and temporary sentiments of wartime and postwar Britain. A period, perhaps, when changing economic and recalcitrant social conditions had perforce to be accommodated in the light of a brave new social philosophy never clearly spelt out but never thoroughly rejected.

In general, this discussion implies that there have been three broad stages in British social policy development: social policy directed at the mass of the population, social policy determined on behalf of the mass of the population, and social policy ostensibly decided on by and for the mass of the population. Looked at in another way, social policy was perhaps first designed primarily to control the masses, then to improve the masses, and finally to liberate the masses from social handicap or disadvantage. Stated so baldly, these can be no more than crude, question-begging assertions. What is apparent, however, is that the development of statutory social policy has reflected at once a growing expertise, a growing confidence, and a steadily mounting ambition with regard to government intervention in social affairs. It has reflected also an increasingly detailed, composite interest in the characteristics of the national population. The population, after all, was in a sense the nation's raw material. The better informed became public opinion, and the more popular became its composition, the more intently and elaborately was the state of the nation identified with the — adjustable — wellbeing and capabiltiy of the populace.

It is against this background of developing social attitudes, in general, and of developing social policy, in particular, that we may now proceed to consider the social and social policy implications of selected waves of mass immigration.

PART II

The case studies

3

Irish immigration
c. 1800-1861

As a first exercise in the study of immigration in relation to social policy, this will be a modest effort in terms of both the evidence referred to and the arguments advanced. The supply of relevant documentary material was in this case somewhat limited — as was, of course, the range of social policy measures in existence. Given both these considerations, it is understandable and even appropriate, perhaps, that this study should draw extensively upon the findings of the 1835 Poor Law Enquiry (Ireland). [1] The quantity and quality of this latter material seemed in any case to justify more than passing reference to it.

We will begin by considering the immigrants themselves, before moving on to discuss the reactions to their presence.

(i) *The nature of the migration*

While it seems:

> 'that a considerable immigration of Irish poor into Portpatrick, and thence to the neighbouring parts of Scotland ... had taken place before the year 1790; ... In no part of England, probably, was there any very considerable number of Irish in the year 1795; although from a very early period some adventurers had crossed the seas from time to time.' (Poor Law Enquiry (Ireland) : iv)

One may wonder at the confidence of the authors of this report, given the dearth of statistics available. Nevertheless, it would appear that large-scale immigration from Ireland to England did not get under way until the early years of the nineteenth century. England followed Scotland in this respect.

Prior to the Census of 1841, no official figures exist as to the numbers of Irish-born residents in Britain. Estimates of those entering the ports do not distinguish between permanent and seasonal arrivals, nor between those destined to stay in Britain and those intending to move on elsewhere. Town-based statistics, moreover, often make it difficult to separate the 'Irish' from the 'Catholic' population — not altogether the same thing (Wilson 1946 : 20). Yet local figures, for what they are worth, give an impression of an Irish population steadily increasing in strength, in Northern and Scottish towns particularly, throughout the first half of the nineteenth century. Notable upsurges in the numbers of permanent settlers seem to have been witnessed in the 1820s (following the famine of 1822) and again during and after the Great Famine of 1846-47 (Wilson 1946 : 8-9). Only after the middle 1850s, apparently, did the greater attractions of North America really command the Irish market (Wilson 1946 : 9).

Thus Manchester, with an Irish population of about 5,000 in 1787, claimed 20,000 Irish in 1805 (Wilson 1946 : 14) and some 35,000 in 1833 (Poor Law Enquiry (Ireland) : vii). Glasgow, similarly, saw its Irish Catholic population rise from some 8,245 in 1819 to 31,000 in 1831 (Jackson 1963 : 7). By 1841, according to the Census, there were over 4000,000 Irish born resident in England, Wales, and Scotland, forming 1.8 per cent of the population of England and Wales and 4.8 per cent of the population of Scotland. By 1851 the respective proportions had risen to 2.9 per cent and 7.2 per cent. By 1861, however, they had levelled off to around 3.0 per cent for England and Wales and 6.7 per cent for Scotland.[2]

The reasons for their coming were not always clear. One of them offered his own, picturesque, explanation:

> ' "The Irish", says Mr. Whitty ... "have a notion that any part of the world is better than Ireland, and consequently are fond of a change. I will say unhesitatingly that nine-tenths of the Irish settled in England did not come over from necessity, but in a wild spirit of adventure." ' (Poor Law Enquiry (Ireland) : v)

There were grounds, nevertheless, for assuming some necessity to exist. June 1798 witnessed a Presbyterian rising in counties Down and Antrim and a far more dangerous revolt of the Catholic peasantry in

Wexford. Both movements failed and in 1800 the constitutional Union of Ireland with England, Wales, and Scotland was effected; a move which, while it frustrated many Presbyterian landowners and lawyers at the time, was to be seen as a far more long-term setback for the Catholic population of Ireland (Curtis 1957). Yet religious and political refugees, *per se*, were perhaps more likely to head for North America than for Britain. Thus while the 1798 Catholic Rebellion might have seemed to many contemporaries to be the cause of the numbers of Irish peasantry flocking to British ports, its significance in this respect may possibly have been overrated (Wilson 1946 : 7).

The obvious, underlying cause of such protracted, almost traditional, population movement from Ireland to Britain was economic. Economic conditions in Ireland virtually demanded large-scale emigration, while the workshop of the world virtually invited footloose labour to come in. Irish wool, silk, and cotton trades found themselves crippled by the effects of Union and consequent English competition (Curtis 1957). A struggling agriculture became less and less able to support a peasant population — partly because of increasing concentration on pasturage (with a consequent drop in the demand for labour) (Jackson 1963 : 3) and partly because of the tendency, repeatedly, to subdivide tenant landholdings in order to maximize rent returns (Curtis 1957). At the same time the population was increasing at what can best be described as an alarming rate. Between 1780 and 1840 the population of Ireland almost doubled — notwithstanding the level of emigration (which, by 1770 was running at about 9,000 a year to North America alone) (Jackson 1963 : 4).

Britain was an obvious resort: not simply as a relatively prosperous economy, but by virtue of the fact that politically and physically she was close at hand. A long-standing tradition of casual, seasonal migration between the two islands was not without its significance in preparing the way for large-scale, permanent immigration. Such an outcome was partly manipulated, nevertheless. That certain landlords actively encouraged their tenantry to set sail for British ports seems without question (Wilson 1946 : 13; Poor Law Enquiry (Ireland) xxxiii). The alleged steamship racket, furthermore, almost bribed individuals to migrate by charging nominal fares — if only in the hope of making a sturdier profit from the Poor Law authorities when asked, later, to re-settle the unfortunates (Wilson 1946 : 12). Whatever the truth of such charges, there seems little doubt but that the rapid expansion of ferry services and the consequent lowering of fares (down to three pence per head, for instance, for a deck passage between Belfast and Glasgow in 1824) (Jackson 1963 : 7), both aided and encouraged larger-scale migration.

The distribution of the Irish-born population in England and Scotland reflected, on the one hand, the direction of such steamship routes (Wilson 1946 : 9-12) and, on the other, the balance of likely job opportunities. Hence by 1835 they were to be found 'in every manufacturing or commercial town, from Aberdeen, Dundee and Greenock, to the central counties of England and the metropolis'. Every place, in other words, 'where there was any prospect of obtaining profitable employment' (Poor Law Enquiry (Ireland) : vii). On the whole, this was a migration of unskilled labourers and their families from a rural, peasant, to an urban, industrial, setting. While some movement of skilled craftsmen was involved (many linen weavers, for instance, came over and took either to silk weaving, or to handloom weaving in Lancashire and Yorkshire) (Jackson 1963 : 82), the great majority of newcomers possessed no marketable skills. Hence one reads that:

> 'Untaught any handicraft, and unskilled in any mechanical art, the Irish immigrant competes only for the coarsest, the least remunerative and generally the most repulsive descriptions of Labour.' (Tennent 1860 : 142)

or that:

> 'the bulk of the Irish population in Great Britain ... consists of common labourers, who are chiefly employed in the towns, at different kinds of coarse, unskilled work, and especially in the several branches of the building trade, as masons; bricklayers; and pasterers' labourers, brickmakers, quarrymen, etc.' (Poor Law Enquiry (Ireland) : 6)

This was not to mention the Irish navvy or the Irish hawkers who 'turn their hands to every description of low trade which is the fruit of industry, and requires almost no capital' (Poor Law Enquiry (Ireland) : viii).

Despite the physical proximity and the formal political union, moreover, this was something of an alien population. Ireland had long been regarded by the English at least as a backward, if not a barbarous, country. Once here:

'The Irishman's clothes, his brogue and general appearance, even when he was not speaking in Gaelic, singled him out from the rest of the community as an outsider, a stranger in the midst. But more potent than the fact that the immigrant lived in a strange and simple way was the fact that he belonged to a foreign church.' (Jackson 1963 : 154)

There were, of course, many English and Scottish Catholics; yet this, apparently, was not the same thing. Not only might Irish Catholicism exhibit a greater puritanism and naivety of outlook, but 'centuries of struggle against the alien and Protestant master' had seemingly produced a 'fusion of religion and nationalism in the Irish mind ... To be a Catholic was to be a true Irishman; to be an Irishman was to be a true Catholic' (Herberg 1956 : 160).

Technically of course the Irish could not be accounted 'foreigners'. Nevertheless they seem to have kept themselves to themselves, whether from choice or from necessity.

'Several witnesses described them as forming a distinct community in the midst of the English, and compared them in this respect with the Jews ... Finding the natives unwilling to mix with them, they naturally herd together in particular quarters or streets of the large towns, and thus associate constantly with each other, and have rarely any intercourse with the natives of the place, except those of the lowest class.' (Poor Law Enquiry (Ireland) : xiv)

The fact that immigration from Ireland was an on-going, rather than a once-for-all, phenomenon must have helped prolong such a separation: the Irish community being: 'constantly kept under the influence of their own countrymen, strengthened, from time to time, by successive relays of new emigrants from Ireland' (Poor Law Enquiry (Ireland) : xv).

(ii) *Host society reaction*

We have, therefore, a picture of Irish immigrants in the first half of the nineteenth century which portrays them as being predominantly poor and unskilled; sufficiently distinctive in their appearance and behaviour as to constitute a separate community within the general community; and sufficiently numerous as to form noticeable settlements in many of the industrial and manufacturing centres of England and Scotland.

Their arrival did not go unremarked. That such a people should ever have entered a country of Britain's stature seemed, to some, a matter for amazement — if not for outrage — in itself. In the words of the Poor Enquiry (Ireland) Report:-

> 'the emigration from Ireland to England and Scotland is of a very remarkable character, and is perhaps nearly unparalleled in the history of the world. It has usually happened that emigrations have taken place from more civilised to less civilised nations, as was the case with the Greek and also the Phoenician colonies on the coasts of the Mediterranean ... with the English settlements in North America, the East Indies and New South Wales; and with the foreign establishments of other European states. In other cases, where a civilised population has not forcibly occupied the territory of a savage race, the emigration has been confined to certain descriptions of artisans, who, though their original might not be altogether more advanced in civilisation than their adopted country, yet were themselves superior in skill and knowledge of their craft to the native workmen with whom they thus came in competition. This was the case with the Flemings, who introduced into England the weaving of fine woollen in the fourteenth century; and with the French weavers, who first established the silk manufacture in Spitalfields ... But the Irish emigration into Britian is an example of a less civilised population spreading themselves, as a kind of substratum, beneath a more civilised community; and, without excelling in any branch of industry, obtaining possession of all the lowest departments of manual labour.' (p.iii)

Given such a view, it is scarcely surprising to find the Irish — as 'less civilized' outsiders — figuring prominently in most areas of contemporary social debate.

Thus, if the living conditions and life-styles of the masses were giving cause for concern, the habits of the Irish were held up — repeatedly — as constituting the very lowest form of life and as an insidious threat, therefore, to national progress. Not everyone went so far as actually to blame the Irish for the spread of disease. Many spokesmen went no further than to bemoan the unhealthiness of the immigrants' lot:

> 'The Irish labourer, on his arrival at his destination in Great Britain, finds dense masses of his countrymen in almost exclusive

possession of unwholesome dwellings, in the most unhealthy portions of a great city ... In their comfortless apartments, domestic enjoyment is little known, and the inmates are inured from infancy to unwholesome influences, damp, miasma and decay.' (Tennent 1860 : 141)

Others, however, were not content to leave it at that. 'The Irish in Birmingham' declared Mr Mouchet, Surgeon of the General Dispensary 'are the very pests of society. They generate contagion' (Poor Law Enquiry (Ireland) : 6). After listening to such evidence, the 1835 Commission itself was of the opinion that, because of their 'wretched' living conditions, the Irish 'are frequently the means of generating and communicating infectious desease' (Poor Law Enquiry (Ireland) : xi).

The dangers of the Irish presence in this respect would appear to have been a matter for some small disagreement. In his Sanitary Report of 1842, Chadwick was at some pains to assert that the Irish were at least no worse than their native counterparts, in matters of public health (p.199). Yet the borderline between public health and perceived public morality was apparently a narrow one. Many of the fiercest critics of Irish living conditions were expressing as much a moral as a medical concern:

' "The Irish", says Dr. Duncan, Honorary Physician of the North Dispensary of Liverpool, "seem to be as contented amidst dirt and filth, and close, confined air, as in clean and airy situations. What other people would consider comforts, they appear to have no desire for: they merely seem to care for that which will support animal existence." '

There was no great distance between this and an assumption that such newcomers must be infecting the native population with their standards. The views of Dr Kay (later Sir James Kay-Shuttleworth) were clear enough:

'The colonisation ... of a large manufacturing town in England by a less-civilised race than the natives is not without its influence on the manners of the resident population, especially in those districts in which the population is mingled together ... I am ... led to attribute a great deal of the discomfort in the habitations of the working classes in Manchester, and the adoption of an inferior diet, to the example of the Irish, because, from extensive opportunities of investigation, I am persuaded that, in some of the neighbouring towns, in all other respects similarly situated to Manchester, but not colonised by Irish, the dwellings of the poor contain more furniture, and are cleaner, and their diet is superior to that of a great portion of the population in Manchester.' (Poor Law Enquiry (Ireland) : xxxix)

Frederick Engels, interestingly enough, was more or less at one with Dr Kay on this point (Engels 1969 : 122-25).

Others, however, were convinced that any influence had been predominantly in the opposite direction and that it had, therefore, been benign. As one Mr Redman, Visiting Overseer to the Poor in Manchester, observed: 'The Irish have gained more in the improvement of their habits than the English have lost by their association with them' (Poor Law Enquiry (Ireland) : xix). An English Roman Catholic priest (Rev. Vincent Glover of Liverpool) even went so far as to assert:

'I think the Irish more apt to learn than the English, both boys and girls ... The children of Irish, born in Liverpool, generally go on well; they learn the habits of the English, are more careful and provident than those born in Ireland. They are willing and active. There is a decided amelioration in the English-born Irish; the longer they stay the more they improve.' (Poor Law Enquiry (Ireland) : 22)

On the whole, the 1835 Commission seemed at least half-inclined to agree. Of Irish immigrants in general it acknowledged that 'there are many on whom a beneficial influence is exercised and whose character and habits are improved' (Poor Law Enquiry (Ireland) : xix). Should this not invariably take place then, even so, the risks of moral contagion seemed limited — if only by the fact that 'the Irish herd for the most part together, especially in the English towns, and have little communication with the natives' (Poor Law Enquiry (Ireland : xxxvii).

Of equal, if not greater, significance than the moral and physical attributes of Irish immigrant households, however, was their economic potential as a labour force. Yet, here again, opinions were divided. Prominent among their critics were those convinced that the presence of the Irish worker served only to depress native wage-levels and hence native standards of living. Local patriotism, in this case, coupled with a lively awareness of popular, economic discontent[4] — would seem, temporarily, to have democratized the interests covered by public opinion. The 1835 Commission seemed convinced that: 'the rate of wages in Lancashire and the West of Scotland has been lowered by the competition of the Irish' (p.xxxiii). Wages in Manchester, indeed were alleged to have declined by two-thirds in twenty years for this reason alone (p.xxxiv). Moreover 'English labourers', says Mr James Holmes of Birmingham, 'don't like the Irish; they say, if it was not for them they would have good wages' (p.xxxiii).

The 'English labourers', so it was said, were not inclined to blame the Irish immigrants for this — so much as the 'gentlemen of Ireland', (for sending them over here), on the one hand and the 'English capitalists' (who strove 'to induce the Irish to come over that they might lower wages'), on the other (p.xxxiii). 'I am at a loss to know whether the Irish gentlemen or the English capitalist has done more for the destruction of the working classes both of England and Ireland' — so said Mr. Richard Sheridan, hand-loom weaver of Manchester (p.xxxiii).

The 'English capitalist', of course, had his own case to put forward:

'Mr. Houldsworth, cotton manufacturer, of Glasgow:- "Wages in the spinning department of the cotton trade have been kept down by the Irish, or rather they have been prevented from rising. If wages were raised, I doubt whether we could meet the foreign competition; even now there is great difficulty, as the Americans export a great deal of cotton goods, and meet us successfully in the Indian and South American markets." ' (p.xxxv)

Indeed the Irish, in so far as they formed a pool of cheap, mobile, labour, were arguably the saving of British industry.

'The demands of the English and Scotch manufacturing districts have been supplied by the surplus labour of Ireland, as their population has been fed by its surplus agricultural produce.' (p.xxxvi)

That the usefulness of the Irish in this respect might make up for their social shortcomings, was occasionally — and cautiously — suggested:

'We ought not ... to overlook the advantage of the demand for labour in England and Scotland being amply and adequately supplied, and at a cheap rate and at very short notice, by Irish, simply because they are a potato-fed and a disorderly population.' (p.xxxvii)

For the most part, however, — just as in the case of public health — it seemed impossible for the economic characteristics of Irish immigration to be considered separately from their moral implications. Once again, it seemed, the Irish constituted a threat to national standards:

> 'by the example they set to English and Scotch labourers; they consent to live on an infinitely lower standard of wages than they have been accustomed to; so that they teach them that it is possible for people to exist, and be tolerably comfortable, so far at least as animal spirits go, upon a much lower scale of wages.' (p.xxxiii)

Such sentiments, apparently in support of higher wages for the working man, sound oddly from the pages of a Royal Commission Report in 1835. Yet the contributors to the Report were concerned far more with the dangerous fecklessness of the Irish than with the plight of the native working classes as such. Self-help was a virtue they looked for in the immigrant and found wanting:

> 'On the whole, it appears that, to a considerable extent, the Irish labourers who settle in Great Britain do not increase their comforts, or improve their style of living, in proportion to the increase of their incomes; that they have a fixed standard of existence, little superior to that which they observed in their own country; and that everything beyond the sum which enables them to live in this manner is spent in drinking.'[5]

Nor was their's a temporary opinion. A quarter of a century later, Sir James Emerson Tennent was making much the same point:

> 'The Scotch or Welsh peasant, who finds his way to the manufacturing towns of England, from a labourer, becomes in his turn an employer, a tradesman, a shopkeeper, a capitalist, a merchant, a magistrate, a mayor; but strange to say, as a general rule, in that humblest of all capacities in which the Irish immigrant lands on the quay of Liverpool or Glasgow ... in that capacity, for the most part, he is contented to continue for the remainder of his life. He lands as a labourer, without a shilling, rarely aspires to any higher position ... and ... leaves the world as penniless and helpless as he entered it.' (Tennent 1860 : 137)

Such fecklessness could be expensive, of course, as far as the host community was concerned. That a Poor Law Commission of Enquiry should have been highly conscious of Irish begging potential was only to be expected, perhaps. Nevertheless the concern expressed went well beyond the implications of an Irish presence for the Poor Law itself. The Irish, it was felt, would 'almost always make an effort to get something for nothing' (p.xxiv). Indeed 'they have no sense of independence, shame, or propriety. They do not mind what means they employ, so that they get what they seek, nor what stories they tell' (p.xxiv). Hence their undue preponderance among applicants for relief from major charities in Manchester and Liverpool in the early 1830s (pp.53, 13). Yet such charities, it was argued, were themselves at fault — in so far as their careless distribution of relief might actually have encouraged this behaviour:

'The large sums distributed by public charities in Manchester and Liverpool, not always with due consideration of the consequences of such indiscriminate relief, have ... assisted in increasing the unthrifty and irregular habits of many of the Irish who flock to England, and doubtless have acted as an attraction to the least valuable part of the emigrants from Ireland.' (p.xxiv)

Decades later, the Charity Organisation Society was to do its utmost to act upon such a belief — in respect of the general, rather than simply this immigrant, population. More immediately, however, Irish fecklessness was reckoned to lead not simply to debt or to begging potential, but to crime — albeit crime of a somewhat trivial nature.

'It appears ... that the Irish in the large towns of Lancashire and Scotland commit more crimes than an equal number of natives of the same place; but that their crimes are not in general of a very dangerous character, being for the most part brutal assaults committed in a state of drunkenness.' (p.xx)

Or alternatively:

'The Irish, not having been regularly trained to house-breaking, are contented with stealing small articles, and this they practise to a very considerable extent.' (p.xxii)

Only in the illicit distillation of spirits were the Irish thought to excel.

'It is to them that the practice is confined, as the English are generally ignorant of the process of distilling, whereas the Irish were much accustomed to it in their own country.' (p.xxiii)

On the whole, any difficulty was seen as much to stem from the inadequacy of local police forces as from the strength of Irish criminality:

> 'The violence to which the Irish are prone when excited by spirits, and the habit of disrespect for the law and resistance to its officers, which they had formed in their own country, are naturally increased when they find themselves under a feebler police and less rigorous administration of the law than they had hitherto been accustomed to.' (p.xx)

The obvious answer, perhaps, was for the Irish to be drafted into the police forces — yet even this daring expedient could produce its own problems:

> 'The force is improperly supplied with men; ... and a great majority of them are of the lowest order of Irish; it is not likely that they can make an effective police; these men are red-hot Irishmen, just imported, who run out and strike every person they meet.' (Wilson 46 : 121)

Such at least had been London's experience.

The one remaining area of interest, both to the Poor Law Enquiry and to public opinion in general, was the Irishman's characteristics as a political — or would-be political — animal. Not surprisingly, perhaps, the evidence on this was conflicting. The position and background of the Irish, as mobile, unskilled, immigrant labour, certainly made them unpromising material for any labour movement in Britain. Inevitably the immigrant was 'more prone to the temptations of wagecutting and black-legging, often through innocence rather than malice', and 'was in any case working in unskilled casual occupations where unionisation was difficult to effect and solidarity was impossible to enforce' (Jackson 1963 : 116).

That employers were not above exploiting such a situation seems obvious:

> 'I consider the Irish as of great value as a check on the combination of the English ... The moment I have a turnout, and am fast for hands, I send to Ireland for ten, fifteen, or twenty families, as the case may be.' (Poor Law Enquiry (Ireland) : 68)

Yet this, apparently, was no more than a response to native unreasonableness:

'The system of combination which has prevailed among English and Scotch operatives has ... contributed to increase the immigration of Irish into Britain. The natives have combined, and turned out, and made unreasonable demands on their employers, and thus have induced capitalists to seek for hands where they were most easily found, that is, among the large unemployed population of Ireland.' (p.xxvii)

There was, however, another side to the picture which, given the feckless, lawless, character attributed to the Irish — and notwithstanding their economic ineffectiveness — seems none too unexpected. While most of the Irish were not tradesmen and were not, therefore, in a position to take part in activities organized by unions of trades, 'they appear to have been, at least, as active as the natives, whenever they had an opportunity of combining' (p.xxiii).

'Thus the Irish bricklayers' labourers were engaged in the general turn-out of the working builders which took place in Liverpool and Manchester in the spring and summer of 1833, and there has been much combination, attended with some riots and outrages, among the Irish hand-loom weavers at Manchester. In Glasgow and its neighbourhood, the formidable union of cotton-spinners was first organised by the Irish.' (p.xxiii)

An Irish Catholic priest, deployed in Manchester, put this in more general terms:

'I have found that the Irish are more prone to take part in trades unions, combinations and secret societies, than are the English.' (p.62)

Certainly, so far as national working-class movements were concerned, the Irish were not without their impact. It was an Irishman, James Doherty, who founded the first (abortive) General Union of All the Operative Spinners of the United Kingdom in 1829; and the National Association for the Protection of Labour, some six months' later (Jackson 1963 : 118). More significant, perhaps, was their influence on the Chartist movement. Given the reputation of the Irish for 'violence in word and action' it seemed no accident to contemporary opinion that the Chartists of the down-trodden 'thirties' and the 'hungry forties' should have boasted Bronterre O'Brien and Fergus O'Connor among their leaders. Nor was it surprising that O'Connor (an Irish barrister) should have been the one to head the militant, northern wing of the movement, whose membership and tone were in such contrast to the workings of the London Working Men's Association or the Birmingham Political Union (Wilson 1946 : 185).

As 'less civilised' outsiders, therefore, the Irish were thought to be setting a bad example to the native working classes in almost every respect. While there were those, of course, who felt that on balance the newcomers were probably benefiting more from contact with the natives than they were corrupting them with their ways and those, in addition, who felt that the newcomers were too different and too isolated for much influence to operate either way, most public spokesmen seem to have seen the immigrants as at least the epitome — if not a cause — of current social shortcomings.

(iii) *Immigration and statutory social policy*

Not surprisingly, the areas of concern encompassed by public reaction to Irish immigration tended, more or less, to correspond to those same social issues as were generally exercising public opinion and prompting statutory endeavour.[6] As the designated least civilized members of the population, the Irish were seen to evince just those unhelpful — or actively destructive — characteristics as were currently regarded as prejudicial to the national interest. While, in the case of public health, or public law and order, immigrant characteristics were seen as adding fuel to an already urgent public debate, in their economic fecklessness they also were seen as impinging directly upon the workings of an existing, statutory service.

To begin with, the Poor Laws — both before and after 1834 — were regarded as a prime inducement for Irish beggars to come in. Since there were, before 1838, no equivalent provisions in force in Ireland it seemed obvious, to many commentators, that the destitute must have been attracted by the prospect of statutory relief in this country. As the Rev. Jonas Brooks of Liverpool was anxious to point out:

'It is well known that many of the Irish come over here for the express purpose of availing themselves of that assistance which they are unable to procure at home.' (Poor Law Enquiry (Ireland) : 36)

Or, in the words of Mr. Thomas Armitt:

'The Irish in Manchester ... have no other aim or plan than to hang on the poor laws; if they ever had any energy, it seems taken away when they have once had relief ... It seems an Irishman's ambition to gain a settlement, or live here long enough to have a claim for relief; he seems raised by it, whereas an Englishman is lowered by it, and at first feels some shame. An Irishman never feels any shame on this score.' (p.48)

However occasional, or idiosyncratic, such observations might have been they were evidently sufficient in number and authority to prompt the establishment, in 1835, of a Poor Law Enquiry designed to examine the state of the poor in Ireland as well as (parenthetically) the state of the Irish poor in Great Britain. Following the voluminous findings of these Commissioners, an *Irish Poor Relief Act* of 1838 effectively extended the English system of unions, compulsory poor rates, and elected Boards of Guardians to the parishes of Ireland. Yet, though the Act was designed primarily to improve conditions in England rather than in Ireland, it failed to have any noticeable effect — either on the numbers of Irish migrating or upon the prevalence of destitution among those already in this country (Wilson 1946 : 143).

So while the poor laws might allegedly have contributed to the magnitude of early Irish immigration they were unable, subsequently, either to stem or to mitigate its effects. The effects were indicative, in one respect at least, of an inherent weakness in the Poor Law system. One of the abiding causes of concern in this period related to the operation of the Laws of Settlement so far as Irish destitutes were concerned. Prior to 1838 it was theoretically impossible to 're-settle' an Irishman in his native parish simply because Ireland, unlike England, had no Settlement Laws in operation. In practice, however, it was a question rather of the long-term profitability and practicability of such a course of action and of who, in the short term, was to meet the costs.

Ratepayer hostility to the presence of vagrants — and particularly Irish vagrants — had long been in evidence. An Act of 1819 empowered parishes, in the aftermath of the Napoleonic Wars, to remove Irish destitutes simply 'to any port in Ireland' under the vagrancy laws. Begging was held to be sufficient proof of vagrancy (Wilson 1946 : 139).

Such removals could be an awkward and costly business however. The evidence submitted to the 1835 Poor Law Commissioners was clear enough — between 1825 and 1828, it seemed, no less than

17,323 Irish persons were returned from Liverpool to Ireland. Of these, moreover, no less than 11,312:

> 'have intruded themselves, or have been driven from other parishes into the county of Lancaster. The charge upon the county in the year ending June 1827 was nearly £37,000, of which this parish [Liverpool] has paid about £700.' (p.11)

Nor was this last an isolated sum. Between October 1832 and October 1833 some 2,975 Irish persons were transferred by the parish of Liverpool to Ireland at a cost of 5/- per head; making a total cost of some £743.15s. upon the parish (p.10).

Nevertheless, the problem of Irish settlement and removal was in reality only a part — if a conspicuous and expensive part — of a more general dilemma. The Laws of Settlement and Removal as they operated within the Poor Law were destined to divide and confuse pre-Victorian and Victorian opinion for decades (Rose 1971 : 191-93). Whatever else it reformed in 1834, the Poor Law Amendment Act largely skirted this tangle — leaving the parishes to continue or to elaborate upon any improvisations they may have worked out (Rose 1971 : 191).[7] Not that the Laws themselves, of course, were unclear in their intentions. The idea that the parish to which the individual 'belonged' should be the one to support him if or when he became destitute, was one that appeared not only just but reasonable to contemporary public opinion.

Even so, the operation of the Laws of Settlement and Removal in industrial, urban parts of Britain had, by the 1830s, become complex. On the one hand, were the employers keen to have cheap, mobile labour at hand whenever and wherever it was required; on the other hand were the ratepayers (sometimes the same people) determined not to pay, either for absent or 'non-resident' poor, the moment such labour became redundant. The Irish — as a noted source of cheap mobile labour, a likely drain on the poor rate, and the most expensive paupers to remove — were bound to figure often as the subjects of such a debate.

Some parishes, inevitably, were more daring or more drastic than others in the remedies they felt bound to adopt. None of these was acting specifically in response to the presence of Irishmen so much as in response to a wider, labour-hungry, or labour redundant, situation. In expanding urban areas there was an obvious need somehow to attract, and retain, a pool of necessary, extra labour. Many parishes therefore contrived to pay out 'non resident' relief — at least on the understanding that they would be re-imbursed by the parish of settlement. Others, such as Manchester and Liverpool, went so far as to allow normal relief to anyone who had resided within their boundaries for a mere ten years or more. The need to retain a labour-force, more or less in spite of the provisions of the Poor Law, seemed paramount. Even so, the 1835 Poor Law Commission felt bound to regard this as both a questionable practice in itself and one designed ultimately to favour Irish immigrants. As the Commissioners put it:

'In Liverpool and Manchester a considerable burden has been entailed on the parishes by the adoption of a rule, that Irish, who had lived ten years in the town, should be treated as if they had a settlement.' (Poor Law Enquiry (Ireland) : xxxviii)

Whether or not such arrangements were designed primarily to accommodate the Irish, rural English parishes were hardly likely to object so long as their own export of surplus manpower to the towns was also catered for. It was, arguably, to appease rural interests (after the Repeal of the Corn Laws) that an act was passed which not only generalized but added to the implications of the Liverpool and Manchester practice. After 1846, parishes were compelled to relieve any destitute persons resident within their boundaries (and not previously in receipt of poor relief) for the previous five years alone.

This was not a measure intended to meet the requirements of Irish immigrants as such. Its impact, nevertheless, seemed biased in this direction. No sooner had the act been passed than manufacturing centres of the country were invaded by the 'Great Famine' influx of Irish manpower of 1847-48. This on top of a national trade depression. It was no accident, perhaps, that the Leeds Board of Guardians, by 1854, should have felt itself peculiarly hard hit:

' "It is difficult to state how much of the increase in relief paid out is to be attributed to the alteration in the law, and how much to the influx of the Irish." Yet "a considerable proportion ... arises from Irish cases." ' (Rose 1971 : 202)

Either way, it seemed, the Irish could be a difficulty. So long as the Settlement Laws were retained in strength, then 'by destroying the field of the Englishman's employment' they 'allured the Irish, and even afforded them bounties to supply his place where he was wanted' (Rose 1971 : 204). If the Laws were tampered with, however, the Irish would be bound to take advantage and saddle their Unions with a mountain of applications for relief (Rose 1971 : 205-6). The dilemma was in essence no more than an emotive illustration of the controversy surrounding the operation of the Laws in general. They were not repealed in the nineteenth century. They remained to embarrass the Poor Law until its own abolition, and the introduction of nationally based Assistance, in 1948.

For all that the Irish figured so regularly in such controversies, no real evidence exists as to what effects the Poor Law had on them: concern centred rather upon what effects they might be having on the Poor Law. Such a bias was only to be expected — given a statutory service designed primarily to control, rather than to assist, the poor. It was not until the next century that comprehensive efforts were made to assess the impact, after the event, of the Poor Law upon the destitute in general and by this time the Irish no longer figured as a separate item for discussion.[8]

Aside from the Poor Law, of course, there was at this time relatively little in the way of statutory intervention, or state-subsidized intervention, for the impact of Irish immigration to be measured against. Even after 1848, public health was still more a matter of debate than of direct government activity, and the impersonal nature of the provisions introduced makes it difficult, in any case, to relate their impact specifically to and Irish population. No legislation was introduced specifically to combat the Irish menace, in other words, and no follow-up enquiries were mounted such as to measure, specifically, the effects of public health developments upon the health of the Irish population.

If we turn to areas of incipient state intervention more directly geared to the promotion of individual well-being, such as factory reform or state-subsidized education, it would seem even more impracticable to try to relate any measures undertaken to the impact or the requirements of an Irish presence. In neither of these cases, interestingly enough, were the needs or attributes of the immigrants a prominent subject of debate. For the most part, one can merely suppose that any improvements in working conditions and any increase in popular education facilities benefitted the Irish population rather less than they did the general population — simply because the former were far more likely to be employed in unskilled and unregulated contexts (see above, pp.46, 54-55) and because, as Roman Catholics, they were likely to find the efforts of either the 'British' or the 'National' societies inappropriate for their children (see above,

Ch. 2, p.18 and note 9).

This is not to say that some individualized welfare service for Irish immigrants was never regarded as desirable or as likely to be constructive. The 1835 Commission was indeed of the opinion that:

> 'their mode of life is very slowly and very slightly improved *unless* some civilising influence descends upon them from above, some external moving force independent of their own volition, as of masters, employers, superintendents, education, municipal regulations, etc.' (Poor Law Enquiry (Ireland) : xx, my italics)

A 'considerable improvement', however,

> 'in their dress and personal appearance ... is particularly observed in the schools and factories where the Irish children, after a short attendance, soon are able to assimilate their outward appearance to that of others, however ragged and dirty they may have been at the beginning.' (p.xix)

Everything seemed to depend, in other words, on the quality of works management and on the availability of schools provision.

While it is impossible to quantify the proportion of Irish manpower in Britain which was catered for either by paternalistic employers, or by enforceable factory regulations after 1833, the matter of schools provision stood as an obvious problem — indicative, to some extent, of a wider, national, dilemma.

As early as 1802, the *Health and Morals of Apprentices Act* had stipulated not only that the hours of work of parish apprentices should be restricted to some twelve hours per day but that these same youngsters should receive daily instruction in the three Rs for the first four years of their apprenticeships. No one ever said, however, who was to provide the requisite instruction. In 1802 this meant an unrealistic reliance upon the availability of make-shift or voluntary arrangements. After the 1833 *Factory Act* requiring, among other things, that children under thirteen attend 'some school to be chosen by the parents or guardians of such children', there were at least the state-subsidized efforts of the 'British' and 'National' Societies to look towards (see above, Ch. 2, p.18 and note 9). For those not already either apprenticed or in full employment, moreover, there were the efforts of the workhouses, particularly after 1834, to make some gesture in the direction of child-inmate instruction.

Little of this, however, could have either much relevance or much

appeal for an Irish Roman Catholic population. Popular education was
very much a branch of religious and hence moral instruction in the
first half of the nineteenth century. As members of a minority Church
which was ill-equipped and nervous, in any case, of embarking too
strenuously on anything which might look like proselytization, Irish
immigrants were in a weak position. Too poor as a community to
provide schools entirely of their own, there were few self-respecting
parents willing to see their children attend Protestant establishments
(Wilson 1946 : 132). Bishop Andrew Scott, of Glasgow, put the case
forcibly enough to the 1835 Poor Law Commission:

> 'There are many charitable schools in Glasgow; but the teachers,
> being all Protestants, always mix up with the elements of education
> the principles of the Protestant religion. This necessarily excludes
> Roman Catholic children from attending these schools ... An
> attempt has been made to get schools for the education of these
> poor people, but that attempt, for want of funds, and the daily
> increasing poverty of the lower orders, will render it impossible for
> them to keep up schools for themselves. To improve the feelings,
> the conduct, the morals, and the loyalty of the Irish Roman Catholic
> poor in this country, it would be necessary that the Government
> should, at least, extend the same assistance for education as is
> granted to them in Ireland.' (p.106)

Such interests were not prominently voiced. That they were,
nevertheless, illustrative of a wider public debate and disagreement
over the role — not simply of the Protestant churches, but of the
reigning Anglican establishment — in the field of popular education,
seems beyond dispute. Why, some asked, 'should not the spirit of the
Repeal of the Test Act and of the Catholic Emancipation Act liberalise
the nation's schools?' (Bagley and Bagley 1969 : 10).

Matters progressed slowly in this respect. From 1836 to 1842,
Liverpool Corporation maintained (on its own initiative) 'two schools
open to, and plentifully attended by, children of all denominations
including Roman Catholics'. Despite the apparent popularity of this
so-called 'Irish system' among local parents (Irish and native),
however, established religious opposition ensured its abandonment
(Bagley and Bagley 1969 : 10). The time, it seemed, was not ripe for so
secular an experiment. From 1846, nevertheless, a Whig Government
decided to support and supervise the educational work of a wider
range of voluntary bodies including, for the first time, the work of the

Roman Catholic Poor Schools Committee (Bagley and Bagley 1969 : 4; Barnard 1961 : 105 (footnote)).

Following such a breakthrough, areas of Irish Catholic concentration — coincidentally or no — evinced a gradual increase both in the number of Catholic schools and in the number of Catholic teachers (Wilson 1946 : 135). By 1858, according to the Newcastle Commission, there were some 24,563 public schools in England of which 743 were Roman Catholic (catering for 60,000 pupils (HM Government 1846-61; Wilson 1946 : 135). Yet the real breakthrough came, arguably, with the 1870 Education Act — whereby the safeguards of conscience clause, state-subsidized education allowed at last for a relatively easy expansion of Roman Catholic Church school provision, along with a safer access for Catholic isolates to other educational establishments (Curtis 1963 : 281).

(iv) *Conclusions*

It would seem evident from this discussion that the opinions voiced and the issues raised over early Irish immigration were illustrative of the scope and ethos, not merely of existing social policy, but of contemporary social policy debate.

That the principal document dealing with Irish immigration in this period should have been an Appendix to a Poor Law Report, would seem significant in itself. The Poor Law (or Poor Laws before 1834) emerges as the single, most talked-about, statutory social provision — which is scarcely surprising, given that this was the only example, at this time, of an intendedly nationwide statutory social policy endeavour. Public health was as yet more a subject for public debate than one for concerted public action; while causes such as factory reform or popular education were still in their infancy as vehicles for government initiative. All this would seem confirmed, rather than revealed, by the documented response to early Irish immigration.

Nevertheless, the illustrative quality of Irish immigration runs deeper than this. Poor Law consternation over how best to deal with Irish fecklessness, for instance, seems little more than an emotive illustration of some of the ambiguities and dilemmas with which this supposedly modernized service was bound to have to contend. The maintenance, however attenuated, of the Laws of Settlement and Removal was not consistent with the needs of an industrializing economy for a mobile labour force. Central Poor Law authorities, moreover, were in no position effectively to dictate to local Boards of Guardians as to how they should respond on this or associated issues (see above pp.58-59). The wandering Irish menace would seem merely to have highlighted such problems.

For all this, the Irish were not likely, at the time, to be accounted a constructive influence upon contemporary social policy. That they should have been the subjects of, but never contributors to, current social policy debate would in itself seem indicative of the ethos of social policy in this period. The destitute were not expected to be consulted about the workings of the Poor Law — any more than were the dirty working classes expected to be consulted about possible public health legislation, or the ignorant masses expected to be consulted over the pros and cons of state-subsidized, popular education. Statutory social policy, and potential statutory social policy, was the perquisite of the voting, rate-paying community. It was theirs to decide upon and theirs, for the most part, to debate.

Hence it was that, when the Irish were accused of exploiting the Poor Law, it was the English rate-payer they were mainly supposed to be exploiting — not the potential English claimant for relief. Hence too the noticeable absence of any attempt systematically to measure the economic benefits of an Irish presence and set these off against any Poor Law expenditure incurred on this account. Members of the voting, rate-paying community were wont to assume a knowledge and understanding of the poor. Even had such knowledge not been assumed, moreover, it is difficult to see how any comprehensive, fact-finding enquiry could have been envisaged — given the dearth of both machinery and precedents for such an exercise.

Nevertheless, the fact that contemporary 'informed' opinion was in a sense so very uninformed, does complicate the consideration of our second and third lines of analysis: namely the extent to which statutory social policy proved on the one hand to be a problem-solving and, on the other, to be a problem-exacerbating resource in the context of Irish immigraiton. Both these themes have to be interpreted in relation to an effective public opinion which was not merely restricted in its interests but apparently mistaken in many of its beliefs.

How far the existence of an English Poor Law system might in fact have encouraged Irish immigration, and hence exacerbated the Irish problem, it is impossible to say. What is clear, however, is that the problem was not to be 'solved' simply by extending the same Poor Law system to Ireland. Informed opinion, in other words, was misguided to this extent. That the Poor Law might have solved some problems from the Irish immigrant's point of view or even, in the long term, from the occasional employer's point of view, was at best irrelevant and at worst a matter for concern. The Poor Law was supposed ideally to deter the able-bodied poor, not support them. Nor was it supposed, save in a narrow, negative sense, to contribute to the workings of the economy.

Other areas of incipient social policy possessed apparent problem-solving potential. Irish living quarters might in theory be rendered less noxious through public health regulation, just as Irish children might be gentled if only they went to school. In practice, however, the newcomers seemed the people least likely of any benefit from early moves towards public health or popular education. For all the consternation aroused by their presence, there was certainly no concerted effort to channel services explicitly in this direction.

Social policy, in other words, might be expected to tackle problems highlighted or exacerbated by an Irish presence, but it was not primarily expected to do so for the sake of the immigrants themselves — any more than for the sake of the native working classes themselves. If Irish families benefited directly or indirectly from any national social policy initiatives this was at best incidental and at worst a matter for annoyance and anxiety.

Furthermore, it might be argued that, had there not been such a public interest in the state of society, Irish immigration might perhaps have been less noticed and less resented — at least at national level. Yet if the workshop of the world was inclined to be a self-conscious, self-examining entity it was also, of course, a society bound both to attract and to benefit from additional cheap labour. It was understandable, therefore, that the Irish should have come — just as it was understandable that their coming should have been so publicly resented.

The most positive feature of this encounter would seem to lie, not in the response of contemporary social policy to Irish predicaments, nor in its response to immediate host-immigrant predicaments (given that the local working classes were scarcely more likely than the Irish to have their interests taken foremost into account), but in the apparent significance of a poor Irish presence for showing up the extremes of current social conditions — together with the limitations of contemporary statutory endeavour.

4

Jewish immigration
c. 1870-1911

The arrangement of this chapter corresponds, in outline at least, to the arrangement of the previous case-study. In other words, we shall begin by discussing the reported characteristics of the immigrants in question. Following this, we shall review the host society reaction to their presence before proceeding, more specifically, to assess the import of this situation in relation to ongoing social policy development. Nevertheless, while the approach might be similar, this will represent a more complex and ambitious exercise than the last, for two reasons.

To begin with, the documentation is far more extensive. More was recorded and subsequently commented upon in relation to Jewish immigration than was ever the case over the earlier Irish influx. At the same time, the scope of contemporary social policy has become both broader and more detailed in its pretensions. Despite the relative abundance of material on both sides, however, there have been few attempts, either at the time or since, to relate the one systematically to the other. Evidence in this respect, therefore, tends to be piecemeal and occasional, and derives more often than not from the efforts of the Jewish Board of Guardians in this period to act only alongside, never in competition with, statutory social policy in the drive to safeguard the interests of alien co-religionists.

This brings us on to the second point of difference with the Irish case. It is not sufficient, this time, to consider immigration simply in relation to its impact upon general public opinion and general, statutory, social policy. The presence, the influence and the activity of the Anglo-Jewish community in this sphere constitutes an additional dimension. As members of a self-conscious cultural and religious community only recently assured of full formal integration into English social and political life,[1] leading Jewish families were at once part of the English establishment and apart from it; at once part of (and in some respects at one with) general public opinion in its reaction to new Jewish immigration and apart from it — anxious to forestall or overcome native Gentile sentiment, both for their own sakes and for the sake of the newcomers. As members of a community long accustomed to provide for its own yet (as English taxpayers and politicians) with an interest also in public authority performance they were bound, perhaps, to view their responsibilities towards new Jewish immigrants very much in terms of trying to ensure a suitable statutory response to alien predicaments and of supplementing, in the meantime, proven statutory deficiencies in this respect.

Such at least was the stance consistently maintained by the Jewish Board of Guardians throughout this period. This being so, one can hardly embark upon a study of the interrelationships between new Jewish immigration and statutory social policy performance without frequent reference to the Jewish Board of Guardians in their role as self-appointed intermediaries and social policy stop-gaps in this context. In dealing with this aspect of the subject, I am much indebted to V.D. Lipman (1959) for his expert analysis of the policies and programmes of the Board from its inception. With so apt and comprehensive a commentary available I may be excused, perhaps, for referring so frequently to its contents.

(i) *The nature of the migration*

During the latter decades of the nineteenth century a series of events took place in Eastern Europe sufficient to prompt Jewish migration westwards on an unprecedented scale. 1870 saw the expulsion of Jews from the Russian border regions and the beginnings of systematic persecution of Jews in Rumania. The Russo-Turkish war cast its shadow in 1875-6. Widespread pogroms occurred in southern Russia in 1881-2. Jews were expelled from Russian cities such as Moscow and Kiev in 1890. In 1900 came the 'exodus' from Rumania and, in 1903, the Kishenov outrage. The Russo-Japanese war broke out in 1904 and the 1905 Russian Revolution left its own trail of pogroms. The happenings are too numerous and too well-documented elsewhere for further description in this context (see Gartner 1960). In response, Jews 'migrated by the million' (Gartner 1960 : 30) and many of them arrived in Britain.

While this country may have been 'but a backwater of immigration' compared to the 'golden land' of the United States, (Gartner 1960 : 15) the volume of East European immigration experienced from the 1870s until after the turn of the century was sufficient to strike, first, the native Jewish community and, later, the mass of English politicians as remarkable (Garrard 1971 : 23). Once again it is impossible to be exact about the numbers of immigrants settling in Britain. With no law (before 1905) to prevent or control the entry of aliens (Gainer 1972 : 23), estimates of the numbers coming in were usually based either on the Aliens Lists supplied by the Board of Trade or on the evidence of decennial Census returns. Both sources, inevitably, were limited.

Thus, while the Board of Trade might require every ship's master to furnish lists of all the aliens ferried to these shores (together with details of their trades or occupations), no satisfactory method was evolved for distinguishing between those effectively en route for elsewhere and those actually settling in Britain. [2] Census returns, moreover, tended to underestimate aliens — whether because of ignorance, inacessibility, or evasion — and could in any case only supply very crude ten-yearly comparisons as a basis for calculating annual inflow long after the event. [3]

There were two special grounds for uncertainty. In the first place Britain, or rather England, was if anything more important as a transmigration point than as a country of settlement for this population (Gartner 1960 : 17; Gainer 1972 : 2). In the second place, not all East European immigrants were Jewish. [4] Government records did not distinguish by religion (Garrard 1971 : 215) while, in the contemporary public mind, 'immigrant' and 'Jew' were roughly synonymous expressions (Gainer 1972 : 3).

Yet, for what they are worth, the Board of Trade's estimates suggest a fairly close correlation between events in Eastern Europe and the numbers of immigrants subsequently entering this country. Large numbers began to arrive in the 1870s, but the first real peak in such immigration seems to have occurred in 1881-3 with an estimated net influx of 5-6,000 aliens per annum. Following this, numbers steadied down to around 2-3,000 per annum until the second great upsurge of 1891 — during which year over 7,000 persons were believed to have settled in England. A subsequent annual rate of 2-3,000 was apparently trebled from 1899 to 1902, while the inflow for 1905 and 1906 seemed to break all records.[5]

Census returns seem to confirm this trend. From a recorded population of 100,638 Russian, Russo-Polish, and Rumanian aliens in England and Wales in 1871, the figure rises to 118,031 in 1881, 198,113 in 1891, 247,758 in 1901, and 284,830 by 1911, by which time they accounted for some 0.8 per cent of the total population.[6] Hardly a massive proportion, if one compares it with the Irish presence at the close of the last period in question (see above, p.44).

Why did they come? At first sight the answer seems self-evident: they came because they were pushed. Whether or not all the emigrés were fleeing actual persecution in Eastern Europe, they were virtually all refugees from what had come to seem intolerable political, social, and economic conditions. Yet this does not in itself explain why they came to Britain, or why Britain came in this period to harbour more East European immigrants than any other country except the United States of America. Was it simply in response to the shining vista of England as 'the haven and protector of freedom?' (Gartner 1960 : 28).

In part this was undoubtedly true. The country's tradition of asylum was by now a hallowed one and entrenched, for instance, as part of the essence of current Liberal Party dogma. The rather less altruistic stance of the English working man, however, — together with the agitation leading up to the *Aliens Act* of 1905 — helped gradually to tarnish this image (Gartner 1960 : 28). More important, perhaps, was the existence of a native Jewish community in England: a community which had not only managed to survive, but seemingly to flourish. Such a presence already established, offered not only general encouragement but the possibility of active assistance for new arrivals — both in the form of general community supports and as a result of inter-family connections.

There were other, more mundane, considerations nevertheless. As with the Irish before them, much could depend on where the ferry-boats would take you, at what cost. In this case the effects of cut-throat competition between companies was to enhance the immediate attractiveness of Britain as the optimum staging-post between East Europe and America. During the 'Atlantic Rate War' of 1902-1904, the fare from England to America was slashed from £6.10s. to £2, while the fare from *Germany* to America remained at 120 marks, (i.e. just under £6).[7] Naturally 'a torrent of emigrants rushed to England to seize the opportunity' (Gartner 1960 : 36) and naturally, too, not all of them went on to America.

Again, even more so than was the case with the Irish (see above p.46), ferry-boat routes helped to influence the pattern of immigrant settlement in Britain. Most of the immigrant ships docked in London (in this case), and between 1881 and 1905 roughly 60 per cent of all aliens in England lived in London. Only 12 per cent lived in Lancashire (mostly in Manchester) and a mere 7 per cent were to be found in Yorkshire (mostly in Leeds) (Gartner 1960 : 3), each of these latter cases being a response, presumably, to the pull of already established Jewish populations. Within London, moreover, most of the immigrants were to be found in the East End and, within the East End, in the Metropolitan Borough of Stepney. In 1901 some 18.2 per cent of Stepney's population was alien and the borough housed the largest immigrant population in the country.[8]

To some extent, such a concentration was no more than a product of immigrant inertia and ignorance. Before 1905 there were no guide-books for Russian immigrants to inform them about Britain as a whole (Gartner 1960 : 27). London was where they arrived and London was where they tended to stay. If an incoming family possessed any advance information, this was as likely as not to be in the form of a personal contact, or address. Such a contact or address would usually be in London. Virtually all of the Russian immigrants were Jewish. Whitechapel was the centre of a long-established Jewish community. It was hardly surprising, therefore, that Russian Jewish immigrants should have 'gravitated to East London as to a second home' (Gainer 1972 : 5).

There were, moreover, sound material advantages to be gained from settling in the East End. As England's largest established Jewish community, it offered the best chance, not merely of fellow-feeling and religious support, but also of gainful employment. 'Immigrant trades' were expanding here and immigrant labour was in consequent demand (Gartner 1960 : 63).

The nature and notoriety of the immigrant trades throws some light both on the social and economic background of the newcomers and on their position in English society. This was a migration of townsfolk rather than peasants: yet they were townsfolk without major resources either in the form of industrial skills or accumulated capital. Having been barred, for the most part, from membership of skilled trades and the professions in Eastern Europe, they came frequently with a background of petty trading or with only superficial vocational skills. Very few of them had ever worked in a factory. When the Poor Jews'

Temporary Shelter made its prolonged inquiry into the callings of its lodgers, it found 29 per cent (out of over 9,000 respondents) had formerly made garments of some sort; 23 per cent had been in 'trade and commerce'; 9 per cent had made boots and shoes; 7 per cent had been carpenters, and 2 per cent had been in agriculture (Gartner 1960 : 57-8).

Where were they to fit in an English, industrialized, already partly unionized, economy? Some of the old trades — such as peddling, hawking, and (to a limited extent) shopkeeping — continued as before (Gartner 1960 : 58-61). What became known as the 'immigrant trades' however were those which depended on workshop, rather than upon factory, production. Workshops drew on the pool of immigrant and female labour and, by subdividing the work process more and more, could utilize what skills were possessed (together with the immigrants' willingness to work long hours for small return) without being hampered by language difficulties or culture shock. Pre-eminently this was true of the tailoring trade (armed with Isaac Singer's sewing machine) (Gartner 1960 : 84-93). It was less and less true of the boot and shoe trade, or of the cigar and cigarette trade — as both of these became increasingly factory oriented.

These then were some of the occupational characteristics. In a way they helped both to compensate for, and to emphasize, the social distinctiveness of the Jewish immigrant community. Unlike the Irish before them, they were technically foreigners. Over and above this, however, linguistic and cultural differences separating the immigrant from the native population were in this case much more pronounced (Gartner 1960 : 73-6).[9]

> 'Immigrant Jewry formed a society apart, with standards derived from other sources than England. In the first generation of immigrant settlement there was a great deal of mutual avoidance; even given good will on both sides, there was so little common ground between the immigrant Jew and his neighbour that it could not have been otherwise.' (Gartner 1960 : 166)

Such a clear, group identity was the product of religion and culture rather than of nationality in the technical sense. The newcomers were all Jews — not all Russians or all Poles or all Rumanians — together. They were, moreover, all immigrant Jews, a characteristic which helped to set them apart, not simply from English society in general, but from Anglo-Jewry as well.

As in the case of Irish Roman Catholicism (see above, p.47), the religious beliefs and practices of the immigrants coincided none too closely with those of their so-called co-religionists already established in this country. Immigrant religious leaders in this case fought to protect and uphold orthodox 'fundamental' Judaism in the new country — against the insidious threat of English Jewry's 'Victorian Compromise' (Gartner 1960 : Ch. 7). Such was the laxity and degeneracy of English Jewry, in the newcomers' eyes, that, 'to our great regret, the foundations of our law have become weakened, and the whole structure of Religion is threatened' (Gartner 1960 : 210). Such strictures were bound, of course, to provoke a counter-reaction.

So purist an approach, at least among the spiritual spokesmen for immigrant Jewry, served if anything to exaggerate the extent to which Judaism could amount, in this context, not simply to a religion but to a highly distinctive way of life. Quite apart from their tendency to patronize what were by Anglo-Jewish standards, 'primitive' places of worship (Gartner 1960 : Ch. 7), the immigrants shared a general cultural background which was, apparently, 'almost wholly Jewish, unmixed with Russian or Polish Gentile components, and it was compounded of Jewish folk elements and normative rabbinic Judaism' (Gartner 1960 : 242). They spoke, not only Russian or Polish, but Yiddish.

(ii) *Host society reaction*

Compared to the earlier Irish case, native reaction to this 'alien horde' is interesting on several counts. To begin with, the immigrants were Jewish and they were refugees. No one who was at all self-conscious on this score would want to be accused either of anti-semitism or of an unwillingness to offer asylum to the genuinely persecuted. Negative observations, particularly by politicians or self-appointed public leaders, tended, therefore, to be couched in careful, or at least ambivalent, terms. Never let it be said that they were against Jews as such, or against refugees as such. This did not of course prevent damning, condemnatory remarks being expressed. It merely ensured that these were mostly prefaced or qualified by some 'enlightened' declaration and that they were usually countered by some sort of Liberal response.

The fact that this immigration was the subject of intense, recurrent, political debate is in itself a point of interest. Perhaps because of the political climate and the make-up of the voting public; perhaps because these refugees were aliens; it was possible in this case to campaign for increased statutory control over the numbers and categories of such people entering the country. Ageing imperial Britain, with its future unsure and its manpower seemingly under pressure, seemed ill-inclined to accept the possibility of unending, indiscriminate, immigration. The existence and the force of such an anti-immigration campaign helped undoubtedly to polarize as well as to publicize opinions about those East European immigrants already present.

Against this background, the fact that the newcomers tended to concentrate conspicuously in the East End of London (together with parts of Manchester and Leeds), must have rendered their presence only the more remarkable in relation to the total numbers of immigrants involved. There was, nevertheless, a striking similarity to be observed between the remarks passed about these new Jews and those previously exchanged in public about the Irish presence. Notwithstanding any ongoing shifts in the make-up or management of British society, in other words, and notwithstanding the obvious differences of background, culture, and economic attributes of these two incoming groups; native, publicized, reaction to their presence as low-status outsiders would seem to have been remarkably consistent.

There is, nevertheless, one special feature to take into account. The presence, the efforts, and the ideas of what turned out to be a well-organized and articulate native Jewish community in response to the new arrivals was at once an important part of effective public opinion and an influence upon it. To compare this performance with the less prominent role played by English Roman Catholicism in respect of Irish immigration would be, perhaps, to compare the efforts of a mere minority church with the strivings of a self-conscious, cultural community (see above, p.62). Be this as it may, it would seem wise in this account to distinguish, specifically, between the general native and the Jewish native reaction. We will deal with the general reaction first.

The themes upon which opinions were exchanged about the newcomers were largely the same, writ large, as those aired earlier over Irish immigration: public health and morals; standards of living; employment conditions and wage-levels; law and order. There were one or two new themes however: principally housing and education. Such a broadening of the areas for debate can be looked at from two points of view. In the first place one can see this as a consequence of the state's being expected to exercise a responsibility in more and more areas of social life. There were more areas, therefore, for necessary or profitable discussion. In the second place, and allied to this, one can interpret the trend in terms of the growing political importance of the common man: of his vote and therefore of his interests. Housing conditions in the East End were, *par excellence*, a subject of popular grievance and concern such as was far removed from the propertied public health unease of the earlier nineteenth century.

How far such reaction might have built up had not the immigrants been so visible and had they not seemed so drastically different from the native population, it is impossible to say. As it was, contrasts of language, dress, and custom between English and Alien were only heightened and rendered the more obvious, and off-putting, by the tendency of the newcomers to crowd together — noticeably in the East End. Such a massing of strangers so strange as this was enough, in itself, to prompt a fearful, defensive reaction. The English way of life — whatever that might be — seemed under threat.

'Now there is no end of them in Whitechapel, Mile End. It is Jerusalem.' (HM Government 1902-3 : 298)

'There are some streets you may go through and hardly know you are in England.'[10]

' ... the presence, especially in London, of thousands of foreign-faced men and women crowding into the dense parts of the poorer quarters of the great city does not so much anger our own people as it saddens them. Quite apart from other questions, their alien looks, habits and language, combined with their remarkable fecundity, .tenacity and money-getting gift, make them a ceaseless weight upon the poor amongst whom they live.' (White 1892 : 87-8)

Mere strangeness seemed, more often than not, to go with other, more specific, complaints. Like that of the Irish earlier, this was the strangeness of the less-civilized, the degrading, the unclean, and the immoral.

' ... there is an aspect, a moral aspect, to this competition ... The alien, notwithstanding many virtues, seems to bring a sort of social contagion with him, which has the effect of seriously deteriorating the life of those of our own people who are compelled to be his neighbour. It is a painful thing to write, but truth compels the statement, that wherever the foreigner comes in any number, the neighbourhood in which he settles speedily drops in tone, in character, and morals. It can be seen most distinctly in those districts in London where the alien is to be found in large numbers.' (White 1892 : 91)

The threat this constituted to the already doubtful condition of the native working classes seemed unmistakable to many. The Earl of Meath was scarcely alone in his conviction that

'if you desire to improve the condition of the working classes of this country ... we must ... do something to prevent this country from becoming the dust heap of Europe.'[11]

If nothing was done, then prolonged association — and perhaps inter-marriage — with the alien could only mean:

'that those working classes would become, to a great extent non-English in character, and that, both in physique and in moral and social customs, they had fallen below our present by no means elevated standard.'[12]

The condition of the people — already a matter of some public concern — was, in other words, being subjected to additional, unnecessary risks. Interestingly enough, the Irish could by now be accounted as part of the people rather than as outsiders themselves — at least in the face of a Jewish invasion. In the words of an East End midwife in 1902:

'I have had about 16 years connection with the Whitechapel Union, and I never met among the Irish people so much coarseness as I have met among these ... '

'Samuel Street ... used to be a street occupied by poor English and Irish people. In the afternoons you would see the steps inside cleaned and the women with their clean white aprons sit in summer time inside the doors, perhaps at needlework with their little children about. Now it is a seething mass of refuse and filth, ... and the stench from the refuse and the filth is disgraceful.' (HM Government 1902-3 : 310)

It was Jewish rather than Irish dirtiness and lack of elementary hygiene which were now felt to constitute a special threat to public health. Whitechapel had hardly been noted for its cleanliness and healthiness before (Hobson 1892 : 59), but even by Whitechapel standards the Jew who threw out offal in his yard, put down sand instead of carpets on his floors, stopped up his fireplaces and 'will not introduce any fresh air' into his house, seemed a particular menace (HM Government 1902-3 : par. 1724).

With such charges commonplace it was remarkable, perhaps, that the death rate in such areas was not noticeably increased by the Jewish presence. If anything, indeed, the aliens seemed to have been more healthy on average than their Gentile counterparts. Only in the incidence of TB and other such complaints as cramped, unhealthy working conditions were likely to foster, did the alien population seem more than usually hard hit (Gartner 1960 : 159-62).

Apart from lowering the tone and threatening the sanitary standards, however, the Jews were accused of aggravating, if not creating, a local housing shortage. Their presence served apparently to drive up rent levels, drive out the native population, and increase the overall rate of overcrowding in the districts where they concentrated. This was stronger stuff than had ever been alleged against the Irish in the first half of the nineteenth century. Yet decent housing, as a right of citizenship and a prerequisite for any satisfactory condition of the people was, even by the turn of the century, still a fairly tentative idea.

That the newcomers' presence had served to increase rents seemed beyond dispute. Indeed the menace seemed twofold. On the one hand immigrant tenants seemed prepared to pay exorbitant rents such as no native houshold felt able to afford. On the other hand it was immigrant landlords, apparently, who were far and away the most ruthless racketeers:

'a good deal of house property has lately changed hands, and been bought up — purely as an investment — by the shrewder and wealthier among the foreigners themselves.' (Lewis 1900 : 17)

'These men come over here and they save a little money and they live in the worst style imaginable, and they get these houses and let them in tenements, and then they buy the property and get £100 or £50, and they mortgage it. They do not pay the mortgage, it is the incoming tenant who has to pay the mortgage.' (HM Government 1902-3 : 309) 'people cannot afford to pay the exorbitant rents that very many of these foreign landlords charge.' (HM Government 1902-3 : 310)

English landlords were not blind to this situation, of course, nor to the possibilities it held out for themselves:

'It is significant that some East End landlords, and not Jewish ones only, have publicly announced that they will not accept Christian tenants.' (HM Government 1902-3 : 230)

Even where they did not go so far as this, landlords were not above raising their rents on the explicit grounds that, if native households wouldn't pay, then there were plenty of immigrants who would:

'There is a street in Mile End ... the houses of which were ... put up for sale ... the rents when sold were 7s 6d per week, after the purchase ... the rents were raised to 15s per week. The mother of a gentleman I know well went after one ... she was informed, ''We do not want English, these are for the foreigners.' (HM Government 1902-3 : 287)

It was not greater wealth, of course, which enabled immigrant tenants to meet the higher rents. Dependent, for the most part, on remaining within the East End of London, in areas whose housing shortages were already pronounced, they had virtually no choice. The least mobile and most vulnerable section of the local population, they had somehow to pay whatever was demanded. The consequences — both of the housing shortage and of the rents charged — were scarcely surprising. Immigrants could pay the high rents, it was alleged, only because 'they were willing to herd together like swine' (Gainer 1972 : 43). Allegations of immigrant overcrowding were legion:

'I think it is an invariable rule in each of the smaller houses ... there is a family in each room.' (HM Government 1902-3 : 310)

Nor was this all:

'It appears they sleep in their beds at night and in the daytime they let them out to some bakers to sleep.' (HM Government 1902-3 : par. 9420)

Given such behaviour, native residents were gradually driven out as much, it seemed, by revulsion from close proximity with the immigrants as by rents which they could not afford. Either way, the process was allegedly dramatic:

'the inhabitants of whole streets in some cases have been turned out to make room for the foreigners, a large percentage in others, and so on more or less until you can scarcely find a street into which the alien has not penetrated.' (HM Government 1902-3 : 286)

Naturally enough this did not go unmarked or unprotested. The *Eastern Post* of 31 August, 1901 voiced what would seem to have been a popular indignation over the fact that:

'Englishmen were compelled to leave their own districts to make way for the scrapings of Russia and Poland.' (Gainer 1972 : 43)

To many, there seemed to be 'nothing but the English going out and the Jews coming in' (HM Government 1902-3 : par. 2535-8).

Such opinions were entirely in keeping with those held about the aliens as interlopers in the labour market. In this last respect, however, their presence was held to be especially pernicious, the more so since its significance seemed double-edged, if not self-contradictory. On the one hand the newcomers were accused of being a horde of unprincipled paupers, here to take advantage of whatever charities might exist. On the other hand they seemed to constitute an unending supply of cheap labour, here to undercut native wages and drive the Englishman out of his job. The dichotomy of judgement was, if anything, even more pronounced in this than it had been in the Irish case.

Declarations on the first score were not hard to come across. Whitechapel, so a parliamentary candidate alleged in 1906 (reported in the *East London Observer* on January 6, 1906):

'was never destined to become a foreign pauper settlement. It is intolerable that we should have unblushingly dumped down among us the very scum of the unhealthiest of continental nations.' (Garrard 1971 : 60)

Nevertheless it was the second score which seemed the more urgent in this case. Whereas the Irish had been regarded as a more or less straightforward case of low value — low price manual labour, the Jews impressed many observers as being a rather different, more singular, kettle of fish. On arrival, they represented a pool of cheap labour, not because they did not aspire beyond the lowest forms of life (as was alleged of the Irish), but because they held no opening to be too meagre as a starting point for self-advancement. Such at least was their ascribed reputation. The Webbs put the case succinctly. Whereas the Anglo Saxon artisan could be expected to demand fairly high minimum conditions of employment and whereas negroes could be expected to evince a fairly low maximum with regard to effort, the Jew, they argued, was different from both of these:

> 'the Jew ... is unique in possessing neither a minimum nor a maximum; he will accept the lowest terms rather than remain out of employment; as he rises in the world new wants stimulate him to increased intensity of effort, and no amount of income causes him to slacken his indefatigable activity.' (Webb and Webb 1920 : 698, footnote)

The notion of the alien Jew as the archetypal economic man was hardly likely to boost his popularity — however much he might seem to epitomize and vindicate the self-help creed propounded so relentlessly by the middle classes of nineteenth century Britain. Crowded into those very parts of London where conditions of employment seemed most desperate (according to Booth) and associated, furthermore, with the notorious sweated trades, they stood for unfair, unwholesome competition and seemed a menace to the native working man.[13]

Nor were these merely popular, local, sentiments. In the hands of politicians and economists of the day, they became a closely reasoned argument. J.A. Hobson, writing in 1892 on *Problems of Poverty*, put the case with notable precision:

> 'From the point of view of the old Political Economy, they are the very people to be encouraged, for they turn out the largest quality of wealth at the lowest cost of production.'

> 'But if we consider it is sound national policy to pay regard to the welfare of all classes engaged in producing this wealth, we may regard this foreign immigration in quite another light. The very virtues just enumerated are the chief faults we have to find with the foreign Jew. Just because he is willing and able to work so hard for so little pay ... because he can surpass in skill, industry and adaptability the native Londoner, the foreign Jew is such a terrible competitor. He is the nearest approach to the ideal ''economic'' man, the ''fittest'' person to survive in trade competition.' (Hobson 1892 : 59-60)

The more the state had regard to the well-being of the populace, in other words, as opposed to the efficacy of business competition as an end in itself, then the less readily could it tolerate an influx of what should, by mid-Victorian standards, have been reckoned ideal working men. Now it seemed, their presence could only undermine, if not negate, any hard-won advances the working classes might have made in terms of wages or living conditions.

'The insistence of the poorer working classes, under the stimulus of new-felt wants, the growing enlightenment of public opinion, have slowly and gradually won, even for the poorer workers in English cities, some small advance in material comfort ... Turn a few ship-loads of Polish Jews upon any of these districts, and they will and must in the struggle for life destroy the whole of this ... when the struggle is between those accustomed to a higher and those accustomed to a lower, standard of life, the latter can obviously oust the former and take their work. Just as a base currency drives out of circulation a pure currency, so does a lower standard of comfort drive out a higher one.' (Hobson 1892 : 61)

Or again:

'The inflow of a comparatively small number of foreigners into a neighbourhood where much of the work is low-skilled and irregular, will often produce an effect which seems quite out of proportion to the actual numbers of the invaders. Where work is slack and diffi-cult to get, a very small addition of low-living foreigners will cause a perceptible fall in the entire wages of the neighbourhood in the employments which their competition affects.' (Hobson 1892 : 61)

If he was not actually displaced from his job, in other words, the English worker was likely to find himself in receipt of lower wages as a result of alien competition. In essence, of course, this was no different from the case made out earlier against the Irish presence. This time, however, a much more powerful, ostensible, concern for the well-being of the masses, together with a much more powerful regard for popular sentiment, added force and urgency to the arguments. That this might seem no more than a capitulation to working-class voting power, was freely admitted by one writer at least:

'The opinion that we should impose some legislative restrictions upon the free immigration of destitute aliens is naturally strongest among the working classes ... who find the rate of wages for

Unskilled Labour sensibly reduced by the competition of foreigners more frugal and certainly more sober than themselves. On the face of it, that is a selfish and almost an ignoble motive. But we must remember, in the first place, that we have made the working-men our masters, and that through their parliamentary representatives, whom they are able to treat as mere delegates, they have the power of giving effect to their views.' (Jeyes 1892 : 179-80)

Nevertheless, he declared, not all the parliamentary supporters of aliens control regulations could be accused of 'mere popularity-hunting'. Some sincerely-held principles were in evidence (Jeyes 1892 : 180).

Be this as it may, it was never actually proved, of course, that the economic effects of an alien presence were such as were so freely described, either in the East End or anywhere else. Given the desperate economic plight of most of the working classes in the areas of immigrant settlement it seemed, once again, to be a case of self-evident truths being exchanged — as much, this time, by the working man as by his political mouthpieces.

Against such a backcloth it was of little avail, seemingly, for others to reiterate cherished Liberal ideals about the moral impossibility of refusing admittance to poor refugees, above all poor Jewish refugees,[14] and about the importance of free trade, in men just as in materials. So far as local, competitor, opinion was concerned, such affirmations much have seemed of doubtful relevance. Indeed, they could seem of doubtful relevance in this case even to those who were normally inclined to regard successive immigration as having hitherto been the key to national success. 'At all events', remarked William Cunningham in 1897, 'we have not much to gain from imitating the institutions of the Polish Jews'. (1969 : 266). Even the attempts of some parliamentarians to demonstrate at least the illogicality of the charges made against the newcomer seem largely to have fallen upon deaf ears. Thus Earl Grey's assertion that:

'If the alien is a public charge it is because he is out of employment: and therefore that he does not displace a British workman. If he displaces a British workman he cannot be a public charge.'[15]

was more a case of impeccable logic than one of political force. Public opinion wanted, and perhaps needed, to have it both ways.

Issues concerning the alien and the law, or public order, brought forth comparably mixed, contradictory, reactions. By local standards at least, the new Jews of the East End had to be accounted exceptionally law-abiding citizens. However much they might be blamed for rendering the 'moral conditions of our cities graver, more menacing and more difficult in every sense',[16] they were, nevertheless, not prone to engage in crime — and even won acclaim in some quarters for cleaning up some of the worst streets in East London by their mere arrival (Gainer 1972 : 52). Yet they were associated in the popular mind at any rate with two particularly unwholesome offences: perjury and the adulteration of food-stuffs (Gainer 1972 : 53). For all their law-abiding appearances, in other words, the characteristics of the immigrant as a morally destructive agent seemed confirmed by the nature of such misdemeanours as he was associated with. Swindling, duplicity, and 'crawlin' under 'and ways' seemed of a piece with his overall supposed degeneracy and degradation (Russell & Lewis 1900 : 14).

Rather more to the point, perhaps, in an age of burgeoning trades union activity and of mass political representation, was the aliens' potential as an organized, working-class force. Yet here again the judgements were ambivalent. Like the Irish before them, the Jews were doomed to be rated poor trades unionists. As a wage-undercutting riff-raff, if nothing worse, they were declared impossible to organize and, indeed, to constitute a serious threat to English trades union organization. The reason for this seemed obvious:

> 'Englishmen who belong to the same trade have a notion that they ought to stand by one another in the interests of all ... That is why, in a strike, decent and generally amiable men will bully and mal-treat the "blacklegs" and the "knobsticks" and the "scallywags" ... Now these resident aliens in London are the "blacklegs" and the "knobstick" and the "scallywags" of the Unskilled Labour market. They will do more work for less wages than their English rivals; they submit without grumbling to the petty tyrannies of the overseer and the mean exactions of the sweater; they join no Trade Union.' (Jeyes 1892 : 180-81)

Few efforts were made, however, to encourage the aliens to join English trades unions. On the contrary it was those unions who felt themselves most affected by the newcomers' presence (the National Union of Boot and Shoe Operatives for instance) who were most vociferous in their demands — not for the recruitment of immigrant fellow tradesmen, but for a simple ban on any further such immigration. Given such rejection, it was scarcely surprising that Jewish unions for Jewish trades should become the order of the day — in so far as these could survive at all with such 'unpromising' material (see Finestein 1971; Gainer 1972 : 30-31; Garrard 1971 : Ch. 9; Fishman 1975 : 137-8, 169 *et seq*.).

Yet however spineless the Jewish workman may have been adjudged from a trades union point of view, the newcomers were assumed, nevertheless, to harbour other, more insidious or disruptive, political ideas. Unlike the Irish before them, it was not violence that these immigrants were associated with so much as wild, dangerous beliefs. Anarchism and socialism had originated on the European continent. European refugees, therefore, were often vaguely supposed to be one or the other or both. Certainly a number of Jewish socialists and anarchists were imported — along with a larger number of non-Jewish fellow-thinkers. This was hardly sufficient reason in itself, however, for the *Standard's* assertion in 1901 that there was 'a huge Anarchist colony' in East London and that the East End anarchist was 'almost invariably a Jewish immigrant' (Gainer 1972 : 105).

Nevertheless, the fact that Jewish socialist and anarchist clubs did exist in the East End could only have confirmed native suspicion and unease. Not only did it seem that the aliens had come to England deliberately:

'to strengthen that spirit of discontent and disorder on which the agitators live and batten, and which in time may pollute the ancient constitutional liberalism of England with the visionary violence of Continental Socialism.' (Jeyes 1892 : 189)

but Jewish revolutionary societies were known to:

'have papers of their own circulated among themselves, written in Yiddish, breathing the vilest political sentiments — Nihilism of the most outrageous description.' (Wilkins 1892 : 47-8)

Once again, this was stronger stuff than anything which had been alleged about the Irish. In part, however, it seemed no more than an extension of a deeper unease. To contemporary observers the Jews were not merely alien in a technical sense. They represented an extreme of otherness such as not only offended local social and religious susceptibilities but gave rise to something approaching panic among a public already on the defensive about their own and the country's prospects. The newcomer was not only strange and, by local standards, unfeelingly irreligious. He was also thought to be clever.

Thus it was not simply a question of the immigrants' flouting local custom ('I think that foreigners, if they come here, should pay some respect to our Sabbath' (HM Government 1902-3 : 297), but of the alien's:

> 'superior calculating intellect, which is a national heritage ... used unsparingly to enable him to take advantage of every weakness, folly and vice of the society in which he lives.' (Hobson 1892 : 60)

It was against this background that the noticeable infiltration of Jewish immigrant children into London's elementary schools could strike contemporary opinion not merely as a liberty, but as supremely ironic:

> 'Thus those of us who are the workers have to assist to educate those who by and by will be in the labour market contending against our own children for the wherewithal to exist.' (HM Government 1902-3 : 286)

The likely outcome of such eventual competition seemed clear enough.

All in all, therefore, the Jewish immigrant was as much feared as disliked by a public opinion partly composed of, and very much mindful of, popular local sentiment. Everywhere they went, the newcomers seemed able to drive out the natives, be this from their houses, their churches (HM Government 1902-3 : 286), their jobs or even their children's schools (see below pp.00-00), if only indirectly. This too in an age when the state was expected to exercise a fairly composite responsibility over domestic affairs and when government was supposed to be nominally answerable to popular complaint.

No one, of course, expressed an opposition to the presence of Jews as such — not in writing, at least, and not at national level. Rather their concern centred on the perceived characteristics of destitute aliens who may or may not be (but for the most part were) of the Jewish religion. Nor was there much evidence of any widespread inclination to lump all Jews — poor Jews and rich Jews; native and new Jews — together. The Socialist Democratic Federation was swimming against the tide, somewhat, when it singled out rich rather than poor Jewry as the target for concern[17] Like so many others of course the Federation had:

'no feeling against Jews as Jews ... but as nefarious capitalists and poisoners of the wells of public information, we denounce them. It would be easy enough to get up a capitalist Jew-bait here in London, if we wish to do so, and the proletarian Jews would gladly help us.' (Silberner 1952 : 43)

For the most part, however, it was immigrant (mostly poor) as opposed to native (mostly better-off) Jewry which struck contemporary opinion — both local and national — as proper targets for concern. As one informant put it to the Royal Commission on Alien Immigration:

'I am not speaking of English Jewish people. Our English Jewish people are comfortable, and we can do with them.' (p.298)

Or again:

'It has been said that "every nation has the Jew whom it deserves". We have, then, our native English Jews — a better, a sturdier stock, a more desirable body of fellow-citizens, it would not be easy to find. They have their faults, but they are English to the core. In patriotism they are not inferior to any of us Gentiles.' (Jeyes 1892 : 187-8)

These were, perhaps, the sort of sentiments which the Anglo-Jewish community was not necessarily unpleased to hear. Native Jewry was in a delicate and a difficult position. Faced with an influx of destitute Jewish refugees from what could only be described as more primitive circumstances than their own, it was moved, on the one hand, notably to assist these unfortunates 'for the sake of the Name' and, on the other hand, to be highly nervous of the possible harm such an influx of destitutes might exert upon its own, hard-won position.

On the one hand therefore there was the abundance of Jewish charitable organizations geared to assist the newcomer (among others) through all manner of predicaments while, on the other, there was the constant drive to ensure that as many as possible of these aliens might either de diverted from coming to England at all or else be assisted to move on elsewhere as rapidly as it could be arranged. An influx of co-religionists, especially of primitive co-religionists (see above pp.71-72) was manifestly not an unmixed blessing.

The ambivalence of response was often all too apparent. While numerous Jewish charities existed — and while the Jewish Board of Guardians had been established expressly, in 1859, for the relief of the 'strange poor' (Lipman 1959 : 1) — one provision normally in operation throughout the Anglo-Jewish charities required six months' residence in England in order to qualify any applicant for Jewish relief.[18] There were to be no grounds for accusing the resident Jewish community of trying to encourage fellow-Jews to come and settle in this country.

Against such a backcloth, the Poor Jews' Temporary Shelter opened to a troublesome start in 1885: even though it confined its attentions to providing bed and board for new arrivals, allowed no one to remain beyond fourteen days, and eschewed any giving of cash relief. For a while it even imposed a labour test upon every able-bodied person; but the Jewish Board of Guardians was not sufficiently impressed — or at least not sufficiently reassured — as to afford recognition to the Shelter for some fifteen years (Gartner 1960 : 53-4). The Guardians' reluctance was understandable. The Shelter could seem an irresponsible enticement to wandering refugees: precisely what the Guardians were seeking to avoid from both a practical and a public relations point of view. They were not alone in their judgement:

> 'the ... Poor Jews' Temporary Shelter ... has fallen into considerable disfavour, even in the community to which it belongs, because, rightly or wrongly, it is believed to attract pauper immigrants to this country. Nor could we be surprised if this were the case, since in 1888 it "provided board and lodging for a period of from one to fourteen days to 1,322 homeless immigrants!' " (Jeyes 1892 : 177)

The Guardians, along with others, were more alive to the importance of encouraging Jews either to remain in their homelands or else to migrate on elsewhere from Britain. Russian Jews, for instance, ought ideally to put their faith in political emancipation in Russia rather than in flight across Europe. Destitute immigrants who did not seem to be genuine victims of persuasion might even be repatriated (prior to the Russian pogroms of 1905) — provided they were known still to have friends or relatives in the home country who might assist them (Lipman 1959 : 94-6). If they were truly bent on flight, however, then such immigrants ought at least to be speeded towards America — provided American Jews 'did not object too vehemently' (Gartner 1960 : 25, 51). The Atlantic Rate War at least gave the Guardians, along with numerous other emigration societies, a welcome chance to clear their books during the bargain years of 1902-04 (Gartner 1960 : 36). Once again, their stance did not go altogether unappreciated:

'the system of charitable relief established by the Jewish Board of
Guardians ... is purely beneficient, that part, at least, which consists
in sending back to their own countries those newcomers who could
not pick up a living here, and in passing others on to America.'
(Jeyes 1892 : 175-6)

The idea of encouraging poor Jews to emigrate elsewhere — and
thereby ease both the financial and social strains on the resident
Anglo-Jewish community — was not really a new one (Gartner 1960 :
49). Nevertheless the efforts of 'such nineteenth century groups as the
Jews' Emigration Society, the Emigration Committee of the Jewish
Board of Guardians, together with the Bevis Marks synagogue' were
especially prominent in this period (Gartner 1960 : 49-50).

It was not charitable aid which was begrudged, therefore, so much
as permanent mass settlement which was feared. English Jewry had
been first to appreciate the possible impact of East European
migration (see above p.68); to argue the case for some restriction of
undesirable immigration (Gartner 1960 : 55); and to sense the
possible social effects for themselves of unthinking immigration
concentrations in the East End. In the words of the *Jewish Chronicle*
on September 28, 1888:

'If poor Jews will persist in appropriating whole streets to themselves
in the same district ... drawing to their peculiarities of dress, of
language and of manner, the attention which they might otherwise
escape, can there be any wonder that the vulgar prejudices of which
they are the objects should be kept alive and strengthened. What
can the untutored, unthinking denizen of the East End believe in
the face of such facts but that the Jew is an alien in every sense of the
word.' (Garrard 1971 : 49-50)

Even so, the bulk of Anglo-Jewish opinion was not necessarily behind
the Rothschilds and other leading families in their conviction that no
material support, other than re-emigration assistance, should be
offered to poor Jewish immigrants on their arrival. Indeed there were
those, particularly the older generation of Dutch and other artisans
resident in the immigrant areas and competing with the newcomers in
the same areas of trade, who were inclined to go even further. Fresh
immigration, they argued, ought positively to be curtailed — not
merely discouraged (Gartner 1960 : 54). Set against this stance, the
Poor Jews' Temporary Shelter was expressive of an opposite point of

view. Conventional Anglo-Jewish support for the principle of an open door on immigration could have little meaning, so this group argued, so long as it was not backed up by at least minimal provisions to aid and comfort destitutes upon their arrival in this country (Gartner 1960 : 51-4). There would be many quick to take advantage of the newcomers' ignorance and vulnerability (Gartner 1960 : 36-7). Anglo-Jewry ought at least to make a gesture in the opposite direction.

Such differences of opinion could not speedily be resolved. Nevertheless, once settled in this country (i.e. once they had survived their six months' qualifying period) Jewish immigrants were at least in a position to benefit from the charitable and social supports of a well-established and much organized native Jewish community.

It is at this point that the discussion enters into the realms of social policy debate and development, rather than being a matter merely of public, or Jewish public, reaction. As an official agent of the Anglo-Jewish community, the Jewish Board of Guardians, for instance, did not decide upon its policies and practices in isolation from contemporary developments in both voluntary and statutory social provision. As its very title implies, this was a case of close, often subtle, interaction. The intricacies of such interaction, however, are best discussed within a broader social policy context.

(iii) *Immigration and statutory social policy*

Once again, as in the Irish case, the issues raised in public over this immigration tended very much to reflect those items currently prominent in general social debate. There were two important differences, however, between this and the earlier experience. To begin with, these tended to be issues close to the hearts, not merely of the policy-making classes, but of the voting working classes who felt themselves most immediately and directly affected by the aliens' presence. If anything, therefore, there was rather more edge and urgency to the debate this time. The areas of debate, furthermore, tended to be much more closely related to the role, or the possible role, of statutory social policy. There was, after all, considerably more evidence of social service activity on the ground, and of developments in the pipeline, than had been the case with earlier Irish immigration.

Superficially at least, the relationship between the new Jews and the Poor Laws would seem, *par excellence*, to be a case of unfounded allegation. However destitute the newcomers may heve seemed — and however available the Poor Laws may have seemed for alien abuse — the 'scrapings of Russia and Poland' made relatively few demands, in fact, upon this umbrella service. The statistics reproduced within the Report of the Royal Commission on Alien Immigration of 1903, seem clear enough:

Rate of pauperism as a percentage of total population

	Native	Alien	
England and Wales	5.0	—	(no figures available)
London	7.9	2.4	
Stepney	7.9	3.7	(p.16)

Given such statistics, it was scarcely surprising, perhaps, that the 1905-9 Royal Commission on the Poor Laws and the Relief of Distress should have refrained from any mention of alien immigration as a separate factor in its review of the workings of the Poor Laws (HM Government 1909). Yet neither was it surprising, in a different sense, that the 1905 *Aliens Act* should nevertheless have voiced so deliberate a concern to prevent 'undesirable and destitute aliens', or persons who were likely to become a charge upon the rates, from landing on these shores. Unless they could prove themselves to be bona fide refugees from religious persecution, penniless aliens were not henceforth to be allowed to land at all. Those who were allowed to land, moreover, might be expelled by the Home Secretary within one year of their arrival, should they be found to be in receipt of poor relief.[19] Whatever the discernable facts of the case, in other words, political priorities seemed to revolve around combatting the menace of alien pauperism.

Such political priorities, of course, were the subject of no little political contention (Gainer 1972 : Ch. 8). Yet, setting this on one side, the reasons why Jewish alien paupers should have figures so sparingly in statutory statistics are by no means clear-cut. One can, of course, interpret their apparent restraint as being no more than an outward proof of the greater self-sufficiency and independence of this striving population. Bentham's forecast that the truly rational, economic, man would turn to the Poor Law only as his very last resort would, on this showing, be vindicated at last. Two factors, however, serve to complicate the picture.

To begin with, the incoming, orthodox, Jew had reasons of his own, over and above those suggested by Bentham, for avoiding the workhouse:

> 'He would avoid it [the workhouse] if he was a right-minded Jew … We do not make provision for their religious difficulties.' (HM Government 1909 : 373)

Workhouse routine was intended to be grim and monotonous, of course, for any able-bodied pauper and his family yet:

> 'From the Jewish point of view, even more important was the virtual impossibility of complying with the Jewish ritual requirements: the dietary laws could have been followed, if at all, only by virtual restriction to bread and water, and the observance of the Sabbath and Festivals was impossible.' (Lipman 1959 : 11)

To be a practising Jew could be a rather more limiting condition, in other words, than to be an Irish Roman Catholic in similar circumstances. In such a context, the efforts of the Anglo-Jewish community both to influence the Poor Law's receptiveness to Jewish immigrant predicaments and to provide alternative, acceptable, facilities of their own proved a second factor of no small significance.

For the Poor Law Board [20] and for the local Boards of Guardians, the issues posed by the presence of destitute Jews were intricate. According to the Principles of 1834, all able-bodied paupers should be treated alike, irrespective of circumstances or location. To bend the rules or vary the treatment of individual claimants, if only to allow for their religious susceptibilities, could seem to be flying in the face of the iron law of less eligibility (see above p.16). How else could one be sure that conditions in the workhouse were less eligible than those of the lowest independent labourer, except by making no allowances? Set against this, however, was the realization that, unless allowances or special provisions were made, of some sort, there could effectively be no Poor Law in operation so far as orthodox Jews were concerned; and the Poor Law was supposed to be a system universally applicable. Indeed as early as 1772 the then Attorney General had pronounced that:

> 'the poor of whatever nation or religion must be maintained by the officers of the parish, where they are found, and no other person is compelled to relieve them.' (Lipman 1959 : 10-11)

The *Poor Law Amendment Act* of 1834 had done nothing to invade this principle — any more than it had invaded the related issues of settlement and removal (see above p.58).

Mass alien immigration gave such issues added point and urgency. Not only were the new Jews a controversial population in themselves for statutory authorities to have to deal with, but they were at once, on average, the most destitute and the most orthodox of the resident Jewish population. In a part of London where Poor Law resources were already possibly strained to their limits (Lipman 1959 : 11), needy outsiders were the last category of persons, perhaps, for whom special arrangements ought conceivably to be made. Indeed, it was argued, the very provision of special arrangements might attract more of them into the country. Nevertheless the 'religious difficulties' had to be coped with somehow.

From the Poor Law's point of view, the situation was saved in the end by development of Jewish charitable provisions with which the statutory authorities could liaise. Clearly, once it was possible to refer all their Jewish cases elsewhere, albeit at some cost to the Unions concerned, then any question of special workhouse or out-relief facilities for alien Jews being provided directly by the Poor Law, was effectively removed. The solution, even so, was not one speedily or easily arrived at. Only after some years of bargaining and negotiation — notably between a recently formed Jewish Board of Guardians, local Poor Law Unions and the Poor Law Board itself — were any conventions consolidated.

The stance adopted by the Jewish Board of Guardians was in this, as in other social policy respects, of no small significance, Established in 1859 by 'A group of young Victorian Jews, imbued with the Benthamite ideas of their time' (Gartner 1960 : 20), the Board stood for ideals of efficiency and co-ordination between all statutory and voluntary effort concerned with Jewish poor relief. Much the same sort of thinking, on a more general basis, was to prompt the establishment of the Charity Organisation Society some ten years later. Despite this common ground, however, the two institutions were to differ in their stance in two interesting respects, each of some relevance to our discussion.

To begin with, while both were wary of encouraging vice or fecklessness by any too casual administration of relief, the Jewish Board could not go so far as did the COS in distinguishing between deserving and undeserving — or helpable and unhelpable — cases.

The all too obvious predicaments facing Jewish refugees recently arrived in this country were sufficient to render such nice distinctions, however rational in principle, more or less inoperable in practice, if any semblance of humanity was to be preserved (Lipman 1959 : 29, 74). For all its early attempts at thorough investigation and individual case recording, in other words, a Jewish Board of Guardians confronted after all by repeated waves of near-destitute immigrants was bound, perhaps, to find itself more a caretaker and spokesman for such a general population than a painstaking administrator of any more selective, personalized, relief service (Lipman 1959 : 109-10). An early ambition 'to draw all the poor to their doors' was realized more completely, perhaps, than had ever been envisaged (Lipman 1959 : 46).

The second point of difference between the Jewish Board of Guardians and the COS concerned the role each thought the State, or local statutory authorities, ought properly to play in the administration of relief, and in the provision of associated services. While both organizations were products of the same general body of opinion — proclaiming the need for systematic charitable effort, based upon thorough case investigation and diagnosis, coupled with centralized case record-keeping — the Jewish Board of Guardians did not share the COS's firm belief in the intrinsic superiority of such voluntary effort, compared to anything the state could attempt. As the representative of a minority community, the Board was bound to insist that, as ratepayers and taxpayers, members of the Jewish community were entitled to expect at least a fair share of the benefits arising out of statutory services — whether these were in the form of the Poor Law or in anything else.[21] Furthermore, as an agency which found itself repeatedly stretched in trying to cope with successive peaks of Jewish immigration, the Board was concerned, not unnaturally, to husband its resources, and never to duplicate unnecessarily any service which the state could suitably provide (Lipman 1959 : 51, 61-3, 132, 135).

From our point of view, the Board's stance was highly significant. Since its policy seems, on the whole, to have been to concentrate its efforts wherever statutory services seemed to be falling short — for just so long as they seemed to be falling short — the history of the Board's activities over this period is in many respects a guide to the speed and efficacy of statutory developments. Moreover, since its policy was not merely to try to make good any statutory shortcomings but simultan- eously to press for their removal, the Board itself, together with the body of Anglo-Jewish opinion behind it, must be accounted an important influence upon statutory policy in its own right — at least so far as London was concerned.

There was, however, one important complicating issue. Wherever Jewish religious requirements seemed to necessitate a specially adapted form of social service provision, the question of whether, in the long term, the state or the Jewish community itself ought properly to arrange for such facilities was not a simple matter to resolve. In itself, perhaps, this furnishes further evidence on the shifting ethos of such statutory social policy in this period. The Poor Law was not the only branch of statutory social policy to have to come to terms with this issue; but, as a longstanding, umbrella institution, it was inevitably the first.

For the orthodox Jewish population to enjoy at least an equal chance, in effect, of utilizing Poor Law facilities, local Unions must establish a separate Jewish workhouse, arrange for Jewish facilities within a general workhouse, or else be prepared to grant out-relief on a much more widespread basis to Jewish paupers. Such at least was the opinion of the Jewish Board of Guardians (Lipman 1959 : 51). For a time it seemed as if Poor Law opinion might also incline to this view. The 1860s witnessed a not unproductive interchange of ideas and action between the statutory authorities and the Jewish Board of Guardians on just this issue.

Initially, the *Certified Schools Act* of 1862 seemed to point the way to a rather different general solution when it empowered the Poor Law Unions to send workhouse children to schools of their own denomination, at the expense of the Unions concerned. Under the terms of this Act, the Orphan Department of the Jew's Hospital was certified, in 1868, as a school to receive workhouse children, as was the Jewish Deaf and Dumb Home in 1874 (Lipman 1959 : 50). The Poor Law authorities were empowered, in other words, to cater for Jewish religious susceptibilities by paying Jewish voluntary institutions to take on Jewish paupers, rather than by providing specialist facilities within the Poor Law apparatus itself.[22]

The precedent, however, was not immediately generalized to cover the able-bodied Jewish pauper. The East London Union, indeed, seemed to set an opposite example when, in 1866, it offered accommodation to victims of the famine in Russian Poland (whom the Jewish Board of Guardians was in no position to accommodate), provided them with Jewish food, and declined to receive any reimbursement of the cost from the Anglo-Jewish community

(Lipman 1959 : 51). The gesture, seemingly, was not lost upon the Poor Law establishment. The 1869 *Poor Law Amendment Act* empowered Unions to put their poor of any one denomination together in a particular workhouse. The Clerks of the Whitechapel and City of London Unions were persuaded to agree that it would be feasible to supply Kosher food in their workhouses, although neither of these Unions was prepared to collect together its Jewish paupers without first obtaining clear direction from the Poor Law Board; since they felt that the presence of such arrangements might very well attract even more pauper immigrants into this country. The Poor Law Board, in response, declared that such provision would in fact serve as a deterrent to further immigration and that, in any case, the Jews were entitled, as contributors, to benefit from the Poor Law to this extent (Lipman 1959 : 51-2).

Everything seemed set, in other words, for the Poor Law to set about making special indoor arrangements for its Jewish clientele. There were, however, other forces pointing in the opposite direction — implying that the Poor Law should think more in terms of referring its Jewish cases to Jewish charitable organizations (as with the 'Certified Schools') than of attempting to lay on special treatment itself. Hence the significance of the famous 'Goschen Minute' of 1869, whereby the then President of the Poor Law Board advocated maximum co-operation (in keeping with the spirit of the times) between voluntary organizations and the statutory authorities in matters of poor relief. Hence also the significance of the establishment, in 1871, of a 'Jewish workhouse' financed from Jewish charitable funds (Lipman 1959 : 51-2). 'Maximum co-operation' seemed thereafter to be ensured simply by the Poor Law's readiness to transfer Jewish cases from its own workhouses to this separate establishment. Coincidentally or otherwise, the question of specialized institutional provision would appear to have been resolved (Lipman 1959 : 52; Gartner 1960 : 20).

After this, the question of more out-relief for Jewish paupers, as advocated by the Jewish Board of Guardians, met with little positive response from the Unions concerned. While the Whitechapel Union promised, in 1876, to do what it could to meet the Jewish Board's 'exceptional' requests, any real chance of flexibility must have been remote — given a prevailing contemporary Poor Law drive to cut back on all out-relief in East London Unions (Lipman 1959 : 53). Those of the able-bodied who did not wish to enter the workhouse must rely upon voluntary charitable effort — if they could find it. The statutory Poor Law authorities were no more inclined than was the Jewish Board of Guardians to duplicate facilities unnecessarily.

On issues where there were no peculiar Jewish requirements to make allowance for, the Jewish Board was of course in a much stronger bargaining and campaigning position. Jewish living and working conditions may have been particularly unwholesome and unhealthy in the areas of immigrant settlement, yet they were no different in kind from those endured by other residents in these neighbourhoods.[23] Accordingly, despite the Jewish community's immediate and traditional concern to take care of its own (Lipman 1959 : 10), the Jewish Board of Guardians at least could view such efforts as purely temporary and expedient: making good immediate statutory deficiencies while indicating to central and local government the directions in which they ought to be moving.

The Board's interest in health matters had not been slow to develop. As early as 1862, conscious of the close link between poverty and ill health, the Board had taken over responsibility for medical relief from the City synagogues. However unnecessary a separate Jewish medical service might have seemed, in principle, there was immediate evidence of immigrants hampered by language difficulties being unable to secure adequate treatment either via the Poor Law's medical officers or via the overcrowded dispensaries of East London (Lipman 1959 : 61). Accordingly the Board appointed two medical officers and ran a dispensary of its own.

The experiment, however, was destined to be short-lived. Concerned by what it felt to be the abuse of this expensive system by those with trivial complaints and by those who could well afford to pay for treatment, the Board decided, in 1873, to close its dispensary for a trial three months. Once this trial had shown no evidence of hardship resulting from the change, the closure was made permanent. The more significant step, however, was to come six years later. In 1879 the Board decided to discontinue its medical relief service altogether since it seemed that 'there was nothing of a specifically Jewish character in mere dispensing of drugs and the giving of medical advice' (Lipman 1959 : 62). Once again, the final closure was only effected after a trial closure period of six months had demonstrated to the Board's satisfaction that no hardship would be caused by this measure.

After such policy readjustment, it was scarcely surprising that the figures reproduced in 1903 by the Royal Commission on Alien

Immigration should have shown reliance upon Poor Law medical relief
to be the greatest single point of contact between the alien population
and this statutory service:

Total relief to aliens [mostly Russians and Poles] : 1901

Total relief:	2,116
Total indoor relief:	512
Total medical relief:	1,590
Total other outdoor relief:	14

(HM Government 1902-3 : 16)

In this case the Jewish Board showed itself unwilling to duplicate
services provided adequately elsewhere — whether statutorily or
voluntarily. On sanitary matters, however, the interaction was more
directly and specifically between the Board and local statutory policy.
At a time when public health responsibility in London remained still
with the vestries and district boards established under the Metropolitan Management Act of 1855; when the inefficiency if not
corruption of such bodies was allegedly notorious; and when the
Board's own medical experience had convinced it of the urgent need
to investigate and improve the housing conditions of the poor; the
appointment of its own sanitary inspector was called for and agreed to
by the Board in 1865 (Lipman 1959 : 63-5). It was a novel and, to
some extent, a tentative departure. Even the term 'sanitary inspector',
rather than 'inspector of nuisances', was a new one, although it was
destined soon to come into general statutory use (Lipman 1959 : 65).

The Board's inspector was appointed initially for a four month
period. His appointment was then renewed for a further six months
and then again for a further six months. All in all he seems to have
proved his worth. In his first six months he inspected some 471 houses
(comprising about 14,000 tenements and amounting to about half the
total dwellings occupied by the Jewish poor under the care of the
Board) and found sanitary defects in 343 of them. It was, arguably, as
a result of such effort that the Jewish poor were reckoned not to have
suffered so extensively from the 1865 fever or the 1866 cholera
epidemics as did their Gentile neighbours (Lipman 1959 : 65).

However this may be, the Board's appointment of a Sanitary

Inspector does not seem to have been renewed between 1867 and 1874. It was not until 1884, moreover, that the Board's famous Sanitary Committee was established. How far this last was simply a defensive move on the part of a nervous Anglo-Jewish establishment galvanized into action by revelations in the *Lancet* about current Jewish immigrant living conditions (Gainer 1972 : 48); and how far it was simply a logical next step on the part of an organization long appraised of East End sanitary problems, long accustomed to a specialist committee form of delegation, but only recently brought face to face with the consequences of mounting alien immigration cannot easily be decided.

The Board's scope for action was limited, in any case. No matter how carefully and constructively its Visiting Committee might act as the 'eyes and ears' of the Board in reporting any sanitary problems they came across, and no matter how zealously the sanitary inspector might inspect, they had no statutory power to act. Apart from exhorting and encouraging tenants to whitewash their homes or to try to keep them clean and tidy, the Board might undertake certain public works on its own account, while its inspector could report house defects either to the landlords concerned or to the local Medical Officer of Health (Gainer 1972 : 66, 126). But the 'inefficient application in some districts of these laws by those who are legally constituted guardians of the public health' (Gainer 1972 : 124) meant that the Board had every incentive to press for a better statutory performance.

Matters improved only slowly. It was not until 1905 that the Board felt sanitary conditions and sanitary administration in the metropolis to be sufficiently sound for it to turn its own attentions away from public and more towards personal health. More than anything else, the improvements noted seemed a consquence of the creation of the LCC and of the London Metropolitan Borough Councils — by the terms of the 1888 *Local Government Act* and the 1899 *London Government Act*, respectively. As public health authorities, they were both more credible and more active than the vestries and district boards they replaced. The replacement, in 1904, of the East London Waterworks Company by the newly formed Metropolitan Water Board seemed at last to complete this long-awaited rationalization (Lipman 1959 : 128-9).

In the meantime, two related sets of development in statutory social policy had been taking place partly again, it would seem, in response to pressure from the Jewish Board of Guardians among others. The Board was hardly alone in expressing concern, from the 1860s onwards, over unfit and overcrowded housing conditions in London's East End (Barnes 1934). Sanitary inspection — and even sanitary enterprise — could be little more than a palliative in such a situation. Yet any more radical action could only be effected on the basis of legislative authority. Hence the significance of successive national housing acts — from the 'Artisans and Labourers' Dwellings Act' of 1868 to the 'Housing of the Working Classes Act' of 1890. Local authorities were, cumulatively, provided with powers to improve, remove, and theoretically to replace insanitary dwellings, if necessary on an area basis (Barnes 1934 : Stages III-V).

Removal was one matter, however. Replacement, with no prospect of central government assistance to support the costs incurred, was quite another. To demolish without constructing alternative accommodation for the families displaced, seemed bound only to aggravate existing shortages and thus add to current overcrowding. In a period that did not seriously envisage local authority house-building on any massive scale, the Jewish Board of Guardians was at one with members of the Charity Organisation Society, for instance, in advocating an extension of voluntary 'model dwellings' projects in the East End as a solution to this problem (Lipman 1959 : 66). The activities of the Peabody and other Housing Trusts had long been noted with approval before the Board itself helped (indirectly) to launch the Four Per Cent Industrial Dwellings Company, under Lord Rothschild's leadership, in 1885 (Lipman 1959 : 128). If the efforts of such enterprises were to amount to no more than the merest drop in London's housing ocean, this was not the way contemporary, informed, opinion was inclined to view the matter (Cook 1974). Model dwellings trusts seemed the only positive response to slum housing, slum housing mentality, and slum housing demolition. They ought, therefore, to receive the maximum support.

The second area of policy developement revolved rather more exclusively around the question of statutory, governmental powers. Workshop sanitary inspection, practised regularly from 1892 by the Jewish Board of Guardians, was arguably of some significance in urging the provision of a suitable water supply and suitable drainage facilities, together with some check on overcrowding, in small immigrant workshops (Lipman 1959 : 127). Yet there were severe limits on what could be done — either voluntarily or via government authority. The workshops, seemingly part-domestic, part-industrial in character, fell on the whole between two stools. The factory inspector had no right to inspect unless there were women or children employed. There was little child labour amongst the immigrants and if the women should declare that they were merely 'visiting' the premises there was not much that the inspector could do to contradict them (Gartner 1960 : 69-70). The sanitary inspector, on the other hand, could hardly tackle the landlord over inadequate toilet facilities, when it was the tenant's numerous employees who were creating the problem. The sanitary inspector had no recourse save to the owner of the property (Lipman 1959 : 127).

The *Factory Act* of 1901 must, therefore, have seemed of no small significance when, for the first time, it tackled the problem of subcontracted workers and their requisite facilities by requiring each principal manufacturer to keep a list not only of all their outwork contractors, but of these contractors' employees (Gartner 1960). This was not a measure passed with specific reference to immigrant trades. Sweated workshops were not, after all, populated exclusively by immigrant workers. In so far as the Act did apply, however, to immigrant establishments, the efforts of the Jewish Board of Guardians had contributed to its coming.

It was with such developments in being that the Board felt not only able but bound to concentrate its activities elsewhere — within the field of personal health services. TB, like sweating itself, was not exclusively an immigrant complaint. It was, however, the one talked-of disease to exercise a disproportionate effect upon an otherwise healthy (or at least resilient) immigrant population. It was also, despite Koch's discoveries in 1882, a disease that local authorities seemed unlikely, speedily, to overcome — given their administrative inexperience together with the multiplicity of their overall tasks (Lipman 1959 : 130).

As early as 1897 the Board appointed a special committee to consider whether the incidence of TB had increased recently among the metropolitan poor. The committee returned a negative opinion yet, by 1902, the Board's Visitors were suggesting a positive, necessary role for the Board when they stressed the urgent need for after-care for TB patients returning from hospital and sanatarium treatment to the same unhealthy work and home conditions as had first occasioned their complaint (Lipman 1959 : 130). The Board was seemingly well prepared for a shift in orientation. When its sanitary inspector resigned in 1903 he was replaced (in 1904) not by a further sanitary inspector, but by two lady health visitors appointed specifically to help check the spread of TB among the Jewish poor. More particularly, they were to help not merely in stemming the dissemination of the disease, but in ensuring adequate after-care. The pressure of work thus taken on was sufficient to necessitate the appointment, in 1906, of two assistant health visitors, together with a clerk. The Board's Sanitary Committee declared specifically that it was now determined 'to aim more closely at ... the prevention of the dissemination of phthisis' (TB) (Lipman 1959 : 131-3).

The Board's efforts did not go unnoticed. Once the Brompton Hospital had started its system of voluntary notification it was accustomed, from 1908, to inform the Board of all its Jewish notifications. Once the London Hospital had taken on its Jewish Lady Almoner it, too, did the same. No longer was it necessary to depend merely on the alertness of its own Health Visitors for news of new cases. By 1909 the Board was aware of no less than 760 Jewish cases of TB in the London area (Lipman 1959 : 133).

Nor did this remain a matter of voluntary interchange alone. The 1908 Public Health (Tuberculosis) Regulations required compulsory notification to the Medical Officer of Health of all TB cases in the care of the Poor Law, while the Public Health (Tuberculosis in Hospitals) Regulations of 1911 required a similar notification of all cases known to hospitals, dispensaries, and other establishments. Further regulations in 1911 and 1912 ensured, in effect, the notification of all TB cases in receipt of medical care — including those in the charge of private practitioners. With such notification procedures in operation, neither the logic nor the convenience of passing on information concerning all London-based Jewish cases to the Jewish Board of Guardians, for after-care purposes, would seem to have been overlooked. The Medical Officer for Stepney, for instance, passed on all the Jewish information he thus received to the Jewish Board (Lipman 1959 : 133).

The volume of the Board's endeavours inevitably increased as a result. By 1911 its TB cases stood at some 1,285 while, by 1913, the figure had risen to a breathtaking 3,015 (Lipman 1959 : 133). The Board's Sanitary Committee was renamed its 'Health Committee', in 1911, in recognition of its now primary duty not simply to:

'take such steps as from time to time they consider desirable to improve the health of the poor and the sanitary condition of their

homes, but ... specially ... [to see to] the supervision of consump-
tive persons and the execution of such measures in connection there-
with as the Board may from time to time decide.' (Lipman 1959 :
134)

Statutory replacement of, rather than use of, the Jewish Board's
efforts to combat tuberculosis, was somewhat late in coming. As late as
1907-12, the establishment of three TB dispensaries in Stepney
seemed more important as additional referral sources for the Board
than as any real replacement for its services (Gartner 1960 : 161). The
Board's Health Visitors attended such dispensaries to record either all
Jewish cases or at least all those who were not insured (together with
their families) (Lipman 1959 : 166). It was only after the First World
War that local health authorities seemed seriously to embark upon TB
prevention and after-care, whereupon the Board, true to its own
traditions, could allow its own efforts to run down. By 1920 it had
given up visiting TB suspects in Hackney, Bethnal Green,
Westminster, and a host of other London boroughs. By 1921 the local
authority had taken over responsibility for the Stepney dispensaries to
which the Board's health visitors had formerly been attached. The last
health visitor employed by the Board was given notice in 1923.
Thereafter the concern was confined exclusively to the after-care of
Jewish sanataria unfortunates (Lipman 1959 : 166-7).

So far in this discussion, the Board's relationships with public
authorities would seem little more than a case of voluntary (albeit
energetic and imaginative) responses to combat and compensate for
what looked like either general statutory rigidity (in the case of the
Poor Law) or general statutory inadequacy (in the case of public
health). There were, however, other trends in evidence, where the
applicability of statutory social policy to Jewish immigrant requirements *per se* was either deliberately or incidentally reduced to a
minimum.

When the Liberal government of 1905-1914 decided to introduce
non-contributory pensions in 1908 for respectable old people of
limited means, the decision to allow the pension only to those elderly
who could show themselves not merely to have lived in this country for
at least twenty years but to be possessed of British nationality into the
bargain (Lipman 1959 : 86-7), was no casual manoeuvre. After the
passage of the *Aliens Act* of 1905, with its distinctive concern to stem
the flow of foreign paupers to this country (Garrard 1971 : Ch. 3), it

would clearly have been unwise politically not to have taken precautionary measures when introducing a daring departure from Poor Law practice no more than three years after this event. How far Jewish aliens might in fact have abused such a pension, if given the chance, was scarcely the point. The pension was introduced, ostensibly, as part of a drive to safeguard the national stock. The needs of non-established aliens could no more be a part of its concern, perhaps, than could the needs of the non-respectable native poor.

In other respects, the irrelevance of Liberal reforms to the immigrant population would seem to have been rather more accidental. 1911 Unemployment Insurance was a cautious new departure. Applicable in the first instance only to six carefully selected 'stable' branches of industry, it could be of little immediate assistance to the great majority of the working population, whether immigrant or native (Gilbert 1966 : 276). 1911 Health Insurance was also restricted in its early scope. As a system designed primarily to safeguard employees against threat of sickness, it was geared to the needs of the employed rather than the self-employed, and to the provision of general practitioner services rather than, for instance, to the needs of TB sufferers *per se*. Its usefulness to aliens, therefore, was bound to be restricted on both counts — as the Jewish Board of Guardians was quick to point out.[24] In both these cases immigrant occupational and environmental characteristics would seem, almost accidentally, to have debarred them from any benefit as a result of these new departures in social policy — in much the same way as Irish socio-economic characteristics seemed to have removed them from the effects of factory reform more than half a century earlier (see above p.60). In neither case was novel social policy attempting really to get either to the bottom or to the fringes of contemporary social predicaments, where the needy outsiders tended to be found.

There was, however, one notable area of statutory social policy development in this period which seemed, not merely sufficiently comprehensive in its scope as to embrace the Jewish population (both immigrant and native), but also sufficiently flexible in its mandate as to allow for the positive adjustment of statutory arrangements, as and where necessary, to suit Jewish religious requirements. We referred, earlier in this section, to the complications any special Jewish requirements might give rise to within the framework of a broad social policy provision (above p.93). Whether such special arrangements ought properly to be provided within the statutory framework rather than by voluntary effort, was a matter of principle which both the Jewish Board of Guardians and the statutory Poor Law Board had found difficult to resolve. Hence their liaison compromise, so much to be copied in matters of public and personal health, where no special Jewish requirements were ever even tentatively alleged to exist.

The suitability of Poor Law workhouses for destitute Jews, however, was not really the same sort of issue as the suitability of state supported elementary schools (after 1870) for Jewish children. In this latter case, the question was answered as much by the readiness of Jewish parents to send their children to the new state schools as by any firm decision on the part of the established Jewish community. Right-minded Jews might shun the statutory workhouse, but they did not shun the statutory school.

The contents of the 1870 *Elementary Education Act* would seem to have been decisive in this matter. Not only was the state committed for the first time to providing elementary schools on the rates wherever voluntary facilities were in short supply (and in London this meant providing many schools), but the education offered, whether by Board schools or by voluntary schools in receipt of central government support, had to be 'conscience free': not exclusively aligned, in other words, to the requirements of any particular religious denomination. The Cowper-Temple clause might have been designed primarily with the rivalries of Roman Catholics, Church of England, and Non-conformist denominations in mind, but its significance for a new Jewish population was obvious.

Even so the results were interesting. While the Act stimulated Christian denominations into an unprecedented burst of school-building activity in an effort to minimize the need for state schools and maximize their own benefit from government grants, (Curtis 1963) the same was not true of the Jewish authorities. Despite Anglo-Jewry's long-established reputation for the quality of its schools, and despite the availability of government grant aid there was no conspicuous expansion of Jewish voluntary schools provision after 1870. The reason is not hard to uncover. For the first time Jewish children could enter non-Jewish schools without being exposed to some form of Christian religious instruction. Apart from the need to lay on its own religious instruction facilities, therefore, there was no real reason why the Jewish community should attempt to meet all the education requirements of the immigrant population — particularly when the latter seemed quite content to use non-Jewish schools. Once again, it seemed, this had become a question of not duplicating unnecessarily any statutory (or other voluntary) provision:

'The Elementary Education Act of 1870 ... removed the need of the establishment of any new Jewish voluntary schools ... there is not the slightest reason why we should not participate in the general benefits which the State is able to confer impartially on all its citizens.' (Levy 1943-4)

With Jewish schools provision remaining relatively static and the Jewish population rapidly increasing over this period, the proportion of Jewish children attending Jewish schools showed a steady decline. By 1911 a mere 20 per cent of the Jewish child population of the City, Bethnal Green, and Stepney were attending Jewish schools (Gartner 1960 : 228). The rest, for the most part, were attending London Board schools, although a significant minority were placed in other voluntary schools within the elementary system.

The 1870 Act had in this respect produced an interesting quirk. Since the Act had insisted that all grant-aided, conscience-clause education must be accounted part of the overall elementary supply in any one area, the London School Board was bound, when short of places in its own schools, to place the surplus population in any voluntary establishment with places to spare. Hence the direction of some 1,628 Jewish children into eight National (i.e. Church of England) schools in East London (Gartner 1960 : 229). In this case, Jewish parents were clearly not enthusiastic:

'We have to drive them into the National schools; we have to compel them to go there. When the other schools are filled up, we must have them in a school; and so we have to drive them in there.' (HM Government 1902-3 : 338)

The operation was helped, however, by the fact that:

'We have on the School Board attendance committee a good number of Jewish ladies and gentlemen; and, of course, when they see them there, and they are told by these ladies and gentlemen it is Hobson's choice, they have to take that school — there is not any other for them — they do what they are told.' (HM Government 1902-3 : 338)

Rights of conscience and the right to receive their own religious instruction were bound to be respected, of course, even by an

Anglican establishment. The consequences could sometimes seem bizarre:

' ... in one of the Church Schools, namely, St. Stephen's Spitalfields, they have practically followed the line of the Board, and they have made provision for the Jewish children, so as to be taught their own religion at the schools. It is a Church school where practical provision is made for the Jewish children to be taught their own religion. About three-fourths of the school are Jewish children.' (HM Government 1902-3 : 338)

For most Jewish children, however, state education meant education at a Board school and, in the case of London Board schools, 'the line of the Board' could stand for far more than a minimum of adjustment to Jewish requirements. One of the notable features of this period, from our point of view, was the extent to which those Board schools catering for a sizeable proportion of Jewish children adapted their teaching, their timetable, and their staffing policies to suit this Jewish clientele. Initially, at least, this seems to have been no more than a common-sense response to what might otherwise have been an awkward statutory dilemma. Enjoined to see to it that the local school-age population not only had sufficient, but also 'suitable' schools to attend, the London School Board was persuaded, apparently, to come to terms with Jewish parental susceptibilities at a fairly early stage in its activities:

'Many years ago the first school that was opened by the Board, I think, in London, was the Old Castle Street Board School, which is in the very heart of the Whitechapel district. That school was carried on for some years, if I may say so, on the Christian system — the non-Jewish system anyhow — and it was an entire failure. We could never fill the school. We could not get the children to come along at all; and after some, I should think four, five or six years ..., the Board had a great debate as to whether they would adopt a different system, and by a majority it was carried that they would. They then selected a Jewish headmaster; the result being that, the system being altered entirely, the school filled. There was then a Christian lady over the girls' department, but it was found that that did not answer; so that practically we had to have a school entirely Jewish; and that is the line that the Board have since pursued.'(HM Government 1902-3 : 337)

So thoroughly, indeed, did the Board pursue this line that, by 1902, the Royal Commission on Alien Immigration could be told of no less than 16 Board schools:

' ... which are practically Jewish — that is to say, we observe the Jewish holidays, and they are carried out to suit the wishes of the Jews, for very few children in these schools are of the Christian persuasion, so that the schools are practically run as Jewish schools. Jewish ladies and gentlemen are on the management.' (p.337)

Nor was this a static situation. In keeping with the general population movement already referred to (see above p.78), the Royal Commission was informed of:

' ... the gradual spreading over of the Jewish population into other schools than those distinctly set apart for Jewish children, and the Board's plan has been, when the larger number of children has become Jewish to add the school to the list of Jewish schools. Practically they run it on Jewish lines.' (p.338)

To run it on Jewish lines could involve quite an extensive adaptation. Not only might such a school close early on Friday afternoons in winter, but its pupils would be eligible for anything up to five hours per week of Jewish religious instruction, while a substantial proportion of the staff, including often the headmaster, might themselves be Jewish. Whatever the initial motivation, in other words, this would seem to have developed into rather more than a minimal, common-sense adjustment.

Such flexibility, remarkable as it might appear, ought not necessarily to be regarded simply as a spontaneous response on the part of a statutory authority towards the special needs of an alien immigrant population. The London School Board had its Jewish member (Garrard 1971 : 117), 'Jewish ladies and gentlemen' were on the management committee of many schools as well as on the Board's own attendance committee, and there was seemingly a ready supply of Jewish teachers and headmasters for deployment in London's schools. With such scope for statutory influence it can be argued that the Anglo-Jewish community had merely shifted its ground in this case from direct to indirect social intervention. As pillars of the rate-paying establishment in London and as sources of both educational and political manpower, English Jews did not need, it would seem, to expand their voluntary schools provision in order to ensure an effective and suitable education service for the children of Jewish immigrants. Both the London School Board and its statutory successor were inclined, certainly, to regard their 'Jewish schools' as very much the product and the operational responsibility of the native Jewish community (Gartner 1960 : 227).

Be this as it may, the effort seemed well worthwhile. The new Jews seemed anxious for their children to learn and not averse to their attending such suitable Board schools. By 1882 the proportion of Jewish scholars at the Old Castle Street Board School had soared to a record 95 per cent, and 37 per cent of all Jewish children at school in London were attending Board schools. By 1894 the proportion had risen to some 51 per cent out of a greatly increased Jewish child population (Gartner 1960 : 227-8). Nor was this all. Board teachers pronounced these children 'bright', 'superior intellectually', 'excellent workers in school', and 'anxious to learn' (Gartner 1960 : 230). Jewish immigrant parents, moreover, were remarked upon for their interest and enthusiasm at a time when their English neighbours had still very often to be bullied or cajoled into sending their offspring to school (Gartner 1960 : 230).

Yet such developments and such prowess was bound, perhaps, to meet with criticism. Popular public reaction tended to focus, not unnaturally, upon three related themes. Jewish children were rapidly replacing (if not driving out) English children in the Board schools of East London; as the children of aliens they had no moral right to be there; as 'clever' children determined and encouraged by their parents, to get on, they threatened native children even more than their numbers might suggest. On the whole it was the crowding-out syndrome which attracted most attention. The *East London Observer* addressed an appreciative public when it remarked, in 1902, that:

'there are 30,000 children of the foreigner in the elementary schools ... in the East End of London.' (HM Government 1902-3 : 286)

No evidence was ever produced to suggest that such numbers resulted in a physical shortage of school accommodation for the overall child population (Gainer 1972 : 51). Rather it was a case of native parents electing to remove their offspring from a board school (and enrol them at the nearest voluntary establishment) once the number of alien scholars had begun to build up, and once the Board school had begun to adapt its routines to suit Jewish requirements. That such adjustments could often seem excessive, not to say irreligious, seems evident enough:

'The English children attending Rutland Street School were deprived of their own Easter holidays, which were postponed for eight or ten days, so as to make them synchronise, or fit in with the Jewish Passover ... It is making them [i.e. the parents] conform to the aliens instead of the aliens conforming to them.' (HM Government 1902-3 : 87)

Even without such aggravation, however, the general movement of native households away from areas of immigrant settlement tended, in any case, to leave Board and even voluntary schools with a predominantly alien clientele. In some cases there seemed no more possibility of a native intake sufficient to fill a National school than there was of a native congregation left sufficient to fill an Anglican Church. Hence the predicament of St Stephen's of Spitalfields (referred to above) in finding itself, as an Anglican establishment having to cater for a predominantly Jewish scholar intake.[25]

Such concentrations, however localized or unplanned, were bound to offend many native sensibilities. Some confusion over who and what elementary education was for, was in evidence. Thus while the 1870 Act had attempted merely to ensure that 'suitable' elementary schooling would be available in some form to every child of school age in the country, there were those who felt that the children of aliens ought properly to be excluded from such bounty, or, at least, that they ought to come last in the statutory queue. Even if themselves native born, such children 'took up space in the country which would never have been occupied if not for the arrival of their alien parents' (Gainer 1972 : 13). They ought not, therefore, to be allowed to take over rate-aided schools or, at the very least, such schools should not pander so dramatically to their alien ways, thereby driving away any remaining Christian clientele. Religious adaptability, it seemed, was a necessary article only in so far as it applied to rival Christian denominations.

The feeling that their local schools were being taken over by the aliens rested not merely on an appreciation (often exaggerated) of the numbers of children involved, but on their apparent educational prowess. Fear of the clever Jew was echoed in the fears, expressed by Gentile school teachers and others, over Jewish children's alleged 'smartness, especially in commercial things' along with their 'perfect want of moral sense' (HM Government 1902-3 : paras. 10359-61). Or, in the words of a more literary commentator:

'The foreign children at the East End Board schools are universally allowed to be sharper and more intelligent than the English, and they carry off a large proportion of prizes and scholarships.' (Russell 1900 : 30)

Such an appetite for learning was no more likely to add to the aliens' popularity than was the economic dedication of their parents. Once again, it seemed, newcomer prowess could be rather too much for local tastes and local confidence. More particularly, their enthusiasm for elementary education highlighted a further ambiguity inherent in the 1870 Act. Popular statutory education had been legislated for as much to gentle and train the voting, working, masses as to guarantee them an outlet for self-advancement (see above p.26). To the perennially poverty-stricken native population in the East End, such education seems very much to have been something forced upon an unwilling, uncomprehending, population by the better-off — forcing families to support their children while at school instead of benefitting financially from any wages they might be able to collect.

Against this backcloth, the apparent determination of alien households to extract the maximum benefit out of state education for their children not merely confounded local norms and expectations of behaviour, but threw the Anglo-Jewish community into some confusion as well. Along with the rest of propertied opinion, native Jewry had seen popular education, whether provided by themselves or by the state, very much as a means of gentling and civilizing the masses — in this case the alien immigrants. These same immigrants, however, showed themselves to be if anything rather more ambitious on their own behalf. In the event, indeed, their children became rather more civilized, or Anglicized, as a result of statutory education than English (or even immigrant) Jewry had envisaged. After 1918, therefore, the overriding concern of the Jewish community was not to Anglicize its Jewish youth any further, but rather to promote Judaization among this population before it was too late (Gartner 1960 : 240).

(iv) *Conclusions*

Like the Irish before them, Jewish East European refugees entered Britain as needy outsiders, whose presence served in many ways to highlight and exacerbate existing tensions and unease within the host society. Superficially, therefore, there are many parallels to be drawn between these two experiences. At the same time, of course, there were obvious differences — both in respect of the characteristics of the immigrants themselves and in respect of the social and political climate into which they came.

Thus, while both sets of newcomers were predominantly poor and unskilled on arrival, and while each was pronounced at the time to be a threat to native living standards and native self-respect, the Jews were feared for their brains and their ambition in a way the 'feckless' Irish never were. Again, while both stood apart from the general population, thanks to their distinctive appearance and behaviour, along with their tendency always to cluster together, differences of language, religion, and culture were that much more pronounced in the Jewish case.

Jewish immigrants, furthermore, were even more confined, and therefore conspicuous, in their geographical distribution than the Irish had ever been. The greater the cultural distance, it would seem, the greater the need to stick together. The Irish may well have been remarked upon for their tendency to form distinct communities within many of Britain's major industrial centres. The Jewish concentration in the East End of England's capital city was even more likely to attract attention, both for its size and its pervasiveness — socially as well as economically. The fact that the new Jews, unlike the Irish, were technically aliens in Britain would appear to have been little more than a formal confirmation of a strangeness much more readily apparent.

The question of popular sentiment illustrates, in itself, a further point of difference between these two experiences of immigration. Effective public opinion, by the later nineteenth and early twentieth century, was much more mindful of popular sentiment — to an extent which might have struck earlier politicians or campaigners as totally immoderate if not actually unsafe. For this reason alone, perhaps, the new Jews were assured of a more volatile public reception than ever the Irish had had to encounter. Any advantage they might have had, as bona-fide refugees or as self-helping individuals, would seem to have been cancelled out, in part, by the effects of public opinion becoming more popularly based. Lofty, liberal sentiments were one matter; mass fear and resentment of a competitive presence was quite another.

In such a context, the careful part played by the Anglo-Jewish community in attempting variously to respond to alien Jewish immigration, provides a further point of distinction. Unlike the Irish, the new Jews had important native backers. English Jewry could hardly ignore either the presence or the needs of its alien co-religionists in this country, nor did it lack either the resources or the organization with which to assist them. All the same, native Jews were placed in an awkward and an ambivalent position. As Englishmen they were largely at one with informed opinion over the dangers and undesirability of large-scale destitute immigration. As Jews still conscious of a need to safeguard their own social position in Britain, they were alive to the impression any unthinking Jewish alien influx was likely to make upon popular attitudes and beliefs. Also as Jews, however, they were determined that the state — to which they as ratepayers and taxpayers had long contributed — should play its full part in helping to cope with bona fide immigrant predicaments.

The fact that English Jewry (or at least the Jewish Board of Guardians) was able to see itself as operating within a context of statutory policies and statutory potential, however, highlights what was perhaps the most obvious point of distinction between this and the earlier immigration. The Irish had entered a country whose statutory social concern did not extend much beyond a desire to control and, if necessary, cleanse, protect, and train sections of the labouring classes. The new Jews, on the other hand, came into a society increasingly conscious of both the wishes and the welfare of a voting populace. Statutory social policy enacted, however ambiguously, on behalf of the working man was designed, ostensibly, to help him rather than control him. Ground level statutory social intervention was increasing and expected further to develop. The state was rather more visible, in this sense, and more was coming to be expected of it by both politicians and populace.

Against this background it is not difficult to see the issues aired over Jewish immigration as illustrative, in many respects, of the current scope and ethos of British social policy development. Ongoing interaction between statutory authorities, the Jewish Board of Guardians, and general public opinion was nothing if not illuminating on this account.

Thus it is possible to view the negotiations in the 1860s and early 1870s between the Jewish Board of Guardians and the statutory Poor Law authorities, over who should provide for Jewish destitutes and in what manner this should be done, as indicative of a broader Poor Law uncertainty. As a destitution authority established (decades earlier) on rational, utilitarian lines, the Poor Law was at last coming to be aware, not only of the political potential of the poor, but also of the variety of circumstances contributing to their poverty.

Precedents of some sort were already being established, of course, for some variation in the strict application of deterrent Poor Law principles. The offer of the workhouse test to every able-bodied claimant for relief had proved, and was proving, itself impracticable. It was too expensive, too inflexible, and too unpopular. The needs of the 'genuinely unemployed', moreover, were coming increasingly to be recognized as being distinct from those of the hard-core ne'er do well. Alongside this, the trend towards more specialized institutional treatment for the traditionally deserving categories of pauper, such as the young, the sick (especially the contagious sick), and the old, served also to boost the Poor Law's scope for flexibility.

There were established grounds, therefore, both for outdoor relief to certain of the able-bodied and for specialized institutional provision for selected other categories of pauper. Jewish alien destitutes, nevertheless, did not readily fill either bill. As impoverished refugees, they may well have been considered deserving by many criteria. Yet they were manifestly not regarded as deserving by the mass of the local native population — nor could their special attributes be accounted dangerously contagious by the Poor Law authorities. There was little room, in other words, for a special Poor Law response — either in the form of more out-relief or in the form of a special Jewish workhouse — to Jewish religious susceptibilities.

As a destitution control authority increasingly uncertain over how far it was now supposed to deter and how far to assist in awkward cases, or over how far it was supposed to function as a last resort safety-net, rather than as a weapon for social control, the statutory Poor Law was saved from embarrassment in this case by the presence of voluntary Jewish facilities with which it could legitimately liaise.

Such liaison, as it was established and extended between Jewish and statutory authorities, was illustrative in itself of a broader characteristic of social policy development in this period. After decades in which it seemed to many that any system or efficiency in the New Poor Law was being undermined always by the lack of any system or co-operation among voluntary relief-giving agencies, the movement for charity organization and for some rationalization of relationships between voluntary and statutory agencies was an influential one. It was only given an added twist in this case by the special position of the Jewish Board of Guardians as the mouthpiece of a minority community.

While the Board had been established initially in an attempt to create some order among the profusion of Jewish charities, it was inclined thereafter to insist upon the primacy of statutory responsibility in a way the COS was never disposed to do.

This being so, the history of the Board's activities stands to some extent as a measure of statutory performance over this period. Not only might inherent ambiguities in poor law policy be exposed by the Jewish Board's reluctance to cater without argument for all Jewish destitutes; the extent of its health and sanitary activity was a response to statutory shortcomings, in as far as and so long as these persisted, just as its *lack* of involvement in voluntary education was a tribute, in effect, to the efficacy of statutory provision in this field.

Jewish informed opinion was no different, necessarily, from general informed opinion regarding how far statutory responsibilities ought properly to extend. In essence, the Jewish Board of Guardians seems to have done little more than urge the enactment of services already implied, at least, in existing legislation. To this extent, the Board cannot be accused of departing from conventional opinion out of a special concern for Jewish welfare, but merely of pressing for its full implementation in this respect. Indeed, the conventionality of the Board's position is well illustrated by its stance over housing construction. Even though local authority demolitions (for sanitary purposes) were widely assumed to be adding greatly to existing housing shortages in East London, and even though local authorities were empowered (although not specially paid) to replace the dwellings they removed, the Board was at one with the bulk of informed opinion when it saw the answer in terms of more voluntary housing endeavour, rather than in terms of large-scale local authority house-building.

Against such a backcloth — of public enterprise requiring no little voluntary supplementation — the field of popular education stands out as a clear exception to the rule, at least so far as the London Jewish population was concerned. This was the one area in which no major, additional Jewish voluntary endeavour seemed to be required after 1870, notwithstanding the numbers of immigrants who were to settle in East London. In itself, of course, such sufficiency was revealing.

Forster's *Education Act* had been nothing if not a careful compromise. Apart from requiring that there must be a sufficiency of elementary school places to accommodate each district's child population, and that such places, whether voluntary or statutory, should not be denominational in any exclusive sense, the Act left matters of detail and contention effectively to the localities (and their school boards) either to resolve or ignore. Just how great was the scope for variation (and misconception) within the terms of the Act, is amply illustrated by the efforts of the London School Board, noted generally for its 'progressiveness' and energy in this period, to make suitable arrangements for its Jewish clientele. In its 'Jewish schools' policy and in its direction of surplus Jewish pupils into Anglican establishments, the Board was acting completely within its rights and within the terms of the Act, so far as these went. Whether so drastic an adjustment was within the spirit of the Act, however, was a matter of opinion. Such niceties had deliberately and necessarily been left less than clear in 1870.

That the experience of Jewish immigration served to highlight the current nature of social policy activity and development would seem, therefore, to have been generally the case. More than this, thanks particularly to the work of the Jewish Board of Guardians, alien immigration seems actually to have promoted policy development, at least in the fields of public and personal health, to say nothing of education. This brings us effectively to our second and third contentions: namely that statutory social policy might function, on the one hand, as a problem-solving mechanism and, on the other, as a bone of contention between newcomers and hosts, once the immigrants had begun to make their presence felt.

In this case, certainly, these were not mutually exclusive possibilities; nor are they easily to be assessed. In a situation of popular anxiety and antagonism (where mass reaction was of no little policy significance), statutory social policy could only function as a general problem-solving mechanism, perhaps, to the extent that it seemed to alleviate social conditions across the board — without favour or disadvantage to either side. Thus one might point to the general improvements in public health machinery (albeit spurred on by the example of the Jewish Board of Guardians) over this period as an example of the social policy development seeming to be of general popular benefit and thereby militating against some at least of the underlying causes both of popular unease and of immigrant hardship. Had statutory policy been even further developed and had large-scale housing replacement been envisaged, for instance, then one might have argued that, by tackling effectively one of the abiding causes of popular grievance as well as of immigrant difficulty, social policy might indeed have functioned as an overall problem-solver in this context. As it was, of course, an increase merely in public sanitary inspection was arguably more important for furnishing additional, emotive evidence on immigrant housing conditions than for promoting significant large-scale housing solutions.

To argue, however, that problem solving capacity must depend on statutory social policy becoming in some way complete or comprehensive within each sphere of its activity, is hardly useful or realistic in this context. Quite apart from the executive and financial limitations of late nineteenth and early twentieth century administration, there were strong political and popular constraints, still, over how far the state should try to go in domestic affairs. Parliament did not wish to undermine the individual's will to help himself. The individual did not necessarily wish to be interfered with. Such principles were neither novel nor transient. In this case, however, they supported a view of statutory social policy which was fundamentally selective — albeit with increasingly 'helpful' intentions. The working classes were no longer, ostensibly, to be controlled; they were, however, to be assisted only sparingly, as their own and the national interest would seem to require.

In such an atmosphere of scarcity, respective immigrant and native claims upon the statutory services were bound, perhaps, to be seen as rival or conflicting claims. Help to members of one group would seem to imply disadvantage and deprivation to members of the other. Hence, for instance, the Jewish Board of Guardians' consistent preoccupation with the notion that the Jewish community should receive its 'fair share' from existing statutory services and hence also the widespread popular assumption that the newcomers, in so far as they received any benefit at all from statutory services, must be benefitting at the expense of native households.

The Poor Law was perhaps wiser than it knew, therefore, when it resolved the problem of Jewish immigrant destitution by seeming not to make any special provision for such people, while in practice passing them on to Jewish voluntary authorities. This was not sufficient, in itself, to assuage popular fears of an immigrant pauper take-over, yet in some measure it may have helped to keep passions relatively muted. The position adopted over old age pensions in 1908 had of necessity to be more openly defensive. A novel statutory allowance for respectable old people could hardly have been extended to include immigrants of less than twenty years' standing, or of non-British nationality. Native public opinion would not have stood for it, even if national demographic concern had seemed to necessitate such a step, which of course it did not.

Even where services were supposed, formally, to be operating on a universal basis, the idea that there must be some rationing involved was not easily to be overcome. Thus a noticeable presence of Jewish children in the elementary schools of East London seemed sufficient reason, in itself, for many to assert that native children were being deprived of education as a result. In this case, of course, there were two additional factors. To begin with, native parents were not necessarily keen themselves on the idea of compulsory school attendance. Jewish enthusiasm in this respect was bound to add to any resentments. More important than this, however, Jewish educational requirements seemed to involve not merely standard but special treatment. Such special treatment could seem not merely a wilful misappropriation of scarce statutory resources, but an effective restriction on Gentile school attendance.

Thus, while statutory social policy over this period might be described as being broadly helpful to the general population and (to judge by the reactions of the Jewish Board of Guardians) broadly helpful to the immigrant population also, it cannot be regarded as 'problem-solving' with regard to host-immigrant relationships. If anything, statutory services seem to have provided further items (along with housing and employment) for host-immigrant competition. Nor was this all. Judging by the record of most statutory authorities over this period, and the tenor of their interaction with Jewish voluntary organizations, there would seem to be no little divergence of opinion between those formulating and administering social policy, on the one hand, and those mainly in receipt of it, on the other. The policies of the London School Board with regard to Jewish education, for instance, were hardly what the local populace in general would have prescribed.

It was not a trivial divergence of opinion. I suggested earlier that this was, broadly speaking, a period in which social policy was enacted on behalf of, rather than by, the working classes (see p.30). In other words, established, informed opinion saw itself generally as acting in the best interests of the voting populace, but not necessarily in direct response to popular demand. In this context, the fact that informed, established opinion tended to include leading Anglo-Jewish opinion was of no small significance. This is not to suggest that there was an Anglo-Jewish conspiracy in operation to bend social policy in this period towards meeting immigrant requirements; but simply that those in positions of influence, whether in Parliament, local government, or on the Jewish Board of Guardians, tended to be the same sort of people, if not sometimes the same individuals.[26]

Quite apart from the influence of Anglo-Jewish opinion *per se*, these were the very classes who might be expected to be most sensible of the apparent self-helping potential of the alien immigrant population (so different from the Irish before them), and least likely to feel threatened by it. This much, at least, would seem to be implied by the nature of statutory social policy performance in the late nineteenth century, and its apparent resilience in the face of popular anti-immigrant opinion.

This is, of course, to state only one side of the picture. Popular sentiment in this respect was hardly devoid of effective political expression. It merely took time to build up on this as on other accounts. The passage of the *Aliens Act* of 1905 was at least a paper triumph for popular opinion as marshalled and interpreted by interested MPs.[27] Existing social policy might soldier on regardless after this event, yet subsequent new policy departures tended effectively, if not explicitly, to rule out extensive alien participation. How far this was a matter of chance (in the case of 1911 health and employment insurance) and how far a matter of deliberation (as in the case of 1908 old age pensions) it was not profitable even for the Jewish Board of Guardians to debate.

This was, therefore, very much a transitional period. Popular, competitor, sentiment was much more blatantly anti-immigrant than were the more measured, self-conscious views of most of the 'informed', detached, responsible classes. In itself this was not necessarily anything new. Effective public opinion, however, was coming to take account of, if not to incorporate, popular sentiment, even if the operation of social policy might still be relatively cushioned from its demands.

5

New Commonwealth
immigration
c. 1950-1971

The approach to this study is designed to follow on from that so far developed in respect of early Irish and East European Jewish immigration. In terms of length and complexity, however, this has to be the most ambitious exercise of the three. For the sake of manageability, it will be divided into four linked chapters, of which this first is intended to set the scene in preparation for the main social policy debate.

The reasons for this more extensive treatment can be summarized readily enough.

To begin with, New Commonwealth immigrants were entering a society which was not merely possessed of an unprecedented quantity of statutory social services: it was a society which saw fit to describe itself as a 'welfare state'. Thus the range and pervasiveness of social policy to be taken into account in this discussion will be not merely more extensive, but qualitatively more challenging, than anything hitherto.

Independently of this, perhaps, New Commonwealth immigration has been the subject of more investigation and documentation (both private and official), together with more literary and pseudo-literary comment, than anything aroused by earlier immigration experiences. How far this has been because New Commonwealth immigrants were mostly coloured; how far because they came from one-time outposts of the Empire; and how far because their presence, as needy outsiders, was bound to appear that much more vexatious (either way) amid the trappings of a welfare state, must all be matters for discussion within this study. For whatever reasons, however, the proliferation of what might broadly be described as 'British race relations literature' from the latter 1950s onwards, has been little short of spectacular.

Even so, the relative profusion of material, relating to social policy on the one hand and to New Commonwealth immigrant circumstances on the other, does not mean that the evidence available was necessarily either complete or appropriate for our purposes. True there is extensive documentation of the environments within which, and the opportunity barriers within which, New Commonwealth immigrants (and their families) tended to live, once settled in this country. True also, there are records relating to the ways in which formal national social policy guidelines have gradually and variously been adjusted to take account, however incidentally, of the coloured immigrant's presence. A welfare state has had, after all, certain pretensions to proclaim.

Evidence relating to the operation of existing local social services faced with a New Commonwealth immigrant presence tends, however, to be far from complete. For reasons of policy as well as of expediency, central government departments do not usually maintain a detailed record of the ways in which local social services (whether local authority or civil service-administered) respond to issues associated with the presence of New Commonwealth immigrants. An assortment of area research studies, variously inspired, might refer in passing to local statutory performances in this respect; yet such evidence, put together, hardly amounts to comprehensive, balanced coverage for our purposes. With the exception of one national survey into the ways in which local education authorities have responded to the presence of New Commonwealth school children within their areas (NFER 1971), there was no generalized evidence to hand regarding local social service response either to the immigrants themselves or to issues possibly associated with their presence.

Much the same might be said, of course, regarding the local operation of such services as existed during the earlier examples of immigration under debate. Yet there are two points of difference. To begin with, given such a relative wealth of statutory social policy in the postwar period, the manner in which such services were administered to actual or potential clients was arguably of greater significance to relative life-chances within this society than could ever formerly have been the case. More immediately, however, the fact that this was a contemporary experience meant that I was not bound, necessarily, to rely upon records already compiled, or books already written, for my raw material.

Accordingly, in an attempt to fill in at least some of the gaps in the evidence, I conducted an exploratory survey (with the help of the Social Science Research Council) into the ways in which local services in the fields of employment, health, housing, and social care have so far responded to the presence of New Commonwealth immigrants within their catchment areas.[1] The number of areas to be covered had inevitably to be limited, as had the scope of the questions to be asked. Nevertheless, the partial reliance in this case-study upon first-hand survey material makes it qualitatively a different exercise compared to either of the earlier two.

Reliance upon the survey material, moreover, makes this case-study stand apart from the others in one further respect. We shall be discussing the impact of New Commonwealth immigration c. 1950-1971. The survey evidence relating to the response of local social services to this influx, however, was assembled after the close of this period, i.e. in 1973/4. We shall therefore be discussing not the services' immediate but, perhaps, their considered response to New Commonwealth immigration. This response, moreover, will have to be examined in the light of those additional national social policy manoeuvres, either directly or indirectly inspired by effects of coloured immigration, which had materialized meanwhile in the 1960s. Thus we shall be considering the novel social policy departures first, before proceeding to the general social policy response.

This may well seem an arbitrary procedure. Nevertheless there are two points to recommend it. To begin with, since the impact of New Commonwealth immigration did not end abruptly in 1971,[2] we shall still be considering the social services' response to a current, albeit an increasingly familiar, phenomenon. In the second place it may be argued that an evaluation of so complex and dynamic a subject may be all the better, perhaps, for coming after the initial period of impact.

However this may be, there remain two points worth noting at this stage: the first concerning the nature of this immigration and the second concerning my approach to the material.

While the terms 'Irish immigration' and 'East European Jewish immigration' were sufficiently broad, no doubt, as to comprehend a wide range of group experiences and characteristics in each case, the term 'New Commonwealth immigration' could have little collective meaning at all, to the groups to which it was applied. This was not merely an ascribed label, but one which was ascribed initially on the basis of a negative definition. The term 'New Commonwealth immigrants', according to the Registrar General in 1966, embraced all those Commonwealth immigrants who did not hail from the 'Old Commonwealth' (i.e. Canada, Australia, and New Zealand).[3] This was, to say the least, a definition that left much scope for variety within the ranks. Even so, New Commonwealth immigrants seemed — at least to some — to share certain common characteristics: they were typically poor, typically unskilled, typically 'less civilized' and, to varying degrees, non-white.

For the sake of simplicity, this study will concentrate initially upon the characteristics of West Indian and Indo-Pakistani immigration to the exclusion, on the one hand, of second-generation immigrants and, on the other, of any smaller-scale branches of New Commonwealth immigration. This has, of course, to be an arbitrary, temporary distinction. Discussion of the New Commonwealth impact upon either host society opinion or upon social policy development cannot in practice confine itself exclusively to the import of first generation Indian, Pakistani, and West Indian newcomers, if only because the reaction to their presence was in no way so specific. To concentrate initially upon these groupings may nevertheless afford some introductory shape and clarity to the approach.

One final point: I have no wish in this case-study to reiterate unnecessarily, or to reinterpret unnecessarily, the findings of what has to be reckoned a formidable body of research relating to the subject of New Commonwealth immigrants in Britain. Both the present and the following chapter will consist, essentially, of a commentary based upon evidence already well demonstrated and documented by others. In both chapters, therefore, there will be extensive reference to such secondary material. It is only in Chapters Seven and Eight, where appropriate material was not already to hand in relation to many aspects of the discussion, that a quantity of primary evidence will be called into play.

(i) *The nature of the migration*

Thanks to the effectiveness of organized political pressure for immigration controls, New Commonwealth immigration can be divided into two periods: before and after the implementation of the 1962 *Commonwealth Immigrants Act*. The Act constitutes a landmark, not simply because it brought about a reduction in the total annual inflow of New Commonwealth immigrants (as was its obvious intention), but because it contributed also to a shift in the balance of this inflow — away from a predominantly West Indian towards a markedly Asian entry.[4] Thus these two periods of New Commonwealth immigration tend to be associated, respectively, with the bulk arrival years of each of our main component immigrant groups.

The period between June 1948 (when the former German pleasure cruiser, the 'Empire Windrush', set sail from Kingston, Jamaica with some 492 intending immigrants on board) and June 1962, can be termed the years of colonial/New Commonwealth entry as of right to the mother country. Just as in the case of Irish immigrants, or Jewish immigrants prior to the *Aliens Act* of 1905, there existed no government machinery either to prevent their coming in, or definitively to compute their numbers. The Home Office was left to produce its own annual estimates of net colonial/Commonwealth immigration, based upon shipping and air transport passenger lists — alongside such figures as were produced, for instance, by the Migrant Services Division of the Jamaican Colonial Government up to 1956, and thereafter by the British Caribbean Welfare Service (up to 1958), and thereafter again by the Migrant Services Division of the Commission in the UK for the West Indies, British Guiana, and British Honduras (Peach 1968 : 10). The figures thus produced were bound, of course, to be little more than approximate. Home Office estimates could no more distinguish reliably between genuine migrants and intending short-stay visitors than could the Aliens Lists of the years before 1905 (see above p.68 and Peach 1968 : 11-13). Migrant services figures, focussed as they were upon organized group arrivals (of which the Division, as a welfare agency, was most likely to be appraised), tended inevitably to underestimate total immigrant numbers (Peach 1968 : 10).

Against this background, decennial Census returns were exposed as providing, not merely a behind-hand record of doubtful relevance (the 1951 returns showing no more than a trivial New Commonwealth presence and the 1961 returns being obviously out of date by the time of their publication), but a seriously inaccurate record in any case. By including, as immigrants, children born abroad to British nationals the Census tended to exaggerate immigrant numbers (Rose 1969 : 94,

Appendix III 3a) by excluding the children born in this country to immigrant parents it tended to give a misleading impression in the opposite sense (Rose 1969 : 95, Appendix III 3b). Most important of all, however, the 1961 Census operation seemed to have under-enumerated those first generation, 'authentic', New Commonwealth immigrants who were resident. Simply by taking the 1951 totals, allowing for deaths in the meantime, and adding on to the remainder the estimated net immigration figures such as existed for the 1950s decade, it was possible to indicate, for instance, that West Indians in England and Wales must, in 1961, have been under-enumerated by about 20 per cent (Peach 1966).

Yet however imprecise the data, the general pattern of (what came to be styled) New Commonwealth immigration over this period would seem obvious enough. West Indian immigration was the first to assume noticeable proportions following World War II. By the mid-1950s it was noticeable anough for the Home Office to begin supplying the House of Commons with annual estimates of the net inward movement of citizens from the West Indies and from Commonwealth territories in East and West Africa, Asia, and the Mediterranean.[5] It was only during the latter 1950s and, more particularly, during the pre-Act scramble of 1960 onwards, that immigration from India and Pakistan began to attract serious attention. West Indian immigration, even so, retained its numerical preponderance right up until the implementation of the 1962 *Commonwealth Immigrants Act.*

Thus, for the years 1955-60 inclusive, the Home Office estimated there to have been a net Caribbean inflow of some 161,450, as compared to 33,070 from India and a mere 17,120 from Pakistan. The subsequent eighteen months of pre-controls desperation pushed the net Indian inflow to some 42,000 for this year and a half, while Pakistani figures soared to a mammoth 50,170 for the same period. Yet no less than 98,090 West Indians (net) were reckoned to have arrived betwen January 1, 1961 and the pre-Act deadline of June 30, 1962.[6] Indian and Pakistani rates might therefore have been catching up by the early 1960s (for whatever reason), yet West Indians remained the largest composite New Commonwealth immigrant group in this country.

The 1961 Census, for all its limitations, could at least confirm this fact. Out of a total enumerated population of some 522,933 'New Commonwealth' immigrants resident in England and Wales in 1961, no less than 171,800 were of West Indian birth, compared to 151,435 (including an estimated 76,000 'white Indians') from India and some 30,737 (including an estimated 5,840 'white Pakistanis') from Pakistan.[7]

Against this background, the introduction of statutory controls in the form of graded employment vouchers would seem to have been little short of spectacular in its effects. Not only was the annual net rate of New Commonwealth immigration cut from an estimated 136,400 in 1961,[8] to an official 57,049 in 1963, for instance; but the introduction of controls seemed to affect West Indian to a much greater extent than it did Asian entry figures. (Only 7,928 net West Indian arrivals were recorded for 1963, as compared to a balance of 17,498 from India and 16,336 from Pakistan).[9]

Why this should have been the case will be a matter for discussion below. The introduction of controls did at least make for a better documented situation however; since under the terms of this and subsequent legislation, annual official statistics concerning the movement of persons between the UK and Commonwealth countries were regularly produced. Not · that such figures were necessarily complete, of course. There was always the problem of illegal immigration, a subject recurrently to the fore in any subsequent debate on the subject of immigration controls.[10] Nor, again, was this improvement in entry recording accompanied by any marked improvement in Census reliability. The 1966 Sample Census, it seemed, was just as likely to have under-enumerated the resident New Commonwealth population, and for much the same reasons, as was the Census of 1961 (Eversley and Sukedo 1969 : 22-5). The 1971 Census attempted to tackle one major area of ambiguity by enquiring, for the first time, into *parental* country of origin. Yet this manoeuvre possibly gave rise to as many anomalies as it removed.[11]

Nevertheless the general trends, so far as West Indian, Indian, and Pakistani immigration was concerned, seemed clear enough once again. Despite considerable fluctuations in overall numbers from one year to the next, at no point after July 1962 did the net annual inflow from the West Indies equal that from India; and at no point after 1966 did it equal even the net annual inflow from Pakistan. In 1971, for the first time, the balance of migration between the UK and the West Indies was to show a net *loss* of some 1,163 persons, as against a net inflow of some 6,584 from India and 5,643 from Pakistan.[12]

The significance of this turn-about in entry patterns after July 1962, was two-fold. To begin with, it meant that, while the majority of West Indians resident in the UK by the latter 1960s must be immigrants of relatively long-standing (having arrived before the implementation of controls), the majority of Indian and Pakistani residents had to be of post-July 1962 vintage (Rose 1969 : 83). At the same time, so marked a shift in entry proportions exercised an inevitable, cumulative effect on the relative strength of these groupings within the resident New Commonwealth population.

Census evidence would seem, if anything, to exaggerate rather than minimize this trend. On the one hand, the 1966 Sample Census (England and Wales) suggests a situation not so very different, proportionally, from that of 1961, estimating there to be some 267,910 West Indians resident in 1966, as compared to 232,400 Indians (including an approximate 68,600 'white Indians') and 73,130 (including some 5,400 'white Pakistanis') from Pakistan.[13] 1971 Census figures, however, suggest nothing short of a drastic turn-about: with a resident West Indian-born population of only 237,035, in England and Wales, as against no less than 321,995 persons born in India and 139,935 born in Pakistan.[14]

Exaggerated or no, this shift in proportions was taking place against the background, furthermore, of an overall increase in New Commonwealth immigrant numbers. From the estimated 522,933 of 1961, the New Commonwealth population was reckoned to have risen to no less than 1,151,090 in 1971, making it some 2.4 per cent of the general population.[14] By this standard the New Commonwealth is to be compared with the early Irish, rather than with the Jewish, case example (see above p.44 and 69).

While the general growth in immigrant numbers may not be difficult to explain, given a decade of continuing, albeit controlled, immigration, attempts to explain the changeover from a predominantly West Indian to an increasingly Asian inflow involve rather more complex considerations. At the very least, it suggests a difference of make-up and motivation between these two broad migratory groups, such as is central to our present discussion.

Generally speaking, there are two ways of interpreting the changeover: either West Indian immigration (being first off the mark) had already spent its force by the time that controls happened to be introduced; or else West Indians were simply less adept than either their Indian or Pakistani counterparts in manipulating the controls once these were in operation. In reality, both these sets of factors would seem to have been in play; although the latter seems, if anything, to have been the more decisive.

The first case really rests on the assumption that there can be some sort of finite, 'natural' limit to a migration movement. This being so, the fact that West Indians had migrated to Britain in such comparatively large numbers during the 1950s is sufficient in itself to make one regard a fall-off in the 1960s as perhaps only to be expected. Such a conclusion seems supported, on the one hand, by the evidence that there was, if anything, a smaller backlog of West Indian womenfolk to be brought in after July 1962 than was the case with Indian and Pakistani migrant groups (Rose 1969 : 88-90) and, on the other, by the evidence (albeit inconclusive) that the more skilled and enterprising West Indian migrants had long since arrived, leaving only the less skilled, less sophisticated and possible less determined islanders to follow in their wake (Rose 1969 : 49-51; Roberts and Mills 1958; Peach 1968 : 38).

Both these latter pieces of evidence, however, are open to a different interpretation. The fact that early West Indian migration included a higher proportion of women than was the case with early Indian or Pakistani immigration, was arguably as much a comment upon the different social structures prevailing between these sending societies as it was either upon initial settlement intentions or upon the possible 'completeness' of pre-controls immigration (Rose 1959 : Chs. 5 and 6). Again, the fact that it was mostly unskilled rather than ostensibly skilled heads of households who were entering Britain from the West Indies by the 1960s, could be taken just as readily as an explanation of their relative collapse in the face of immigration/controls, rather then as proof of this migration's being already past its peak. There were, after all, far more unskilled than skilled heads of households in the Caribbean. Even if all the skilled intending migrants had already long since arrived, this was hardly proof in itself that the migration movement was running down.

Most telling of all, however, was the fact that, far from tailing-off in advance of controls legislation, West Indian immigration actually leapt to unprecedented heights over the January 1961 — June 1962 period. If these were simply stragglers dashing in, in other words, there were plenty of them. If they were unskilled, moreover, they were at least no more unskilled as a group than were the bulk of their Asian counterparts in the same period. One is bound to conclude, therefore, that Indian and Pakistani immigrants must in some way have been more sucessful in their response to controls machinery after 1962.

The facts are not difficult to summarize. Three categories of employment voucher were introduced: 'A' for those who had specific jobs to come to; 'B' for those with specific, marketable skills; and 'C' for unskilled workers without definite prospects of employment. Thanks, for instance, to London Transport and the British Hotels and Restaurants Association's recruitment schemes, West Indians managed initially to do quite well so far as 'A' vouchers were concerned (Rose 1969 : 86). They did not do very well, however, in the competition for 'C' vouchers — securing only 10 per cent of the available places (as against 75 per cent to India and Pakistan) before this (over-subscribed) branch of vouchers was formally discontinued in 1965 (Rose 1969 : 84). In the competition for 'B' vouchers they fared worst of all — scarcely surprising, perhaps, in view of the dearth of skilled migrant West Indian personnel in this period — particularly those doctors, teachers, and graduates in science or technology such as were singled out for special 'B' voucher treatment from August 1965 (Rose 1969 : 84-7).

Asian, particularly Gujarati, menfolk may indeed have been disproportionately skilled along the lines last mentioned (Desai 1963 : 8). Early Asian dominance in the 'C' as well as the 'B' voucher market, however, is suggestive more of better organization than of any intrinsic superiority of skill or migrant suitability *vis à vis* West Indian or other New Commonwealth groups. It is at this point, of course, that one falls back upon well-worn truths alleging the greater resilience and resourcefulness of Asian village-kin, backed up by commercial (and often factory personnel) organization — as compared to the relative vulnerability of 'individualistic', 'uncoordinated' West Indian immigration (Rose 1969 : 70-71, 419; Patterson 1969 : 6-10). Even so, there were perhaps as many points of similarity as points of contrast between these groups.

This was, to begin with, primarily an economic movement of peoples in every case. West Indian islands might vary in the extent to which they had diversified their economies (or in the extent to which they had ever been dependant upon a slave orientated, plantation system), yet in no case were there now sufficient jobs or prospects or landholdings to go round (Parry and Sherlock 1968 : Ch. 18). No less desperate, however, was the landholding situation in the Punjab (aggravated by the flight of Sikhs from the Western to the Eastern Punjab following Partition), or the pressure on the land, coupled with unemployment, in Gujarat, or, again, rural poverty in hill districts of (one-time) East and West Pakistan (Rose 1969 : 52-9). 'Push' factors, in other words, were present in every case.

Early West Indian immigrants, even so, were presumed to be entering Britain out of something more positive than sheer economic necessity. West Indian ex-servicemen[15] were apparently quick to report the attractions of a life in Britain, and subsequent early immigrants were drawn as much perhaps, by the image of the mother country as by any hopes of short term monetary gain. They came, so it was said, as committed settlers rather than as mere migrants in search of a job (Patterson 1969 : 6).

Set against this image, was the picture of early Asian immigration as being essentially a case of menfolk travelling far (and often in rotation) in search of jobs or higher wages with which to support their extended families back home, before the final, hoped-for return with sufficient capital to rejuvenate or initiate a local family business. Sikhs were long noted as 'perhaps the most mobile and versatile people in the whole of India' with a long tradition of purposive migration behind them, yet the image seemed applicable to Sikh, Moslem, and Hindu, or Indian and Pakistani-immigrants alike. All seemed firmly attached to a home-based extended family system and the pull of the mother country, as opposed to the job opportunities she might seem to offer, seemed little in evidence (Patterson 1969 : 6-7; Rose 1969 : 52).

Several factors, however, serve to modify this picture of settler West Indian versus job-hunting Asian immigration. An apparent intention to settle, for instance, was hardly incompatible with a fine, preliminary awareness of available job opportunities in Britain. Indeed West Indian immigration from the middle 1950s was if anything far more responsive to the fluctuating state of the British labour market than was Indian or Pakistani immigration, prior to the 1960-62 scramble (Peach 1968 : Ch. 4; Rose 1969 : 77). Whatever the original contrasts of intention, moreover, West Indian and Asian ideas seemed dramatically to have converged by the middle 1960s, thanks to the disillusionment of West Indians, on the one hand, with the manner in which they had been received and thanks, on the other hand, to the effects of control legislation in forcing Asian (particularly Indian) immigrants to opt at least for semi-permanent residence in this country and to bring over their dependants (Rose 1969 : 445, 461). Neither group, on balance, was happy at the prospect of a permanent stay in Britain; yet neither group, on balance, expected to be in a position to leave within the short-term future (Davidson 1966 : 106-7; Jones 1971 : 116).

So far as their geographical and occupational distribution within this country was concerned, there were again broad points of similarity, as well as smaller points of divergence, between these groups. For all the variety of background, they were after all mostly poor outsiders within an ageing, developed economy.

Thus, in so far as virtually all New Commonwealth immigration started off as a search for employment opportunities, New Commonwealth immigrant settlements tended to build up in those areas where labour, particularly unskilled labour, was reputed to be in shortest supply. More specifically, early immigrants tended to gravitate towards those areas where not merely jobs but housing was fairly freely available. Hence the rapid build-up of immigrant settlements not in the New Towns,[16] for instance, but characteristically within declining, twilight, inner city areas whose native population was apparently already on the move out (Jones and Smith 1970 : 55). Later immigrants tended, naturally enough, to wish to settle alongside fellow-nationals and relatives; so that settlements once started could be expected to grow (Jones and Smith 1970 : 55-6).

Thus by 1961 roughly 80 per cent of all West Indians in this country were reckoned to be conurbation dwellers — as against 59 per cent of all Indians and Pakistanis (Rose 1969 : 100). But the difference between the two was not without interest. West Indians had been the first to begin arriving. They tended to settle either within Greater London itself or (to a lesser extent) within other metropolitan areas such as Birmingham or Manchester, which were traditionally short of labour and within easy, obvious reach of the capital city.[17]

Large scale Indian and Pakistani immigration was somewhat later in getting under way, but once again the migrants were in search, initially, of the most convenient areas of employment (and housing) opportunity. Inevitably there was some overlap in the broad areas of settlement. Greater London, the West Midlands and Manchester witnessed a growth of Asian communities in addition to their West Indian settlements. Apart from this, however, Asian immigrants seemed inclined to move around and spread themselves somewhat further afield.[18] The booming manufacturing centres of the East Midlands or the textile towns of West Yorkshire, for instance, both experienced significant Asian settlement.[19]

If it was the availabiltiy of jobs and houses that determined the initial pattern of New Commonwealth settlement in this country, the jobs and housing actually obtained tended, not surprisingly, to be amongst that least attractive to the general population. Once again we have the picture of an immigrant population having initially to make do with what they can get — which is what other people do not particularly want. Hence the evidence, by 1961, of the New Commonwealth population's being concentrated disproportionately in the least skilled, least desirable, worst remunerated urban occupations, where the demand for labour was understandably at its highest, as well as being housed, on average, in the most obsolete, overcrowded accommodation. Given the Irish and the Jewish experience this was, perhaps, no more than to be expected. West Indian and Asian characteristics were not altogether identical, however, within this spectrum.

To begin with, while the New Commonwealth population as a whole displayed a higher rate of economic activity than did the general population (just as the Jews had done half a century before), West Indians were the most economically active of all — owing to the greater tendency of West Indian, as compared to Indian or Pakistani, women to go out to work. Between 1961 and 1966 this gap narrowed somewhat, but not sufficiently as to remove the differential in this respect (Jones and Smith 1970 : 32, Table 8). At the same time, however, (and partly as an effect of higher female employment) West Indians seemed if anything the worst off in terms of the nature of the jobs they held.

This is interesting, since the available evidence on 1950s immigration would seem to suggest that the first West Indian arrivals included a higher proportion of skilled townsfolk, as compared to an Indian and Pakistani migration consisting largely of village craftsmen and peasants (Rose 1969 : Ch. 5). How far the discrepancy between prior qualifications claimed and jobs actually secured, in the West Indian case, was the product of racial discrimination over here and how far it was simply a comment on the non-comparability of trade labels between a developing and a long-developed economy, cannot easily be determined. That blanket terms such as 'skilled mechanic' were capable of more than one interpretation, however, seems clear enough.

West Indians, at any rate, might be expected to be the more disappointed group occupationally, simply because they seem to have expected more than did their Asian counterparts. In the event, there was not so very much to distinguish New Commonwealth immigrant groups from one another so far as the socio-economic status of their occupations was concerned. All were overrepresented (in comparison with the general population) in semi-skilled and unskilled manual work, just as all were under-represented in non-manual occupations. [20] Within this picture, however, there were points of variation.

Thus particular groups of immigrants tended to be associated with particular fields of work in the various settlement areas — West Indians with bus conductoring in London Transport, for instance; Indian and especially Pakistani men with the textile mills of West Yorkshire; West Indian women with counter service in the catering trade; and Indian women to some extent with clerical posts. West Indian nurses made a strong showing, of course, but then so did Asian doctors. All in all, Asian immigrants seemed the more successful in securing white-collar positions, while West Indian males appeared if anything the more successful in the skilled manual categories.[20]

One further point of distinction concerned the propensity to enter into self-employment, or rather family business, particularly within the catering and retail market. Extended family traditions, coupled with extensive village-kin networks in this country, may well have inclined would-be Indian and Pakistani entrepreneurs in this direction. West Indians, in contrast, made virtually no showing in this field.[20]

So far as housing conditions are concerned, the evidence can readily be summarized. West Indian, Indian, and Pakistani households tended to occupy the most densely populated housing (partly by virtue of their greater than average household size and partly as a consequence of their fewer than average rooms per accommodation unit); they were more likely to be living in shared accommodation; they were more likely to be in units which lacked one or more of the basic amenities (and to be paying more for less in this respect); they were more likely to be resident in an area of general social deprivation; and they were less likely to be in local authority accommodation than were members of the general population (Rose 1969 : Ch. 12).[20]

Set against this, however, New Commonwealth households (Indians in particular) were far more likely than were working-class native households to be purchasing their own homes (Rose 1969 : 134, 137). This might, of course, be interpreted as no more than further proof of the limited options otherwise open to coloured immigrants in the housing market. Certainly the type of properties thus purchased were likely to be at the less desirable, not to say risky, end of the market, just as the loan facilities obtained could be far removed from any building society norms (Burney 1967 : 48-50). At the same time, however, a greater tendency towards house purchase could be seen as part of a broader striving and saving propensity on the part of these newcomer groups.

All three, West Indian, Indian, and Pakistani groupings seemed, in other words, to be inclined to save (or send home) a far higher proportion of their weekly earnings than their native counterparts at similarly low income levels (Rose 1969 : 193-5). This might, of course, have been no more than a consequence of the immigrants' constituting a much younger population than the native average (Rose 1969 : 195). A marked propensity to save, nevertheless, would seem to conform with the (by now) traditional image of the economic migrant — to which perhaps the Irish in early nineteenth century Britain were no more than a starting exception.

Despite such general propensities, however, there was little inherently to unite New Commonwealth immigrants, or West Indian, Indian, and Pakistani immigrants, as a group. As has already been suggested, these newcomers were drawn from a wide range of ethnic and cultural backgrounds, all one-time subjects of the Empire, perhaps, yet hardly with a common experience of Empire (or indeed with any common social or religous traditions) behind them. Thus, on the one hand, there was the variety of Caribbean inheritance while, on the other, there were the intricacies of the religious, linguistic, and geographical affinities evident between immigrants from the Indian subcontinent, along lines which by no means coincided with any neat distinction between those from India itself and those from Pakistan.

Neither the Caribbean immigrants on the one hand, therefore, nor the Asian immigrants on the other, could be described as culturally or ethnically homogeneous populations. Nor was their heterogeneity of the same order or implication in each case.

To talk of a West Indian culture was, in a sense, to talk of an artifact in which things European, things African, things Asian, things Oriental, and of course things British were all variously to be traced, yet all subtly modified by their particular island contexts (see Parry and Sherlock 1968; Carley 1963; Henriques, 1953; Herskovitz 1947; Kerr 1952). So composite and varied an inheritance could at once provide points of affinity, and immigrant expectations of affinity, with British society and, at the same time, furnish ample proofs of differences between host and colonial (or ex-colonial) norms.

The scope for such mutual misunderstandings was less apparent in the Indian and Pakistani case. Moslem, Sikh or Hindu allegiances, for instance, amounted to far more recognizable, predictable, and internally consistent patterns of behaviour, albeit conspicuously alien patterns of behaviour, for the host society to come to terms with. Nor, in this case, was there the confusion of a so-called common first language to contend with.[21].

(ii) *Host society reaction*

Superficially at least, New Commonwealth immigration seems to have given rise to much the same range of sentiments, writ large, as had earlier been expressed about the Irish and about the Jews. Irrespective of the changes in social, economic, and political conditions over this period, there seems to have been a notable consistency of opinion where mass, 'less civilised'[22] immigration was concerned.

Even so, stereotyped impressions of newcomer characteristics did tend to vary in certain particulars. Thus, while every mass immigrant group was liable to be pronounced unconventional, unclean, unprincipled, and generally unwelcome, the clever alien Jew had aroused a somewhat different package of sentiments than those earlier expressed over the so-called feckless, pseudo-citizen Irish. New Commonwealth immigrant stereotypes were slightly different again. They tended to distinguish, for instance, between West Indian and Asian, and, to a lesser extent, between presumed Indian and Pakistani, characteristics.

So varied a typology was no more than a response to the obviously mixed characteristics of this so-called 'group' of immigrants. Yet the variety of response does in itself point to more specific parallels between this and earlier experiences. Thus West Indians, as supposed cheap casual labour, carefree, low-living, immoral, disorderly colonial subjects, seem in many respects to have been perceived as some sort of coloured equivalent of the Irish (who were, after all, still in evidence). Sikhs, Moslems, and Hindus, on the other hand, seem to have been caricatured as a poor, low-living, yet ambitious population; prone to inscrutable underhand dealings; set apart from neighbours or fellow-workers not merely by language but by alien religions, customs, and appearances; and inclined very much to keep themselves to themselves: more reminiscent of the East European Jew, if anything, than of either the Irish or the West Indian.

Like the Irish, but unlike the East European Jews, however, New Commonwealth immigrants were distributed between most of the major urban/industrial centres of the country. Their presence, therefore, was much more generally apparent than had been the case with Jewish (predominantly East End) settlement. In addition, they were possessed of one notable and unifying characteristic: they were virtually all non-white, albeit to varying degrees.

The appearance of coloured individuals, or even of small local coloured populations in this country, was in itself nothing new. The onetime negro slave population of London, for instance, had seemingly melted into the background, following emancipation (Patterson 1963 : 36-7). Colonial subjects of suitable rank or breeding had regularly been invited to visit Victorian and post Victorian Britain (Glass 1960 : 109). The coloured seamen's quarter of Cardiff, Liverpool, and elsewhere were by now traditional features of the local landscape (Little 1947). The presence, nevertheless, of a coloured population sufficiently numerous and widely distributed as to constitute a noticeable proportion of most major urban populations, was a novelty.

This is not the book in which to attempt to analyze the dynamics of colour prejudice, any more than it is the book in which to try to unravel the nature of anti-semitism. Both are subjects in themselves, each with their own extensive literature. However it is worth asking, in this context, how far the existence of colour prejudice as a factor contributing to host society reaction is to be compared, in its implications, with anti-semitism and its effects in the case of East European Jewish immigration. Like the new Jews, New Commonwealth immigrants were to meet with deep-rooted, irrational hostility of a nature quite distinct, it would seem, from the brands of familiar dislike and distaste metered out to the Irish.

Anti-semitism in the East European Jewish case and colour prejudice in the New Commonwealth case shared at least two points of significance. In each instance the potential strength and distribution of such prejudice was assumed, with some reason, to be considerable. In neither case, however, was the open expression of prejudice (or any blatant appeal to prejudice in others) deemed politically respectable.

Three sets of consequences followed from this situation. Leading opponents of immigration, though emboldened by what they doubtless felt to be a weight of popular opinion behind them, would be careful always to disassociate themselves, personally, from any taint of prejudice, however seemingly prejudiced might be the drift of their remarks.[23] Yet the mere expression of such sentiments, however 'reasonably' presented, was sufficient to prompt an answering 'liberal' response. Hence we have the third consequence of apparently widespread but politically non-respectable racial prejudice: a prolonged and often virulent political debate over the question of whether or not the immigration in question should be curtailed. It took some thirty-five years of Jewish alien infiltration, and accompanying debate, to secure the passage of the *Aliens Act* of 1905. It took considerably less time for the first Commonwealth Immigrants Act to reach the statute book although this last, as we shall see, was no more than a statutory beginning.

The parallel, however, should not be stretched too far. One is bound to ask why it was that controls legislation was so much more speedily introduced in the New Commonwealth as compared to the Jewish case and why, after 1962, the controls lobby should this time have lost none of its momentum and effectiveness. Particularities apart, there are at least three general considerations worth bearing in mind.

The first has to be the most obvious. British governments' having embarked on systematic (if limited) alien immigration control from 1905, and having maintained officially throughout the 1930s and 1940s, for instance, that Britain was definitely not to be considered a country of immigration (wartime refugees from Hitler's Germany, Polish ex-combatants, and European Volunteer Workers imported specifically to man the labour-hungry sectors of the country's postwar economy, being specific, limited exceptions to this rule) (Foot 1965 : Ch. 6); it was surprising, perhaps, not that New Commonwealth immigration should eventually have been made the subject of government controls, but that such controls were not more promptly introduced. Only the thinking and unthinking ties of empire, coupled with continuing postwar labour shortages in the 1950s, can explain the temporary free for all in this case.

Against this background, moreover, the state, as a welfare state, was potentially answerable for the social consequences of New Commonwealth immigration to an extent quite removed from its responsibilities in the Jewish, let alone the Irish, case. There was that much more to talk about, in other words, and that much more which ought conceivably to be effected either way in relation to this newcomer presence.

On top of this was the enhanced political importance of popular opinion. By this token, the views of those who felt themselves most immediately to be threatened by the immigrants' presence were not merely of greater numerical significance (given the much wider distribution of the New Commonwealth, as compared to the new Jewish population), but were inherently of greater import, given a system of government that was supposed to act not merely on behalf of, but as the spokesman for, the mass of the people. So competitor unease was a factor to be reckoned with, as never before.

Leaving all this aside, there is one further, obvious, point of difference to note between the Jewish and the New Commonwealth case. Unlike the new Jews, New Commonwealth immigrants had upon first arrival no long-established native community of co-religionists or ex-nationals to turn to. In this sense they had no automatic, and universally credible, native backers.

The consequences of this were interesting. Thanks to the undoubted emotional appeal of any battle against colour prejudice (and thanks also the strengths of colonial and Commonwealth association) (Foot 1965; Katznelson 1973 : 175-6), part of the deficiency in this case was made good by the efforts of what can best be described as a native, pro-immigrant lobby. This was not merely a political coming together (as in the Jewish case) but a body of effort which attempted, albeit in a piecemeal, sporadic, fashion, to respond to the social and economic predicaments of New Commonwealth immigrants, both locally and nationally (Patterson 1969 : Ch. 8). Such efforts were bound, perhaps, to receive a mixed reception on both sides — precisely because they did not constitute automatic, and therefore universally credible, native backing. Nevertheless, we have in this case to evaluate host society reaction, once again, in terms of a two-way distinction: general popular reaction and (for want of a better term) pro-immigrant reaction. We will take the general reaction first.

Once again, the mere strangeness of the immigrants, their unfamiliar appearances, patterns of speech and styles of behaviour, was sufficient to make any area of immigrant settlement seem like a threat to the English way of life. If the Whitechapel of the 1900s had seemed like a latter-day Jerusalem to the 'untutored, unthinking denizen of the East End' (see above p.87), then the Brixton or the Notting Hill of the 1950s, or the Southall of the early '60s, seemed not a whit less transformed beyond alleged local recognition (Patterson 1963 : 3).

The fact that these newcomers were mostly coloured, was of double significance. A darker skin colour was in itself a mark of difference and strangeness. In addition, however, it served as an easy, obvious identifier of those whose characteristics were otherwise to be subsumed under the umbrella of 'typical' New Commonwealth behaviour. There were inaccuracies inherent, of course, in assuming every Black to be a typical immigrant, or indeed in assuming every Black to be an immigrant at all; yet such niceties were no different in kind from those earlier ignored when every Catholic might be presumed an Irishman (above p.44), for instance, or when every poor Jew might be presumed an immigrant — and every East European immigrant might be presumed a Jew (above p.68).

The availability of a colour label for New Commonwealth immigration clearly makes it difficult to separate popular reaction on the score of believed immigrant behavioural characteristics from popular colour prejudice *per se*. Much the same, however, could be said concerning the impossibility of distinguishing between reaction to earlier Jewish immigrants on account of their alleged undesirable qualities, and anti-semitism *per se*. The line between out-and-out race prejudice and specific, 'rational' complaint is in both cases impossible to draw — and there were, in both cases, political opponents of immigration only too ready to capitalize on, and promote, this very ambiguity.

Mere strangeness (and colour) apart, the areas of complaint and misgiving voiced over New Commonwealth immigration have a familiar ring, in the light of earlier experience. Once again, the newcomers were deemed to be a low class, low living, unclean, and therefore unwelcome addition to the nation's stock. Thus, just as the new Jews had 'lowered the tone' of areas into which they moved, so now it seemed the coloureds were doing the same. The Smethwick housewife of 1961 might have been the East End midwife of 1902 (see above p.75) revisited when she declared:-

'Edgbaston Road use to be a *lovely* road ... you used to have nannies up that way, you know. Really good class people used to live there, and it was a pleasure to walk in that area. Now *they've* taken over and the place is a slum. It's horrible ...'

'Their habits are pretty terrible. They use the front garden as a rubbish dump, and heaven knows what they do in the toilets.'[24]

The local Irish, once again, were often portrayed as being almost respectable in comparison with these latest, lowest immigrant arrivals (though Jews, significantly, were rarely mentioned at all in this connection).[25] Yet, however familiar and predictable the general drift of distaste and denunciation, allegations in the New Commonwealth case tended, if anything, to be both more specific and more vehement than those voiced earlier, over earlier immigrants. Perhaps this was only to be expected. Given social services more pervasive than ever before and given working-class expectations of a higher standard of living than ever before, it was at least a more informed, a more questioning, if not a more querulous populace with which the New Commonwealth immigrants had to contend.

The presumed relationship between immigrant living standards and the public's health was a case in point. Both the Irish and the Jews had, in their day, been proclaimed a health hazard, in a general sense. The case against New Commonwealth immigrants, however, could draw not merely upon the evidence of more detailed public health statistics than ever before but upon the vexed question, also, of comparative access to and benefit from National Health Service facilities.

Thus, apart from the general hazard of living alongside 'These people [who] do not know the basic principles of hygiene',[26] West Indian males were known to be statistically more likely to contract (and hence transmit) VD, for instance, while Indian and Pakistani males were known to be unusually susceptible to TB. Indeed, to quote one Medical Officer of Health: 'The concern in this case is valid: TB would probably cease being a problem at all if there was no immigration.' (Jones 1975 : 32)

Whatever the careful, expert arguments put forward to suggest, for instance, that a rise in VD statistics might stem principally from the English girls with whom these West Indian males associated (BMA 1965), or that Asian TB susceptibility might be as much a consequence of Asian living and working conditions in this country as of any imported, inherited predisposition (BMA 1965), the facts, so far as the general public were concerned, seemed all too clear. This was a case of additional 'objective' information serving actually to fuel subjective beliefs.

Where immigrant susceptibilities were not thought to be catching and/or immoral, there was of course not the same public concern. If immigrant children figured disproportionately among cases of rickets and anaemia (Yudkin 1965 : 9-10), then this might be proof of backwardness but it was not in itself a threat to the public's health and morals; though it threatened, of course, to place additional burdens upon the workings of the National Health Service, which brings us to our second point.

The general public, when roused, was not merely more health conscious than ever before; it was also very jealous of its health services. Any seeming threat to these could seem like a health hazard in itself. Hence the uproar, in the mid-1960s, over the so-called take-over of maternity beds by immigrant mothers in the Wolverhampton area particularly (Rose 1969 : 336). This despite the fact that, so far as hospital services in general were concerned, New Commonwealth immigrants appeared to be making well below average demands, as well as supplying the hospitals themselves with a sizeable proportion of their much-needed medical and ancillary staff (Rose 1969 : 337-8).

Many of the so-called health susceptibilities of immigrant house-holds were demonstrably the product of, and a commentary upon, their housing circumstances in this country (Skone 1968 : 13; Dodge and Myers 1969 : 57-64). Yet immigrant housing, naturally enough, figured as a bone of contention in itself. Here again, the public was concerned, not with the adequacy or otherwise of immigrant living conditions *per se*, but rather with the apparent threat to its own housing interests, and to the workings of its own housing services, presented by the immigrants' being here at all.

The association between immigrant households and the least satisfactory, most exploitative housing conditions (whether for house purchasers or for private tenants) could of course be interpreted as no more than a comment on the current shortcomings of the housing market in Britain. Indeed the association was so interpreted by a succession of expert commentators throughout the 1960s.[27] In addition, it could be regarded as proof of the extent and strength of racial discrimination as it bore upon this vital determinant of life-style and life chances in the host society (Milner Hollard Report; Burney 1967 : 10-11).

Nevertheless, so far as the general public was concerned, this was once again (as with the Jews in the East End) a case of primitive newcomers moving into vulnerable areas in force; driving up local housing costs and increasing the rate of overcrowding by their competition for available units; lowering the tone of such neighbourhoods by their mere presence, let alone their patterns of behaviour; and driving out native residents unable to compete with them on a cost basis and/or unwilling to stomach their proximity. If the immigrants themselves were indeed the victims of exploitation then, once again, it was fellow-immigrants who were among the most ruthless racketeers, in their haste to acquire and profit from substandard properties, at their tenants' (be they black or white) expense (Burney 1967 : 25-7 and see above p.76).

Compared to its comprehensive responsibilities in the field of health care, the role of the state in matters of housing was far less clearly spelt out and seemingly far less extensive (see below pp.186 and 237-38). If anything, however, this restricted state responsibility served to make matters more, rather than less, explosive. On the one hand, public imagination could run riot over the effects immigrants were having on the private housing market while, on the other, local authority housing departments could hardly take relevant action of any sort without this appearing to be in some way controversial — local authority housing in such areas being a scarce and much competed-for commodity (see below p.239; also Burney 1967 : Ch. 5).

State responsibilities in the employment field, traditionally the most notable area for grievance over mass immigration, were arguably no more clearly spelt out (and if anything even more marginal) than in the housing sphere (see below p.186). In this case however, while the general remarks in circulation, concerning the deleterious effects of New Commonwealth immigration upon the labour market, were no more than might have been expected, the role of the state was controversial not because its services seemed the subject of fierce competition between immigrants and hosts, so much as because these services seemed, at least indirectly, to be attempting to influence local employment policies in general, to the advantage of the immigrant.

The 'general remarks', needless to say, ran along lines already familiar. Predictably, the immigrants were accused on the one hand of coming here to sponge off social security (the modern replacement for the Poor Law) and, on the other, of prejudicing native job prospects by their willingness to accept even the meanest terms of employment.

Thus on the first account: 'These people are bribed to come here by doles, National Assistance[28] and all the amenities of the Welfare State free.'[29]

So: the Irish had crossed the Irish Sea in order to live off the English Poor Law; the West indians had crossed the Atlantic in order to live off the British Welfare State: not an irrational progression, although hardly a proven one in either case.

The reputation of the immigrants as newcomers to the labour market shows a different kind of progression. Citizens of a welfare state ideologically committed to the notion of full employment were inclined to view coloured labour, not as an immediate threat to their jobs, so much as a menace to their longer-term job security and prospects. The days were long gone, it seemed, when a ruthless or desperate employer might dispense with awkward labour on any scale and replace this with gullible newcomers. Nor were wage rates, where established, to be openly undercut. New Commonwealth immigrants, by constituting a pool of cheap, mobile, undemanding labour, undermined rather at one remove.

Clearly their arrival had helped reduce labour shortages in the British economy in the latter 1950s — a fact of double significance. On the one hand it suggested that if bad times, and large-scale unemployment, should return, then more native workers might be thrown out of work than if this additional labour force had never descended on the country. On the other hand, and more immediately, the existence of an immigrant labour force helped arguably to perpetuate poor employment conditions, since the newcomers seemed prepared to take up the least attractive jobs on terms which fewer and fewer British workers seemed willing to accept. London Transport's direct recruitment of Barbadian labour in the 1950s seemed a blatant illustration of this reality. Were it not for coloured labour, it was alleged, wages and conditions would have had drastically to be improved in this, as in other sectors of employment (National Committee for Commonwealth Immigrants 1967 : 98-9). To a population which was coming, increasingly, to expect rising standards of living as of right, the newcomers seemed a drag on the market.

Nor, once again, was the argument left solely to the populace or its spokesmen to propound. In the hands of professional economists, the issues emerged as, if anything, even more intricate, and potentially doom-laden, than those so carefully proclaimed in the Jewish case (see above pp.79-80). The scope of the discussion had been considerably enlarged. Yet, by the same token, the scope for disagreement between professional economists was correspondingly the greater. For every writer who alleged that an influx of cheap, unskilled labour must have delayed the introduction of modern labour-saving plant into British industry, there were those who declared that, without such an influx

of extra manpower in the 1950s, British industry would have ground
to a halt. For every economist convinced that the capital costs of such
immigration must outweigh any short term economic advantages,
there were those equally convinced that the newcomers were in fact
merely taking up some of the slack in the system — their expectations
and demands being far from comparable with the equivalent
expectations and demands of their native peers. Again, for every writer
who proclaimed that mass immigration must retard capital formation
there were those no less convinced that the greater saving propensity of
immigrant households must constitute an asset, in this respect, to the
British economy. And so the argument went on (see Wilson 1970;
Jones and Smith 1970).

In the meantime, and quite apart from such intricacies, employer
and employee notions as to what to expect from 'the typical' New
Commonwealth worker were varied to say the least. This was not
simply a case of typical West Indian versus typical Indian or typical
Pakistani characteristics, but a range of stereotypes dependent
apparently upon the nature and location of the business, the size of
the total workforce, the numbers and distribution, as well as ethnic
composition, of immigrant workers, the structure of management,
and so on.[30] Thus West Indians might be regarded as over-qualified
and therefore awkward to deal with, or as under-qualified despite
their nominal qualifications. If they were slow this could be because
they were lazy, or because they were incapable of anything faster; if
they were truculent it could be because they had chips on their
shoulders, or because they were simply strong and aggressive by
nature. Asians, again, might be regarded as more tractable than West
Indians as a workforce; yet less flexible when it came to any changes of
work routine; less reliable when it came to sheer physical stamina;
and in need of far more extensive works supervision than anything
required in the case of West Indian/or native employees. This last
need not simply be a consequence of language barriers. In the words of
one employer:-

'Asian workers do not know many things which are just taken for
granted with whites. This causes a strain on supervision time. The
firm employs more supervisors than usual and pays them higher
wages than normal. It is an invisible cost of employing Pakistanis.'
(Wright 1968 : 96)

Such a variety of impression (extending well beyond the range of the illustrations offered above) was perhaps only to be expected, given the heterogeneous nature of New Commonwealth immigration and the widespread distribution of its members. It was against this backcloth, that the role of statutory employment and youth employment services, with their commitment, informal before 1968 and formal thereafter, to promote 'equality of opportunity' between coloured immigrants and hosts in the employment market, could seem so crude, so unwelcome, and so artificial to those who felt themselves, whether as employers or as workers, to be on the receiving end.

For all the modesty of its intentions, the *Race Relations Act* of 1968 (in so far as it applied to employment and employment services) furnished both sides, management and labour, with particular grounds for complaint. Confusion, real or apparent, over its scope and objectives was seemingly widespread. Native workers, protesting the non-existence of race prejudice amongst themselves, could denounce the Act as a device to secure the coloured man preferment and security just because he was coloured. Employers could declare that they were bound, henceforth, to appoint and promote blacks rather than whites, wherever there was a choice, or at least that they must tread much more carefully where blacks were concerned, than they need do over whites (c.f. below pp.232-33).

Employers' organizations and trades unions had been at one, of course, in their oppostion to any prospective race relations legislation such as would seek to interfere, statutorily, with traditional free individual and collective bargaining in industry. How far this stance represented a reaction against the prospect of increased governmental interference as such, and how far it represented an antipathy to race relations regulation as such, is difficult to estimate. But it was only when they were faced with the prospect of possible race relations legislation touching upon employment, that both the CBI and the TUC set about formulating policies to deal with racial discrimination as conceivably practised by their members, instead of contenting themselves, as the TUC had done hitherto, with mere declaratory statements on the subject (see Rose 1969 : 529-32; Patterson 1969 : 102-3; Abbot 1971 : 171). It was in part consequence of this stance that the *Race Relations Act* of 1968, as it eventually emerged, allocated such a prominent role to voluntary machinery in industry for the initial handling of employment complaints (see below p.171).

Formal policy at TUC level was not necessarily the same thing, of course, as individual trades union policy which, in turn, was not quite the same thing as local shopfloor practice (Hepple 1970 : 134-5; Rose 1969 : 311-17). Bearing this in mind, the effective response of the movement to New Commonwealth immigrants can be described as a mixture reminiscent, at least in its negative aspects, of the reception accorded and the reputation ascribed to both the Irish and the Jews in their day.

Thus, if the Irish had been declared a riff-raff impossible to organize and wide open to employer manipulation, and the Jews had been dismissed as spineless, selfish, blackleg material (above p.54 and pp.82-83), coloured workers were often liable to much the same sort of local image. They too might be pronounced impossible to organize effectively, in the low-level occupations in which they were likely to be found. They too were said to lack the resources, the will-power, the self control, and the understanding to make good trades union members. They too, therefore, could be denounced as a threat to the movement.[31]

At the same time, once again, there was little evidence in the early 1960s of any widespread enthusiasm to promote trades union membership among the immigrant population. With a few notable exceptions, the coloureds seem to have been no more welcome at shop-floor or branch level than the Jews had been before them. Once again the 'unpromising', 'unsuitable' material was left very much to sink or swim on its own[32], at least before the threat and then the actuality of race relations legislation eased one branch after another into a more cautious, self-consciously correct 'integratory' posture, on paper at least.[33]

Many of the attributes variously ascribed to sections of the New Commonwealth population by local trades union members were little more than extensions of the newcomers' overall reputation as supposed suspect members of the community. Law and order seemed the field in which parallels between West Indian and Irish, or between Asian and Jewish, reputations were at their most obvious. Like the Irish before them, West Indians were associated in the public mind with spur-of-the-moment violence — quite apart from their leanings towards drugs and sexual offices. Like the Jews before them, the Indian and Pakistani immigrants were associated with fraud, attempted bribery, and generally underhand ways. All in all the coloureds' was not a savoury reputation.[34]

The public's impression, nevertheless, was more understandable than accurate. Police dealings with and expectations of the immigrant community might seem to confirm the general picture; yet members of the police force were also members of the general public even though, like the Blacks, they might be instantly distinguishable from it, at least when in uniform. New Commonwealth immigrants tended to reside in twilight areas noted for a higher than average crime rate. It mattered little, seemingly, that the immigrants themselves manifested a lower than average criminal propensity. Such offences as they were associated with at all might not be of the most serious but they were amongst the least popular, or the most despised, varieties, once again. Furthermore, most Blacks with which roving police officers came in contact were those either connected with or suspected of a possible offence. So far as police dealings with the coloured community were concerned, therefore, police expectations of the immigrants would seem to have been as self-fulfilling as were immigrant expectations of what treatment to expect from the police. Two readily identifiable, vulnerable groups were, in a sense, taking it out upon one another. [35]

That such a polarization of police-immigrant relationships should have reflected somewhat on contemporary recruitment, deployment, and training of police manpower, to say nothing of complaints procedures, would seem to have been a truth eventually and very publicly taken note of (Lambert 1970; Johnson 1970). The realization would seem to have come too late, however, for any far-reaching shift in police-immigrant relationships. There has been no dramatic increase in the level of immigrant applications to join police forces since the latter 1960s; while immigrant organizations profess, if anything, an increasingly militant stance against police 'interference'. [36]

The dividing line between law and order and political propensity has, as before, to be a difficult one to define. New Commonwealth citizens were initially regarded as an awkward and unpredictable commodity but not, in the last resort, as an essential, coherent, immigrant voting lobby. It was the strength of ex-colonial traditions that perhaps allowed for a prolonged political debate over the impact of New Commonwealth immigration which did not in itself look for more than token participation from the immigrants themselves (Katznelson 1973 : 176-7). The possible extent, consistency, or significance of a Black vote, if called upon, was not something that English politicians, conscious rather of the possible extent, consistency, and significance of a native anti-immigrant vote, seemed inclined to explore. It was only the hardening and polarization, eventually, of organized immigrant versus native points of view, that inspired the association in the public mind between coloured immigrants and extreme sectionalist demands (see below, p.149).

It is at this point, however, that we should examine the role of the mediators in this situation: the pro-immigrant lobby, such as it was.

That New Commonwealth immigrants possessed no automatic backers, in the sense in which Anglo-Jewry might loosely be termed the automatic backers of new Jewish immigration, has already been remarked. There was no section of native society, in other words, that might generally be expected to regard itself both as British, on the one hand, and as fundamentally akin to the immigrants, on the other. No one who was one of us could, in any real sense, be one of them also. Whatever the difficulties attached to the position of Anglo-Jewry during the period of new Jewish immigration, the absence of any equivalent group in this case was to prove of no small significance.

New Commonwealth immigrants tended to arrive in this country short of resources — whether in the form of capital, relevant skills, or relevant know-how. Naturally such immigrants made efforts to help themselves and their fellows by pooling many of such resources as they possessed. This was most noticeable in the case of Indian and Pakistani religious and village-kin networks; though it was hardly confined to these alone (Patterson 1969 : 315-22). Once the process of migration had resulted in there being a pool of experienced, established immigrants in this country, these efforts tended to become both more effective and more ambitious.[37]

Yet, to begin with at least, such newcomers seemed in obvious need of ear-marked support and asistance from members of the host society. Given that there was no significant body of Anglo-kinsmen or co-religionists to turn to, such support as was offered came essentially from groups of self-selected individuals — or ex-officio from a range of public figures — whose motivation for offering their services fell roughly into two categories, themselves not mutually exclusive. To begin with, individuals (or public figures) conscious and perhaps proud of Britian's imperial tradition could see it as their duty to make some effort to help our colonial or ex-colonial brethren feel at home and adjust successfully to life in Britain. In the second place, those who felt that some response was long overdue for the years of colonial exploitation together with those who regarded colour-stratified disadvantage as unacceptable in any form, could see their purpose as one of fighting to prevent coloured immigrants and their families from being treated as in any way second-class citizens in this country.[38]

Naturally matters were nowhere near so clear-cut as this implies. Given a subject so charged with emotional overtones and of such explosive political potential, motives publicly stated could be little more than an approximate guide to real intentions. Even so, the two broad types of motivation do seem to correspond to two distinctive styles of support.

A desire to assist our colonial brethren, or mother-country maternalism, seemed on the whole to find expression in a range of local friendship councils, liaison committees, Anglo-Caribbean or Anglo-Asian social clubs, and inter-cultural tea-parties all designed, fundamentally, to help the newcomer familiarize himself with British ways and British standards. The newcomer was to be helped to make the most of his opportunity and to make the least of any short-term difficulties he might be encountering, for his own sake (Ruck 1960). A desire to promote equal status for blacks alongside whites, however, seemed to point more towards political than social activity. The newcomers had a right to be accepted as they were, rather than as they might become, given suitable instruction. Adjustment by hosts as well as by immigrants was therefore required. Integration rather than mere benign assimilation was the target. The Campaign against Racial Discrimination was an obvious, though hardly the sole, illustration of this stance (Patterson 1969 : 308-15).

Not unnaturally, these two types of approach differed chronologically in their years of peak appeal. Early West Indian arrivals who, as colonial subjects of the Crown, both saw themselves as British and were anxious apparently to be received as such by members of the host society, were obvious targets for neo-colonial welfare.[39] The subsequent expansion in the numbers of Asian Commonwealth disembarkations, together with the mounting evidence of the difficulties and complications apparently surrounding coloured immigration on any scale, served gradually to shift the balance of pro-immigrant manoeuvres away from hopes of painless assimilation towards more remedial objectives. West Indians were seemingly becoming disillusioned in the face of manifest non-acceptance. Asians, somewhat later in coming, had never laid claim to any desire either to be regarded as 'British' or, by their own efforts, to render themselves more acceptable to British opinion.

Thus while the 1950s witnessed a flowering of neo-colonial-style welfare arrangements, the first half of the 1960s witnessed a noticeable shift towards what were, in the circumstances, more drastic integrationist postures. The very word 'integration' — hitherto a blanket expression embracing, apparently, most well-intentioned, pro-immigrant objectives — took on a new precision. 'I define integration', declared Roy Jenkins, in his now famous Home Secretary speech of 1966:-

> ' … not as a flattening process of assimilation but as equal oppor-
> tunity, accompanied by cultural diversity, in an atmosphere of
> mutual tolerance. This is the goal.'[40]

He was addressing the committed, and the committed were by this time well prepared for such a definition. Nevertheless, for all its seeming simplicity and benign common sense, the stated goal was to prove both ambiguous and elusive.

To stand up for equality of opportunity was hardly a daring manoeuvre in itself. Equality of opportunity, enshrined more or less as an article of faith in the post-war Welfare State, was not something that many would speak openly against, even where coloured immigrants were concerned. Much depended, however, on what exactly was meant by equality of opportunity and on how, precisely, such equality once defined was to be engineered. The difficulties already implicit and becoming apparent in reconciling the ideal of equal opportunity with the no less cherished ideal of equal treatment, when dealing with a socially and economically unequal population, were inevitably highlighted and exaggerated by the presence of an outsider, but citizen, newcomer population.

The two integrationist accompaniments to equality of opportunity, namely the maintenance of cultural diversity amid an atmosphere of mutual tolerance, were necessary if only to allow for something, at least, of that differentiation of treatment that equality of opportunity within a host-immigrant situation would seem to require. Cultural diversity and mutual tolerance, however, were objectives problematic in themselves. Immigrants, particularly poor immigrants, moving from one society to another, might be expected to find certain aspects of their cultural background more essential than others or more appropriate than others or more functional than others, in the new setting. Quite what is considered essential or appropriate or functional has, by its very nature, to be a private, personal decision, within the constraints imposed by a particular host-immigrant situation.

Similarly a host society may find certain immigrant traits more desirable than others or less intrusive than others or more tolerable than others. The two sets of variables are not necessarily symmetrical, or at least not necessarily reconcilable.

Hence the imponderable problems faced by the committed integrationist. Ought equality of immediate opportunity to be insisted upon to the extent of making special allowance for differences of background and hence for disparity of experience and training? Was cultural diversity something merely to be tolerated so 'long as it persisted — or something positively to be allowed for and encouraged; even when the views of the immigrants themselves (and particularly second-generation immigrants) might be less than clear-cut and when the perpetuation of such differences might seem prejudicial at least to the immigrants' short-term economic and social prospects in Britain? How was an injunction in favour of mutual tolerance to be reconciled with the individual's (*any* individual's) sacred freedom privately to like and dislike whomsoever other individuals he chose?

Given the social policy sophistication implicit in the idea of a Welfare State, it was only to be expected, perhaps, that issues such as these should have been highlighted by the experience of New Commonwealth immigration, in a way that they never were in the Irish or the Jewish case. The fact that such questions were being aired and to some extent answered did not mean, however, that the immigrant population in this case felt itself necessarily to be in any more secure or hopeful position relative to its predecessors. On the contrary, the 1960s were marked by more voluble expressions of immigrant discontent and by more 'intransigent' immigrant demands than had ever previously been experienced by Britian as a host society.[41]

There are many possible ways of explaining this phenomenon. One might argue that, as citizen immigrants to a democratic society, New Commonwealth immigrants were uniquely placed both to voice their grievances and to expect to be listened to, in a way that neither the Irish (as citizen immigrants to a non-democratic society) nor the Jews (as alien immigrants to an increasingly democratic society) ever were. The 'permissive' 1960s, moreover, seemed conducive generally to the expression of sectional popular protest and complaint, to an extent that conventional, hierarchical, Edwardian society (for all its formal democratic insititutions) most certainly was not. Nor could New Commonwealth groups be expected, in their discontent, to compare their own position dispassionately and accurately with the plight of earlier newcomers. Even had the information been to hand, why should they have accepted any such comparison? Indeed one might argue that, as coloured citizen immigrants to a populist welfare state, their position was relatively the more desperate and frustrating than that facing any earlier influx of newcomers.

Nor was this all. Immigrant opinion seemed to harden and become more outspoken to the extent that *pro*-immigrant opinion showed itself incapable of delivering the goods, where equality of opportunity amid cultural diversity backed up by mutual tolerance was concerned. Escalating immigrant demands may themselves have determined this verdict; yet the 'failure' of pro-immigrant opinion, if such it can be termed, merits further exploration. At one level, the reasons seem obvious enough: there were no easy answers to such indeterminate objectives within such an unequal, unharmonious, unclear social setting. At another level, a less facile explanation hinges upon the nature and inherent limitations of pro-immigrant opinion as a mediating or buffer force within this host-newcomer context.

The weakness of pro-immigrant opinion (in all its variety) lay precisely in the fact that it was a matter of opinion. There were no pre-established ties either of blood or religious belief such as might persuade sections of the immigrant community, on the one hand, and the bulk of the host society, on the other, to accept an association between certain members of the host society and certain groups among the immigrant population as fundamentally natural, predictable, or reliable — in the sense that the strength, motivation, and reality of such a two-way loyalty was unlikely seriously to be questioned by either side. As a self-selected group of varying motivation, the pro-immigrants had constantly to demonstrate and to vindicate their position both to hosts and to immigrants alike.[42]

The consequences were as might have been expected. The immigrant's cause, the immigrant's difficulties, the immigrant's grievances were put with sufficient force and conviction as to render the host society not merely self-conscious but actively defensive. The pro-immigrants were accused of overstating their case; of adding to current difficulties by ill-timed publicity; of making no allowance for the run-of-the-mill disadvantages which *any* immigrants to a more developed economy might reasonably be expected to encounter; and of putting ideas and a sense of grievance into potentially peaceable immigrant heads. 'Every West Indian must know by now that he is supposed to be alienated', to quote one disgruntled youth employment official.[43]

All in all, pro-immigrant opinion seems to have struck the bulk of the host society as a mixture of the unbalanced, the unrealistic, the gullible — if not, in the last resort, the unpatriotic.

So far as the immigrants themselves were concerned, the pro-immigrants seem increasingly to have aroused a no less than equivalent suspicion. They were said to protest too much with too little result. As members of an oppressive white society, themselves with an obvious stake in the status quo, they were more interested, so it was said, in purging their own souls by verbal denunciation and disassociation, than in working radically to alter the social structure and conventions upon which they, like the rest of white society, depended. Any moves described by them as in aid of better race relations were little more than attempts successfully to integrate the black man into a subordinate position within the social structure. True integration, apparently, could only be upon a fifty-fifty basis.[44]

Against such a background of mounting defensiveness (if not outright hostility) on the one hand and mounting disillusion coupled with suspicion, on the other, credible leadership of coloured immigrant communities seemed more and more to necessitate a severing of ties both with integrationist whites and their 'go-between' black associates;[45] at the very time when legislative and institutional manoeuvres in the name of better race relations were becoming thickest on the ground. Hence the crises first in CARD (Rose 1969 : 543-46; Heinemann 1972; Glean 1973), and subsequently in the Institute of Race Relations.[46] If there was any place for whites in the Black peoples' struggle, there was no place at all for so-called dispassionate and would-be mediatory opinion (white or black). In so polarizing a situation there was less and less room, apparently, for the men in the middle.

The implications of this development may emerge rather more clearly when we come (in the following chapter) to discuss specific race relations policy manoeuvres within the Welfare State. At this stage, however, it seems worthwhile to refer back to the contrast earlier suggested between the role performed by Anglo-Jewry in relation to new Jewish immigration and that performed by pro-immigrant opinion in relation to New Commonwealth immigration. Both sets of immigrants were poor and strange. Both were the subjects of racial prejudice and of a prolonged political campaign to prohibit or curtail their further entry. Yet there was not the same, well-publicized polarization of immigrant versus native opinion in the Jewish, as there has been in the New Commonwealth case.

Quite apart from the special features of New Commonwealth immigration as a black, citizen influx to a democratic welfare state, one of the explanations for this difference of outcome (so far) would appear to lie in the fact that, as a mediating influence, Anglo-Jewry at the turn of the century was everything that pro-immigrant opinion in the 1960s was not. To begin with, the strength, permanency, and motivation of the former's two-way loyalties were not seriously to be called in question. Members of the Anglo-Jewish community were seen by both sides as occupying a midway position irrespective, almost, of individual choice or individual reputation. They belonged both ways in part; and they belonged completely in neither camp.

Hence, on the one hand, there was the concern of English Jews over the possible harmful effects of unthinking mass Jewish immigration upon English public opinion and upon their own hard-won position (see above p.87). Hence, on the other hand, there was their concern at least to safeguard the interests and the wellbeing of those immigrants already established in this country (see above p.88). This last they were well placed to do — as a community well represented among the businessmen, the politicians, the ratepayers, and the taxpayers of the local community — in an age when popular opinion as such could to some extent be disregarded. Altogether, moreover, this was a role which both sides expected them to perform.

In the light of this example, one may wonder how different, or how much more tempered, New Commonwealth reception might have been, had there existed comparable, well-established Anglo-Moslem, Anglo-Hindu, or Anglo-West Indian communities for all sides to look towards, be it with approval or disapproval, automatically. No single established bridgehead could have sufficed, of course, for so varied a collection of immigrants. In the absence of any, we are left with an interesting series of questions.

Immigrants moving in numbers from a less developed into a more developed and more complex economic and social structure can expect to have to start at the bottom, more or less, and can expect to have a pretty thin time of it, initially at least. Such certainly is the impression to be gained, not only from the study of earlier immigration to this country but from the study, for instance, of successive ethnic waves of immigration to the United States (Herberg 1956 : Ch. 2). As true middle-men, with their feet genuinely in both camps, Anglo-Jewry had sought, in effect, to moderate and humanize this situation for the new Jews, but not fundamentally to challenge the idea of 'natural' newcomer disadvantage. As middlemen with their bona-fides thoroughly accepted by neither side, the pro-immigrants of the 1960s were in no position to exercise any comparable, stabilizing influence. They proclaimed the immigrant's case, furthermore, not in comparison with the situation of other immigrants, past or present, but in comparison with other citizens; and were duly discredited by the one side for extremism and by the other for posturing ineffectiveness, as a result.

To draw such comparisons, however, is to ignore one obvious additional factor. The treatment of coloured people within a white-dominated society has emerged as an issue of moment scarcely confined to the situation of New Commonwealth immigrants in Britain. It was only to be expected, perhaps, that questions of racial discrimination, racial prejudice, and even racial segregation as experienced or institutionalized elsewhere, along lines broadly dictated by colour of skin, should have had their impact upon a Britain which was for the first time coming to terms with the consequences of possessing its own, sizeable, urban, coloured population (the product, furthermore, of Britain's own imperial past). Nor was it surprising that demands and achievements witnessed elsewhere in the name of civil rights and civil sanctions for under-privileged coloured populations, should have influenced both the horizons and the immediate objectives of New Commonwealth opinion in this country.

All the same, the lessons of South Africa and of the USA exercised what might, with some reason, be described as a distorting influence.[47] Black leaders came to set their sights, understandably, not upon what might be due to immigrants, but upon what should be due to blacks in a white-orientated society. Host public opinion, similarly, reacted not simply against the presence of New Commonwealth immigrants as such, but against the implications of harbouring any sizeable, and potentially permanent, Black citizen population. Coloured immigrants by the 1960s could not, in other words, be regarded and treated simply as immigrants. The same was not true of Jewish immigrants in the 1900s, if only because anti-semitism then had not emerged as the full-fledged, fully-documented, international debating rapier which colour prejudice has since become.

This is not to suggest that mass immigrants *ought*, by some natural law, to have to accept some quantifiable measure of difficulty as the price of settlement in a more advanced economy; although such an argument might plausibly be advanced. It does suggest, however, that the arrival of coloured newcomers in a welfare state, of all states, could be particularly problematic. Potentially the most demanding group of 'less civilized' newcomers had arrived in the midst of the most ambitious, vulnerable, and potentially the most exclusive social policy network — at least within British experience.

Against this backcloth, it was perhaps not surprising that large-scale coloured immigration should have prompted a specific national response — not merely in the form of eventual immigration controls (as in the Jewish case) — but also in the form of novel social policy manoeuvres designed ostensibly to influence and safeguard the position and prospects of those newcomers already present in this would-be welfare society. Such innovations represented both an addition to the total stock of statutory social policy and an influence (both intentional and otherwise) upon the workings of already established social services. The net outcome would seem, abundantly, to illustrate both the strengths and the inherent limitations of the Welfare State in this context. We will look first at the ear-marked innovations in statutory social policy, before proceeding to evaluate the workings of ongoing social servicves partly in the light of such departures.

6

Ad hoc policy responses
to New Commonwealth
immigration

There are two themes of interest intrinsic to the subject of this chapter.

To begin with, the fact that novel, immigration-inspired policies were called for and embarked upon at all would seem to amount to an admission, in principle at least, that the existing machinery of the Welfare State was somehow insufficient or inappropriate to cope well enough on its own with the consequences of New Commonwealth immigration. So the Welfare State was not, after all, the comprehensive, open-ended, recipe for social reconstruction that its champions had originally forecast (or at least implied).[1] Ongoing service development and adjustment in the light of changing circumstances was seemingly not enough. Additional lines of government policy were called for. Quite where and why such additional standpoints seemed necessary should become evident in the course of this chapter. Quite how specific, in principle, were the issues raised to the situation of New Commonwealth immigrants *per se*; and quite how constructive, complementary, or compatible were such new policies alongside existing social services operation may become clearer in the course of both this and the following chapters.

In the second place, the introduction of immigrant-inspired additional policy constitutes an example of novel social policy formation from within a conspicuously divided social and political context. As such it may usefully be compared with earlier examples of so-called controversial policy formation and may shed some light, therefore, not merely upon the general processes of social policy formation but, more specifically, upon the relationship between social conflict (and/or political controversy) and social policy development.

There are points of definition, nevertheless, which require clarification at the outset of this discussion.

One may question, for instance, how far measures introduced (roughly speaking) in the name of racial integration ought in any sense to be regarded as mainstream additions to the stock of national social policy. Such measures may very easily be interpreted as no more than short-term political gestures designed, above all, to placate certain sections of voting opinion and/or to preserve some semblance of consistent political morality within the context of a tricky electoral situation. Yet much the same might have been said of many earlier statutory policy departures in their day. Time will presumably tell whether racial integration machinery is to develop as a major, permanent aspect of governmental intervention in domestic affairs. It behoves us, at this stage, to assume that such might well turn out to be the case, if only because any discussion of the recent statutory response to New Commonwealth immigration, which did not take this factor into account, could hardly make much sense.

This being so, we have still to define what is meant and implied, in this case, by racial integration policies. To say that governmental gestures in this direction, and the *Race Relations Act* of 1968 in particular, were directly inspired by the fact of New Commonwealth immigration is not to say, necessarily, that such innovations were confined, in their import, to dealing with New Commonwealth or coloured immigrants alone. The promotion of 'harmonious community relations', for instance, was potentially a very generalizable objective (Hartford 1972). The outlawing of public acts of discrimination was, again, an innovation not confined in its implications to a battle against colour prejudice *per se*.[2] The specific measures, in other words, could be of more than specific significance.

Yet race and community relations policies were at least intended, initially, for application in specifically New Commonwealth, or coloured immigrant, contexts. The same could not be said of one further, arguably immigration-inspired, social policy development in this period: namely positive (area) discrimination. Hailed as a framework for the rational allocation of additional, national, social policy resources between deprived urban areas and via existing (local government) machinery, positive discrimination may have been inspired, if not seemingly necessitated, by the presence of New

Commonwealth immigrant groups and the social tensions that seemed so frequently to be associated with their settlement; yet when various strands of positive discrimination were drawn together into the Urban Programme, this could hardly be described as specifically immigrant-centred policy.[3] Successive governments, indeed, were insistent that, while the presence of a sizeable coloured immigrant community within an inner-city area may constitute one among several indices of such an area's likely deprivation (coloured immigrants being disproportionately associated, after all, with substandard environments), such a presence was not to be considered a social problem nor a cause of social problems in itself: any more than were coloured immigrants to be considered the sole intended recipients of any positive discrimination policies (below p.181).

Positive discrimination, therefore, constitutes something of a hybrid in this context. On the one hand it represents a series of national policy innovations inspired, at least in part, by the fact of New Commonwealth immigration and settlement. On the other hand, it reiterates very firmly the line taken by, and on behalf of, established statutory services in this context: that the presence of New Commonwealth immigrants merely highlighted (and added to) existing social problems; and that the needs of New Commonwealth households were, so far as these services were concerned, no different in kind from those of native households similarly placed.[4] It is for this reason that we shall deal with positive discrimination policies in the final section of this chapter, as a bridging passage, in a sense, between the discussion of specific racial integration policies, on the one hand, and the discussion of ongoing social services response, on the other.

(i) *Integration policy development*

There were two separate, but in a sense converging, strands to integration policy development in the 1960s: moves to promote inter-racial harmony, or better race relations, on the one hand, and moves to prohibit acts of racial discrimination on the other. That both such strategies should have begun to take shape in the 1960s, rather than before, seems readily understandable, since it was only during the 1960s that the full impact of New Commonwealth immigration seemed to be making itself felt, upon both hosts and immigrants (above p.147). The first of these strategies, being the less dramatic and the less controversial of the two in its initial stages at least, was not surprisingly the first to develop.

Here we have a fairly rapid, incremental, progression: beginning with the establishment, in 1962, of a non-statutory Commonwealth Immigrants Advisory Council (CIAC) to advise the Home Secretary, as and when requested, on matters affecting the welfare of Commonwealth immigrants in this country. In 1964, thanks to CIAC recommendation, the first National Committee for Commonwealth Immigrants (NCCI) was brought into being, to support the work of an Advisory Officer specially appointed to co-ordinate and invigorate the efforts of statutory and voluntary bodies across the country in the field of immigrant welfare. In 1965 a larger and altogether grander NCCI took over the responsibilities of both the CIAC and the NCCI mark one, until it too was subsumed, in 1968, under a new, statutory, Community Relations Commission (CRC).[5] The latter's responsibilities:-

'(a) to encourage the establishment of, and assist others to take steps to secure the establishment of, harmonious community relations and to co-ordinate on a national basis the measures adopted for that purpose by others; and

(b) to advise the Secretary of State on any matter referred to the Commission by him *and* to make recommendations to him on any matter which the Commission consider should be brought to his attention.'[6]

(my italics)

seem a far cry from the cautious CIAC beginnings of 1962. Not only had the moves to promote inter-racial harmony become more ambitious, elaborate, and expensive within a fairly short period of time; they had, by definition, become more controversial also.[7]

Meanwhile, moves to outlaw acts of racial discrimination had, as it were, been catching up. For all the bitter controversy surrounding the introduction of the 1965 *Race Relations Act*, as the thin end of a particularly unwelcome wedge, the Act itself was extremely limited, even nugatory, in its scope. The Act made it unlawful to 'practise discrimination' in (certain specified) places of public resort; little more.[8] It was a beginning, nevertheless, and as such could lead on to bigger things, as the opponents of this legislation had been only too aware (Kushnick 1971 : 243) and as the chairman of the newly appointed Race Relations Board, Mark Bonham-Carter, was committed from the start to try to bring about (Kushnick 1971 : 249;

Patterson 1969 : 89-90). The findings of the PEP Report on *Racial Discrimination* (1967) and of the Street Report on *Anti-Discrimination Legislation* (1967),[9] together with the Race Relations Board's own experience of receiving some 327 complaints of discrimination between the date of its first operation (February 17 1966) and March 31 1967, of which only eighty-nine fell within the terms of the Act, the remainder being mostly concerned with employment (101), housing (37) and publications (24),[10] made the case for further legislation in this sphere seem virtually overwhelming.

Accordingly, the 1968 *Race Relations Act* was directed towards prohibiting acts of discrimination in the spheres of employment, housing, and publications, along with prohibiting discrimination generally in connection with the provision of goods, facilities, and services, and the conduct of trade unions, employers, and trade organizations.[11]. The Race Relations Board was, *pro rata*, extended both in size and scope — the new twelve man committee being empowered for the first time actually to initiate investigations where it had reason to suspect that discrimination had occurred, instead of being dependent altogether upon the receipt of formal complaints. [12] The Board, furthermore, could now take its recalcitrant cases direct to one of a number of specially designated county courts — instead of waiting upon the Attorney General for any legal action.[13]

Much ground had been covered between 1965 and 1968, therefore, on the matter of legislation against racial discrimination. Given such progress and given the legalistic complications inherent in any drive to outlaw acts of racial discrimination, it was only to be expected, perhaps, that anti-discrimination provisions should occupy pride of place in the contents of the 1968 *Race Relations Act*. It would seem no accident, nevertheless, that 1968 should also have witnessed the statutory inauguration, within the same Act, of procedures designed to promote harmonious community relations. Here too there had been conspicious policy development over a relatively short time-span and here too the end product could not but be controversial. The inclusion of both strands of integration policy within a single legislative framework in 1968 would seem significant in itself.

It was significant, to begin with, that both sets of strategies should by this time have seemed to require this legislative action. Both had proved themselves to be necessary and both, by the same token, had shown themselves to be flying in the face of apparent majority opinion. Voluntarism, however preferable in principle, was patently not enough in either case.

There was a certain logic, moreover, to the bringing together, at last, of both strategies within the pages of one formal policy document, since these were, after all, supposed to be complementary and interdependent lines of approach. Thus one may posit an overall policy for racial integration which by 1968 consisted, on the one hand, of moves to promote inter-racial harmony and understanding in the long-term and, on the other, of moves to prohibit acts of outright racial discrimination in the present; the whole being consistent, it would seem, with the overall integration objectives as spelt out by Roy Jenkins in 1966.[14]

Even so, this formal coupling of strategies was not necessarily constructive. It could be argued, for instance, that by tacking Community Relations provisions onto an Act which was primarily concerned with (and resented for) the statutory prohibition of racial discrimination, the government of the day merely ensured that the pursuit of racial harmony would henceforth be regarded with as much suspicion, by the mass of the population, as were the regulations against racial discrimination.

Of far greater significance, however, was the fact that integration policy as a whole had from the start been associated in the public mind (both immigrant and native) with that other conspicuous aspect of governmental reponse to New Commonwealth immigration: namely Commonwealth immigration control. If this was, at a broader level, a two-pronged approach which sought to placate both sides of public opinion by taking parallel action on both 'control' and 'integration' fronts, it was to prove more deeply counter-productive than any attempt merely to draw the separate strands of integration policy together.

That the general public should have come to regard control and integration policies, respectively, as being opposite sides of the same governmental coin, was scarcely surprising. The two lines of action had indeed been linked together from the start. By the end of the 1950s, and after the 'race riots' of 1958 (Glass 1960 : Ch. 4, Section 3) in particular, public and parliamentary opinion was divided between those who saw the answer to such inner-city unrest in terms of New Commonwealth immigration control (if not wholesale repatriation), on the one hand, and those who urged the need for positive integration policies, on the other (Glass 1960 : 151). The controls lobby was thought to represent the majority of electoral opinion, at least after 1959,[15] yet the integration lobby (given the disreputable connotations of any sideways appeal to colour prejuduce) was to be seen as representing influential 'progressive' opinion.

In the event, the governmental answer (not confined, as it turned out, to government by any one political party) lay in a policy package designed, as far as possible, to placate both sides. Immigration control, in other words, was declared to be necessary in order that those immigrants already present might be the more thoroughly integrated into this tight-packed island society. Controls were unavoidable if integration was in any sense to succeed.[16] Once propounded, such a formula was not readily to be set aside. The passage of the first *Commonwealth Immigrants' Act* was accompanied by the no less novel, though far less spectacular, creation of a Commonwealth Immigrants Advisory Council. Thereafter, any moves to tighten immigration controls tended to be accompanied or closely followed by moves proclaimed as being in aid of racial integration.

Thus, once the Labour Party had recognized the political necessity of abandoning its outright opposition to the principle of Commonwealth immigration controls as embodied in the 1962 legislation,[17] it took care in its 1964 Election Manifesto to link the promise of continuing controls with the promise also of legislation against racial discrimination and incitement in public places.[18] After this, 1965 proved not surprisingly to be an eventful year. A White Paper on 'Immigration from the Commonwealth'[19] argued the (Labour) Government's case for even tighter immigration controls (including the formal abandonment of 'C' voucher issue) on the one hand, and for a more vigorous drive towards integration (spearheaded by a reconstituted NCCI with increased public funds at its disposal) on the other. This was also the year in which the first Race Relations Act, prohibiting acts of discrimination based upon colour race or creed in places of public resort, was to reach the statute book.

In terms of legislative output, however, 1968 was if anything even more spectacular. This was the year of the second *Commonwealth Immigrants Act*, the one which (in response to the Kenyan Asian Crisis) set about categorizing British passport-holders, for the first time, into those who themselves (or at least one of their parents or their grandparents) had been born or naturalized or adopted in this country, and the rest: the first group being free to enter Britain at any time and the second being subject, henceforth, to immigration controls.[20] Yet this was also the year of the second *Race Relations Act*, referred to above, as well as of the (May Day) Urban Programme announcement (see below p.180).

For all the care obviously taken in this period to make no obvious move in one direction without making some countervailing gesture in the other, the net impact of this two-way policy stance was quite as unimpressive as might have been predicted. Any mass support to be expected from the tightening of immigration controls in 1965, for instance, was cancelled out in part by the spectre of legislation against racial discrimination.[21] Similarly any immigrant or pro-immigrant reassurance to be expected as a result of stronger anti-discrimination regulations in 1968 was allegedly neutralized in advance by the passage, earlier in the year, of the second *Commonwealth Immigrants Act* (Abbott 1971 : 429; Rose 1969 : 614-19).

Not that the balance struck was quite so even as this might suggest. It was not a case of appeasing, and antagonizing, both sides equally. Immigrants and pro-immigrants would seem to be justified in their contention that, once the initial precedent had been established, action to limit New Commonwealth immigration was pursued with far more energy and determination by successive governments than was any ostensible drive to promote racial integration. Could the establishment of a non-statutory CIAC in 1962 be regarded as of equivalent import to the passage of the first *Commonwealth Immigrants Act*? Could even the second *Race Relations Act* be accounted the legislative counterpart to the second *Commonwealth Immigrants Act?*; and what about the *Immigration Act of 1971* above, note 20)?

Politically, of course, there was some reason for this imbalance. There were far more votes to be won, so it seemed, from immigration control than from the pursuit of integration, whatever that meant (Foot 1965 : Chs. 7 and 8). The relative imprecision and intangibility of 'integration' as a policy objective, moreover, was enough to constitute a handicap in itself. Whatever the practical difficulties intrinsic to the effective, selective control of Commonwealth immigration, the limitation of new arrivals was at least a concrete, measurable target, in a way that the integration of those immigrants already here most certainly was not.

Even within the field of racial integration itself it was, once again, the negative policies rather than the so-called positive programmes which tended to furnish the more tangible and therefore the more practicable objectives. Even immigrant and pro-immigrant opinion, in all its variety, could never agree upon precisely what type (if any) of 'integrated' society it wished to see develop in this country; nor upon how, or how far, such a dream might best be brought about. It was much simpler to agree upon what, in the short term, should be fought against. The outlawing of acts of racial discrimination seemed a clear and immediate policy objective: everything that the promotion of harmonious community relations was not. It was unfortunate, of course, that the clearer and more immediate the policy objective in this case, the more certain was it to provoke a hostile native reacton.

Yet not all the difficulties encountered by integration policies, whether 'negative' or 'positive', are to be explained simply by reference to their particular host-immigrant context. It is necessary, indeed, to try to distinguish from the start between those problems intrinsic to *any* new departure in government-sponsored social policy and those seemingly peculiar to the integration case.

Virtually all radical departures in statutory social policy, for instance, have had to grapple with three linked sets of difficulties: a more or less deep-rooted public suspicion of any marked extension to government powers which must, seemingly, be at the expense of individual liberty;[22] a lack of government understanding as to what it is really about and/or how this might best be effected; and a lack of appropriate machinery, or appropriately trained personnel, upon which to draw (see Ch. 2). Where a government was merely following on from, or filling in, a long-established, proven, voluntary tradition then of course all three sets of difficulties tended to be that much less in evidence.[23] Where a government had, so to speak, stepped in early, as in this case, then these same difficulties must appear at their most obvious.

Governments step in early not out of masochism, presumably, but because they perceive or are influentially informed that the situation in question requires urgent treatment. Thus if the threat of cholera was sufficient to prompt 'premature' statutory public health departures in the first half of the nineteenth century (above p.19), the threat of race riots, or at least of unacceptable levels of social conflict, was sufficient apparently to push successive governments towards racial integration (along with immigration control) as an equivalent political necessity.

The question of social conflict, however, raises complications all its own. Hitherto, it has been precisely upon those issues where deep-rooted disagreement, or at least effective public opposition, had made itself felt, that governments were most likely to desist from early action (above p.21). In this case, however, it was social conflict itself which made up the so-called urgent problem. It is in this respect that integration policy has to be regarded as unique.[24] Statutory social policy was, for the first time, to be directed against social conflict *per se*, and in circumstances within which the pay-off for the majority (which *was* public opinion) seemed to say the least indirect, unless an early blood bath was to be accounted a serious risk. One could always go for repatriation after all.[25]

(ii) *Policies to promote harmonious community relations*

It is against this backcloth that we must approach, firstly, the efforts, culminating temporarily in the *Race Relations Act* of 1968, to promote inter-racial harmony in Britain. We will deal first with the central, national, initiatives. Coming as it did after the CIAC and the NCCI marks one and two, the Community Relations Commission inherited what was perhaps their most significant collective and cumulative characteristic: a dual responsibility, to advise the government, on the one hand, and to support and co-ordinate voluntary efforts, on the other. So the Community Relations Commission, like its non-statutory predecessors, was seen as occupying some sort of midway, liaison position between government responsibility and private endeavour in the field of race relations.

In its way, such a positioning made complete sense. One could not proclaim harmonious community relations as a social policy objective, without an implicit assumption that all the interests concerned were fundamentally reconcilable and that what was needed, therefore, was the fullest exchange of views, information, and experience at every level — rather than any directive imposition of statutory policy from the top. Harmony could only be encouraged, not ordered, to prevail. In a sense, therefore, the establishment of the Community Relations Commission was a piece of statutory non-policy: statutory because central government wished to support, to participate in, and to monitor the progress of such manoeuvres; non-policy because it did not wish, on principle, to be seen to direct them.

Such an interpretation, however, is open all too easily to attack as being at best naively charitable and at worst actively misleading. Given an existing community relations situation which was anything but harmonious — where sectional views seemed if anything to be drawing further apart rather than closer together by 1968 — there were three predictable lines of criticism of the government's stance.[26] To begin with, it could be argued that central government was simply opting out of involvement in a contentious situation with its talk of harmony and hence (conveniently) of non-direction as being the policy ideal. The establishment of the CRC with its limited funds and its two-way ministering role was at best a piece of window-dressing, nothing more.[27]

Not far removed from this position were those who argued that, given the current blatant inequalities between immigrants and hosts in this society, harmony could only ever be achieved, not by scrupulous non-partisanship, but by actively taking sides in support of disadvantaged (immigrant) groups. Only one step removed, again, were those immigrants and pro-immigrants who came increasingly to declare that the whole idea of 'harmonious community relations' as a social target was misconceived in any case. Interests were *not* necessarily reconcilable, indeed there was every evidence that they were fundamentally opposed. What was needed, therefore, was a social policy programme geared openly to the support and compensation of Blacks in Britain, so that they might at least be in a position eventually to battle for themselves on more equal terms (Hill and Issacharoff 1971 : Ch. 1; Abbott 1971 : Ch. 11).

Against this backcloth of immigrant and pro-immigrant opinion, the very opinion with which it needed most obviously to come to terms, the CRC's efforts were in a sense doomed from the start. It was established and empowered to service others: the government (in the shape of the Home Office) on the one hand and organized voluntary effort together with interested or implicated individuals on the other. It was not equipped with any open, independent policy-making function, though with its powers to vet (and pay towards) local Community Relations Officer (CRO) appointments and its powers selectively to subsidize Community Relations Councils' activity in general, it could be said to exercise a policy directing influence at this level, comparable for instance to the influence of central government as a whole upon local government activity.[28]

Within its limits and according to its statutory terms of reference, the Community Relations Commission has since had much to show for its activity. Its publications list has to be accounted impressive — covering everything from rudimentary information about minority groups and their social characteristics to independent (or sponsored) academic comment on various aspects of the current race relations situation; regular bulletins on (for instance) the practicalities of education in a multi-racial context, along with the publication (from October 1971) of its own journal for the committed — *New Community*. Nor has it been inactive, of course, where the arrangement of conferences or the subsidizing of local CRO appointments and specific local CRC activities are concerned.[29]

In the circumstances, however, who was likely to be impressed? Interested whites who had either opted for, or found themselves in, a position necessitating frequent contact with immigrant individuals or groups, perhaps; but not the more determined self-declared or popularly appointed leaders of immigrant opinion[30] and not, therefore, the more energetic and committed of pro-immigrants. A two-way servicing role (servicing government, on the one hand and 'government-approved' integratory initiatives, on the other) was not, in the latter's opinion, what was required. The mere acceptance of such a role in such circumstances by the members and paid officials of the CRC, could be interpreted by these critics of the CRC as constituting prima facie evidence, in itself, of these same members and paid officials' questionable good faith.

The Commission, not unnaturally, strove hard to counter this image. It could not move far, however, without provoking an opposite hostility. The mere suggestion in 1970, for instance, that the CRC was proposing to grant-aid not an 'integratory' organization but a reputed Black Power house in central London, was sufficient to provoke a public and parliamentary outcry.[31] This was not what the CRC was supposed to be about. So the CRC, as a would-be integratory force within a non-integratory context, was effectively on a hiding for nothing.[32]

Yet if the Community Relations Commisssion was to find itself caught between two stools,[33] much the same sort of predicament was even more apparent in the case of its local counterparts: the Community Relations Councils (or their equivalents). To be recognized, and hence grant-aided, by the CRC (or the NCCI before it), local committees had not merely to be demonstrably non-partisan in both their formal membership and in their activities; they had also to be assured, in effect, of substantial local authority backing.[34] Right from the start, therefore, there was a potential two-way tug of loyalites: between the central Commission on the one hand and the local authority on the other.

Nor was this all. By insisting, from 1965, that each such committee or council 'should have the support of a wide variety of local organisations as a ''non-sectarian and non-political body'' (Government White Paper), central government (via the NCCI and then the CRC) was demanding, in effect, that such bodies be composed, not merely of local individuals actively interested in and committed to racial integration, but also (via their named representatives) of all those bodies conceivably implicated in and essential to the realization of racial harmony objectives. [35] The pursuit of consensus, after all, could not be less than all-embracing.

Nevertheless there were two predictable consequences arising out of this stance. To begin with, any immigrant or pro-immigrant who consented to serve (in whatever capacity) on a local Community Relations Council was open to attack for being either a time-server or, at the very least, a political innocent in allowing himself so to be used. For local police chiefs or LA housing managers to take part was one matter; for so-called immigrant or pro-immigrant spokesmen to co-operate was quite another. Knowingly or unknowingly, the latter were, some argued, merely being Uncle Toms: allowing themselves and their following to be bought off in true colonial fashion (Nandy 1967 : 38). This added to the fact that, in social class terms, the average Community Relations Council could not, by the wildest stretch of the imagination be termed 'representative' of the full spectrum of local interest and opinion. [36]

This being so local community relations policies could hardly rest assured of full-hearted local backing, least of all from those immigrant quarters with allegedly the most to gain from any integration manoeuvres. Decisive policies, however, would seem the product least likely to emerge from the average fully recognized and fully supported community relations council. Which brings us to our second point.

Unlike the statutory Community Relations Commission, local community relations councils *were* half expected to exercise an independent local policy-making function, in their capacity as non-statutory, multi-representative, and multiply-financed voluntary bodies. If one seeks to pursue harmony by drawing together a range of interests from within an unharmonious situation, however, one may expect some increase of fellow-feeling but one ought not to expect radical policies to emerge as a result. The more representative the

Council, indeed, the less might it be expected to agree on anything approaching the controversial.[37]

Not that this was the only type of policy-making problem with which local community relations councils had to grapple. Sandwiched as they were between the territory of the Race Relations Board, on the one hand, and the workings of established statutory and voluntary social services on the other, it could be no easy matter to decide, in each case, upon which types of activity (and to what extent) they might most properly and profitably devote their attention. Hence the understandable tendency of so many councils to concentrate on the non-spectacular: on what might best be termed individual welfare work, for instance; on 'non-specific' community development projects; and on public education programmes and facilities — to name the most obvious lines (Hill and Issacharoff 1971 : Ch. 7; Butterworth 1972 b).

In this respect of course, local community relations councils had the services of paid officers — CROs with or without Assistant CROs, paid for partly out of central CRC funds — to draw upon. Here again, however, they were to find themselves enmeshed in a difficulty — in this case what might be termed a classic, novel social policy, difficulty. It was all very well for central government to decide, from 1965, that it would, via the NCCI and then the CRC, meet the salary bills of approved professional appointments in the service of local committees. This did not of itself create a pool of suitably trained (what was suitable training?) and suitably experienced (what was suitable experience?) personnel upon which local councils might henceforth rely (Taylor 1972). The heterogeneous backgrounds from which CROs were and have since been appointed cannot but have added to the uncertainties apparent over what, in fact, their job was supposed to be about (Hill and Issacharoff 1971 : 254).

Hence the evident confusion between CROs, between their committees and among their public over whether these officers ought in fact to be regarded as special social workers for Blacks; whether they ought rather to be seen as public relations officers or community action organizers, operating within the local context for the sake, primarily, of the resident coloured community; or whether they ought simply to be regarded as an extra resource for community development in twilight immigrant areas (Baksi 1970).

All of which harks back, of course, to the underlying uncertainty over what, precisely, the community relations movement itself was supposed to be all about. Was it intended simply to be a social service for Blacks — to shore them up, as it were, from the midst of their disadvantage — or was it intended as a service for everyone with a public grievance or handicap who happened to reside in an 'immigrant-infested' area, and even, potentially, for those with 'community' grievances not resident in immigrant areas (Taylor 1962)?

(iii) *Legislation to prohibit acts of racial discrimination*

So far, and not surprisingly, there has been no definitive answer to such queries. It is against this background that we have to consider what may, by comparison, seem an enviably clear-cut field: the prevention of acts of racial discrimination. Here at least the 1968 *Race Relations Act* implied an acknowledgement, on the part of central government, not merely that some form of statutory presence was appropriate in this field of race relations, but that some form of policy direction was also required, from the top. The practice of racial discrimination would not necessarily disappear, or disappear speedily enough, as a result of the mere encouragement of harmonious community relations (this in itself being an admission, perhaps, of the impracticality of harmonious community relations as a serious policy objective). The effects of racial discrimination upon those who were likely to experience it were far too damaging in any case for matters to be left to sort themselves out over time: the more so since this was a field in which the government could, if it chose, take immediate action. The outlawing of racial discrimination, furthermore, might contribute positively to an improvement in the climate of race relations, by forcing a change in habits and thereby promoting gradually a change in accompanying beliefs.

Such at least was the case in support of this anti-discrimination legislation. Predictably, however, it was scarcely a case to command general support. There were four main lines of opposing argument. [38] To begin with, there were those who declared, with some passion, that the extent of outright racial discrimination in this fundamentally fair-minded country could be nothing like so great as had been alleged; that charges of racial discrimination were often no more than the disappointed outbursts of those whose lack of training, experience, or capital placed them at an inevitable disadvantage in a post-industrial society; and that to introduce legislation to prohibit acts of provable discrimination, therefore, would be like using the famed sledge-hammer to crack the alleged nut.

It took no great leap from this position to argue, in the second place, that the introduction of legislation against so-called acts of racial discrimination must not merely be unnecessary but, by the same token, actively damaging to the race relations climate — since it would antagonize whole sections of the host society and place them needlessly on the defensive. More specifically, it could in the third place be argued that any crude legislative attempt to interfere in the field of employment, at least, must do untold damage to the sacred concept of free individual and collective bargaining in industry.

Most telling of all, however, was the argument that in practice no such attempt at legal regulation could conceivably work — Street Report or no Street Report (see above p.159). How could the factor of racial discrimination, even if present, be separated from its socio-economic and individual context and thus be rendered provable within the limits of normal legal convention? To legislate ineffect-ively, it was suggested, must be worse than not to legislate at all (see Kushnick 1971 : Ch. 9 for general discussion of background to legislation).

The significance of such arguments should not be under-estimated. They may not have prevented the 1968 Act from reaching the statute book; but they did influence the content and wording of the legislation in its final form and they did contribute to the climate of public opinion amid which it was launched. Moreover they seemed to forecast (having in part determined) what were to emerge as the Act's principal weaknesses, once in operation.

It was a fine awareness of the Act's alienatory potential, for instance, which made its framers tread so warily where the definition of its scope and sanctions was concerned. True the general prohibition on racial discrimination was extended this time to cover the provision of goods, facilities, and services; employment; trade union and employers' and trade organizations; housing accommodation and business and other premises; together with advertisements and notices (*Race Relations Act* 1968 : Part I, Sections 2-6). Yet, as the list of exceptions to the general rule bears out, there was to be no needless provocation. Employers, for instance, were entitled to keep an eye on the 'racial balance' of their current workforce when making further appointments; sea-going appointments were exempted from the terms of the Act 'if compliance ... would result in persons of different colour, race or ethnic or national origins being compelled to share sleeping rooms, mess rooms or sanitary accommodation'; resident landlords of 'small premises' were entitled to select their 'sharing' tenants on whatever basis they chose; and so on (Sections 7-8).

Far more fundamental, however, was the Act's implicit philosophy over how best to deal with complaints of discrimination which did fall within its terms of reference. Should a complaint, upon investigation, appear to be justified then the answer, ideally, should be conciliation. Only if conciliation failed, should the possibility of legal proceedings ever arise. Hence the network of conciliation committees to be constituted by the Race Relations Board 'for such areas as the Board consider necessary' (Section 14, sub-section 5); and hence also the provision that, in the case of employment complaints, all matters were to be referred in the first instance to the Secretary of State for Employment and thence to the appropriate voluntary liaison machinery in industry, should any exist. Should such machinery not exist, or should conciliation fail, then, and only then, the Race Relations Board might be asked by the Secretary of State to proceed further with the case (Schedule 2).

So the government was only too aware, it seemed, of the inflammatory potential of any rash and over-ready resort to legal sanctions in cases of racial discrimination. Even so, the emphasis placed upon conciliation arose out of something more than a simple reluctance to antagonize those most likely to be implicated. If the prevention of racial discrimination was in truth to contribute to racial integration and hence to harmonious community relations, then conciliation rather than litigation (with one party inevitably coming off the loser) was on principle to be preferred. Even at individual case level, moreover, conciliation was more likely to produce immediate, practicable results than was any paper victory either way.

By according pride of place to conciliation, however, the regulations against racial discrimination seemed to slide inevitably away from the seductive idea of a straightforward, clear-cut, no-nonsense legal framework. We are back, once again, in the indeterminate, awkward territory of trying to estimate how best to promote racial harmony from out of an increasingly divided racial context. Yet one thing at least seemed clear: however preferable conciliation might be in principle, it could never work sufficiently in practice without the reality of legal sanctions in the background — or such at least had been the assumption underlying this Act.

Effective sanctions were necessary, so it was argued, to reassure the immigrant on the one hand and to deter the potential discriminator on the other. There were merely three linked sets of difficulty in this connection. How strong did such sanctions have to be in order to rank as 'effective' (and how counter-productive might they therefore be in terms of alienating host opinion)? How frequently must they be seen to be used in order to constitute an effective deterrent (and how much was *this* likely to alienate host opinion)? How feasible, in the last resort, was it going to be to employ them (and how destructive of immigrant confidence might be any 'failures' in this respect)?

Faced with such conundrums, the government of the day would seem to have taken what can only be described as a cautious way out. True, an enlarged Race Relations Board was now empowered, not merely to initiate investigations, if necessary, without waiting for formal complaints, but to take substantiated cases directly to court. The Board had no power to subpoena evidence, however and racial discrimination even if proven, was to constitute only a civil, not a criminal, offence. If this was what was meant by 'effective sanctions', therefore, there were many, understandably, left unconvinced.

In the event, however, it was not so much the limited sanctions open to the Board as the Board's apparent inability convincingly to deploy such sanctions as it possessed, which was to draw the most criticism. There were two linked difficulties here. To begin with, the proliferation of exemption clauses within the *Race Relations Act* itself, coupled with its general philosophy of attacking not what might be termed personal private acts but only impersonal public acts of discrimination, was bound to create endless problems of definition. At what point, for instance, ought a so-called private and personal appointment to be more aptly described as a public, impersonal job? Or at what stage should a so-called private association be re-termed a public facility for the purposes of the Act?[39]

In itself this was difficult enough. Yet even without such complications, the process of demonstrating, to legal satisfaction, that an act of racial discrimination had beyond all reasonable doubt taken place, was to prove quite as daunting as the Act's opponents had originally alleged.

The evidence would seem to speak for itself. Out of 1,050 cases disposed of by the Race Relations Board during the year 1974, for instance, opinions of discrimination were formed in 224 of these cases, of which 183 were then disposed of by conciliation (HM Government

1975 para. 5). So far so good perhaps. Over the same period, however, the Board considered seventy-one cases in which conciliation had failed. Of these the Board decided to bring proceedings in thirty cases. Twenty-two of these cases were still outstanding at the end of the year, (although in two cases embarked upon in the previous year, the Board obtained judgements in its favour); while in the remaining eight cases the determination to bring proceedings was either rescinded or else the proceedings were discontinued (paras. 6, and 10).

There would seem to be three main points of interest here: the fact that in over half of the 'non-conciliated' cases legal proceedings were not resorted to; that where legal proceedings were resorted to this seemed to produce no speedy settlement; and that, in over one quarter of the cases initially selected for legal action, the decision to proceed was subsequently dropped. If this was the deterrent, in other words, it would seem an exceeding low-profile deterrent.

Naturally enough, the situation was nowhere near so clear-cut as this implies. As the Board itself points out, failure to secure a settlement by conciliation could sometimes be 'due to unreasonable claims by the complainant, rather than the respondent, and ... proceedings would therefore not be justified'. In other cases however, it was significant that, 'while a committee may be justified in forming an opinion of discrimination, the evidence may be insufficiently strong to satisfy the burden of proof faced by litigants in court' (para. 7). Acts of racial discrimination, in other words, might be quite as difficult to prove as was originally suggested.

Nor could the current Race Relations Board be described as complacent on this or on associated points. The prevention of racial discrimination would be better effected, in the Board's opinion, by the establishment of an Equal Opportunities Commission 'with wide powers of investigation, the power to issue non-discrimination notices, and to make recommendations and publicise them' than by any mere 'complaint-based' procedure; where the onus rests effectively with the individual to complain — and where trade unions and employers in particular have no clear incentive to do more than tackle each individual case as it might arise (paras. 83-4).

In the meantime, the Board had further, more immediate complaints — all of which relate effectively to the issues raised above. So far as the pursuit of legal proceedings was concerned, for instance, the Board needed powers of subpoena since without these 'our investigations often take far too long' (para. 85). More generally, it questioned the wisdom of allowing 'the 4,000 or so clubs of the Working Men's Club and Institute Union and thousands of clubs linked to other organisations' to remain beyond the purview of the Act (para. 18). Furthermore, it questioned the wisdom of ceding pride of place, as it were, to voluntary industrial machinery for the initial handling of employment complaints, since such (purportedly independent) machinery seemed not to command confidence among complainants (para. 39).

That further or more deliberate action was required against racial discrimination seemed self-evident. Not only was the Race Relations Board faced with a mounting burden of complaints, but the PEP Reports of 1974 on racial discrimination and disadvantage in the fields of housing and employment respectively, seemed amply to confirm the Board's impression that discrimination, far from being on the decline as a result of the measures of 1968, was if anything on the increase. Nevertheless, it was in its support for a broader-based Equal Opportunities Commission (as proposed in the White Paper 'Equality for Women') to replace the present complaints-based, anti-racial discrimination structure, that the Race Relations Board showed itself fundamentally critical of the system — not merely of the means provided for its operation. The Board's view has to be accounted significant coming as it does from what can only be described as a committed quarter and after some six years' experience of attempting to operate the 1968 regulations.

The notion that one might, at one and the same time, both prevent and / or punish acts of racial discrimination *and* promote the growth of inter-racial understanding by the single expedient of a specialist, but soft-pedalled, system of so-called last resort legal constraints seemed to have proved itself to be quite as misconceived and quite as mutually counter-productive as the Act's critics had originally forecast. The mere fact that a low discrimination prosecution rate could be read in one of three ways: as proof of the low incidence of racial discrimination as proof of the efficacy of conciliation techniques; or as proof of the ineffectiveness of litigation in this field, would seem evidence enough of this single specialist expedient's being unable (whatever the additional powers with which it might be vested) convincingly to perform its dual function.

The Race Relations Board's response was to call, in effect, for another type of multi-purpose structure; one geared to discrimination on grounds of sex as well as of race and one geared to general regulation, information, and education rather than primarily to the handling of post hoc complaints. Such a body, it is argued, might be much better placed to perform the dual prevention and promotion function than the present Race Relations Board which can, after all, take concrete action only after the event. By advocating a widening of the field, moreover, to include sex as well as race discrimination, the Board seemed to be hoping that one might thereby escape from the predicament in which both the Board itself and the Community Relations Commission had so far found themselves, as specifically immigrant (and only immigrant), associated bodies obliged to try to exercise a dispassionate, mediatory role within a specifically host-immigrant conflict situation. A less specialized machinery might conceivably be less open to attack from either side as being allegedly partisan.[40]

The notion, however, that there should still be one mediatory, nonpartisan service of some sort, rather than a range of single-sided, 'championing' facilities, was far too deep-rooted to be questioned. The Welfare State, after all, was nothing if not committed to the idea of fundamental common interest and obligation. If interests and obligations were not, by now, fundamentally common or reconcilable then this, moreover, was a situation not necessarily peculiar to the host-immigrant context *per se*, any more than were its consequences liable to be experienced by so-called integration services alone.

(iv) *Integration policies reconsidered*

It is at this stage, of course, that we come back to the question of how far and how usefully one may relate integration policy development to the general pattern of British social policy experience. It was suggested, earlier on in this discussion, that social policy measures introduced specifically in response to coloured immigration were bound to face certain problems common, albeit mostly less pronounced, to any novel statutory departure. One may go further than this and suggest that in its response to such inevitable problems, integration policy development took on certain classic characteristics.

The whole idea of statutory policy to promote racial integration, and in particular of statutory policy to prohibit discrimination, had been attacked and attackable from the outset as being, on the one hand, yet another invasion of the individual's sacred liberty and, on the other, a wholly impracticable, pointless manoeuvre in any case. It was all very well, perhaps, to talk about the desirability of racial harmony and integration but, in the absence of any convincing evidence as to how this might (if at all) be engineered, the introduction of anti-discrimination legislation amounted, allegedly, to no more than a short-sighted, gratuitous attack upon native sentiments and freedoms in the hope, apparently, that this might appease immigrant opinion for a time. The relationship between possible discriminatory acts and racially prejudiced attitudes was no more thoroughly explored and proven, it seemed, than had been the relationship, for instance, between dirt and cholera in the early nineteenth century. In each case the evidence could only be described as circumstantial and in each case, understandably, the influential public was not willing to move far or sacrifice much in such a questionable cause.

It was against such a background and amid such divisions of opinion that governments tended, not unnaturally, to tread ultra-cautiously in the integration field, just as earlier governments had done in the field of public health. That such caution might in itself prove counter-productive is as evident from the experience of the Race Relations Board as it was earlier from the experience of the 1848-52 General Board of Health (see above Ch. 2 p.19).

More specifically, however, the governmental response on integration has been significant for its emphasis throughout on the primacy of voluntary activity. The Community Relations Commission, and the NCCI before it, was conceived of essentially as being an instrument for the better coordination of government interests and (in many cases long-established) voluntary effort. The Race Relations Board was arguably more important for its powers to create voluntary conciliation committees as and where needed than for its residual powers of prosecution. All in all the rationale seems clear: that in such a controversial and exploratory field it was vital, in the first place, to seek as far as possible to persuade rather than to direct and, in the second place, to utilize whatever unofficial expertise and/or resources that were there, or potentially there, to be drawn upon.

This was buck-passing of a sort, perhaps. Yet once again there are parallels to be drawn between this and earlier experience. Nineteenth century popular education, for instance, had been nothing if not controversial as a social policy subject, with all its much-disputed religious and political overtones, and the state in this case had been nothing if not conscious of, and ultimately reliant upon, the appropriateness of established voluntary effort as something which it might, without taking sides, support. Once not merely the value of popular education but the admissability of the state's taking an active part in popular education had been generally accepted, then the relative importance attached to voluntary efforts inevitably declined. It remains to be seen, of course, whether a parallel process will eventually occur in the field of race relations (a statutory Commission, itself a fairly recent departure from non-statutory beginnings, at the head of an altogether statutory list of community relations councils, for instance?).[41]

Such parallels, however, must not be stretched too far. The prevention or reduction of social conflict *per se* was not really the sort of target familiar to British social policy experience (see above p.164). While one might argue, certainly, that the existence of social conflict or social tension has been a factor of vital significance in British social policy development (above p.24), social policy itself has hitherto been grounded upon two associated beliefs: that any social tensions must be the product of social conditions which are in themselves alterable and that, second, it must be in the interests of effective public opinion (whomsoever that might embrace) to take action against such conditions and hence against the tensions they produce (see above Ch. 2). Neither assumption was necessarily applicable in this case. The social conflict in question might well be more than the simple product of frustrating social conditions. Effective public opinion (whether this be taken to mean majority host, or host plus immigrant opinion) was not necessarily going to regard its interests as best served by some form of conflict-containing or conflict resolving compromise (above p.164).

(v) *Positive discrimination*

Given such a situation and such a background, it seems scarcely surprising that successive governments should have trodden ultra-warily when it came to trying specifically to contain racial conflict or to promote better race relations. Nor does it seem surprising that they should have been so consistently concerned to play down the significance of the racial element in any case and emphasize that far more familiar and manageable theme: that such tensions were almost wholly the product of adverse social conditions affecting all those in a vulnerable position — hosts and immigrants alike.

In itself, of course, this last was not necessarily an easy way out for governments to take. It meant admitting that the Welfare State was far more deficient, and in far more crucial respects, than might otherwise have had to be admitted. Hence the argument which came eventually to possess the status virtually of a self-evident truth: that poor, conspicuous immigrants, moving into a more complex and seemingly more prosperous society, will tend to show up all its weakest and least reputable points, in 'dye-test' fashion.

Of no less significance, however, was the fact that, however minimal a role one sought to ascribe to racial tensions, or colour prejudice, *per se*, the dividing line between specific race relations problems and 'incidental' social problems was never going to be an easy line to draw. Nor would it ever be an absolute line, since the impact of the last set of factors upon the first was hardly to be denied.

Initially of course, the insistence that most 'immigrant' problems were purely incidental, and therefore no different in essence from those faced at other times or in other parts of the country, could be interpreted as little more than a convenient, conventional reaction on the part of governments that, from the mid-1950s onwards, showed every sign of not wishing to become embroiled in the day-to-day (or even year-to-year) problems of immigrant reception (Foot 1965 : Ch. 7-8; Rose 1969 : Ch. 16). By the mid 1960s, however, this had at least been elevated into a deliberate policy position, as the 1965 White Paper on 'Immigration from the Commonwealth' was at some pains to spell out (Rose 1969 : 346).

So long as governments adhered to the principle that local authorities and existing social services could and should be expected to cope as a matter of course with any issues arising out of New Commonwealth immigrant settlement in their areas, then the notion that a coloured presence merely highlighted existing social needs and social policy shortcomings was at least logical in principle, if often difficult to defend in practice (in the face of 'embattled' LAs demanding recompense for extra burdens).[42] However, once central government conceded the possibility that the presence of New Commonwealth immigrants in their areas might constitute grounds, or partial grounds, for such local authorities to receive additional funds, then the 'more of the same' position was increasingly difficult for central government to maintain with any clarity.

Hence the significance, in this context, of the 1966 *Local Government Act* proposal to allow a 50 per cent rate support grant to local authorities in respect either of additional staff appointments or of increased staff loads, arising out of the presence within their areas of Commonwealth immigrants having a different language or culture from the rest of the community (Section II). This was a far cry, it would seem, from the studied pronouncements of the 1965 White Paper, yet it was destined to be only the first of several comparable departures.

In 1967, for instance, the Plowden Report on Primary Schools came out with (among other things) its eye-catching demand for the institution of Educational Priority Areas, the criteria for whose selection was to include the proportion of school-children within an LEA area needing special English teaching (HM Government 1967 : Ch. 5, para. 153h). The institution of the Halsey action-research project of EPAs (Halsey 1972, 1974, 1975), together with the DES policy of allowing enhanced teacher quotas to immigrant-implicated LEAs and the Burnham Committee's policy (from 1968) of allowing salary bonuses to qualified teachers employed in 'schools of exceptional difficulty' (McNeal 1971 : 121-22), were as logical a follow-up to Plowden, perhaps, as was the idea of Housing Priority Areas to the revelations of Milner-Holland and others on the state of the housing market (Rose 1969 : 697).

Three points would seem significant in relation to the developments outlined above. To begin with they all had the appearance, at least, of being separate, spontaneous developments. Certainly there was the persuasive force of mounting host-immigrant tension in the country and certainly there was the example (perhaps as misleading as it was helpful) of the US War on Poverty Programme (Abbott 1971 : 396). Nevertheless each individual British departure could be explained quite logically as being also the product, in each case, of internal service problems internally responded to.

Against this background and in the second place, there seemed no little confusion over the significance formally to be ascribed to the presence of New Commonwealth immigrants within such target areas. The 1966 *Local Government Act*, for instance, had made its additional grant-aid conditional upon the local presence of a linguistically and/or culturally alien immigrant community. Would-be Educational or Housing Priority Areas, however, could count such a non-English-speaking immigrant presence as being merely one prima facie indicator of need among several others.

Third, and perhaps of greatest significance, was the confusion all too apparent over how far the role of central government should extend in such policy departures. That central government must decide, in the first instance, upon which areas to lavish its 'positive discrimination' was scarcely to be denied. Having once done this, however, to what extent should it attempt to direct local authorities as to how precisely they should spend the extra money? The answer, in this case, seemed to depend largely upon the nature and affiliations of the programme in question. Thus the 1966 *Local Government Act* provision, left it essentially to the potentially eligible local authorities to decide for themselves what were their most pressing priorities. Hence the interesting discrepancy, for instance, between the majority of eligible LAs, who decided to claim principally for additional staffing expenses in respect of education, and Manchester, which saw its prime needs, apparently, in terms of additional public health personnel (Rose 1969 : 346-7). Education and Housing Priority Areas seemed, in contrast, to imply at least a modicum of central direction. The Halsey action-research programme might have been committed in principal to the notion of locally varied EPA experiments (Halsey 1972 : 181), yet it was the DES which in the last resort decided upon LEA teacher quotas, just as it was the Burnham Committee which laid down precisely which schools were to be regarded as schools of exceptional difficulty.

It was against this background that, on May Day 1968, the Urban Programme was formally announced. To many, it seemed no more than a logical, consolidatory follow-on from activities already separately begun. Yet in the event, despite its massive-sounding title, the Urban Programme was to prove rather less than the sum of all earlier positive discrimination manoeuvres. It seemed bound, however, to encounter much the same range of problems as these had done, regarding the significance to be ascribed to the presence of immigrants, on the one hand, and the responsibilities to be assumed by central government, on the other.

Thus on the first count, for instance, there seemed widespread public confusion from the outset. Local authorities, not unnaturally, were inclined to view the promise of an Urban Programme as being a more substantial version of the 1966 (*Local Government Act*) initiative and as an acknowledgement, therefore, of their long propounded case: that local authorities faced with the burdens of an immigrant presence should receive additional, ear-marked support from central government to help them cope with the extra load (Rose 1969 :

622-23). This was not at all, however, how the government intended the Programme to be seen.

True, the formal authorization for this Programme — as embodied in the *Local Government Grants (Social Need) Act* of 1969 — went no further than to declare that:-

'The Secretary of State may out of moneys provided by Parliament pay grants ... to local authorities who in his opinion are required in the exercise of any of their functions to incur expenditure by reason of the existence in any urban area of special social need.'

'Special social need', however, was to be rather more explicitly defined in practice — as government circulars to local authorities were prompt to point out:-

'Broadly, [special social need] is intended to refer to multiple deprivation in urban (not rural) areas: localised districts ... with old, overcrowded, decrepit houses without proper plumbing and sanitation; old and inadequate school buildings; persistent un-employment; family sizes above the average; a high proportion of children in trouble or in need of care; or a combination of some or all of these. In addition, the presence of a large number of Commonwealth immigrants is only one factor, though a very important factor, in the assessment of social need. The Urban Programme should not be thought of as an immigrants' pro-gramme, but a programme mainly concerned with urban need wherever and in whatever form it exists.' (Home Office : Notes on the Urban Programme : 1)

The pattern to be followed, in other words, was more reminiscent of the EPA than of the 1966 *Local Government Act* example. The Urban Programme was to tackle social problems with which the presence of immigrants may, incidentally, be associated.[43] So the traditional line was to be upheld, in principle at least.

So far as the role of central government was concerned in relation to the manner in which approved moneys were to be spent, however, the pattern followed was very much that of 1966. Central government was not to initiate policy. It was merely to approve (or disapprove) projects submitted by local authorities within the terms of the Act.[44] Once again, therefore, one might be justified in talking of a deliberate statutory non-policy, as in the community relations case (see above p.164). Government wished to demonstrate good faith and concern, perhaps, without becoming implicated in the details of policies embarked upon, which ought on principle, it might be argued, to be worked out at ground rather than at national level.

The only qualification to this stance lay in the overall phasing policy adopted for the Urban Programme. Under this, local authorities (or, through them, voluntary organizations eligible for local authority support) were bound to submit proposals only for such projects as might be interpreted as falling within the current Programme guidelines. Phase One (relating to 1969/70), for instance, was to concentrate on the provision or improvement of nursery schools and classes, day nurseries and children's homes, and on the additional staff and equipment for them.[45] Subsequent phases have broadened the Programme's scope to include, in principle, all age groups and most aspects of urban social need. Nevertheless central government has still to approve, just as local authorities have in the first instance to decide between their own range of likely statutory and voluntary options.

All in all, however, this seems more a case of showing the flag, as it were, than one of embarking on any deliberately far-reaching new line in statutory social policy. Indeed the emphasis all along has been for central government to play-down rather than play-up the long-term significance of the Urban Programme. Not only was this declared from the start to be no more than a temporary, 'crash' attack on urban problems; its projects were in no way to be regarded as fundamentally competitive with, or supplantive of, permanent Welfare State facilities. To quote the Home Office itself:

'The Urban Programme is not intended to do the work of the major social services like education or health; it does not build primary schools, houses or hospitals. It tries, rather, to encourage projects which have a reasonably quick effect and which go directly to the roots of "special social need" (i.e. acute multiple deprivation).' (1969 : 2)

This stance was, to say the least, understandable. Quite apart from the budgetary implications of undertaking any larger-scale or longer-term commitment, to have done so would have been politically unthinkable. Having asserted, in the first place, that problems associated with the presence of coloured immigrants were for the most part no more than symptomatic of current short-comings in the Welfare State and, in the second place, that such shortcomings were more superficial than fundamental, a temporary, 'extra' well-publicized Urban Programme would seem entirely appropriate.

Such a policy, nevertheless, was open to precisely the same range of criticisms, on the grounds of superficiality, irrelevance, complacency and so on, as were the avowedly integration policies themselves. Once again it seemed, the fundamental wisdom or right-mindedness of the Welfare State itself was not after all to be called in question either by the mere presence of New Commonwealth immigrants nor by any social problems which they might happen to highlight.[46]

It is at this stage, clearly, that we must consider the Welfare State itself.

7

General policy responses to New Commonwealth immigration

One point at least seems clear from the previous chapter: neither integration policies nor positive discrimination polices were intended to be in any way supplantive of normal Welfare State machinery. They were intended as additional devices. Everyday social needs and social problems were still to be the business of the everyday Welfare State, immigrants or no immigrants. This being so, we must begin the present discussion by considering some of the characteristics of the Welfare State, as they seem to bear upon its functioning in this context.

(i) *The Welfare State*

We have already suggested, earlier in this study (above pp.36-37), that the Welfare State started off with two outstanding characteristics. On the one hand, it epitomized the country's drive for social reconstruction: a reconstruction which would (it was hoped) ensure a new, fairer, more open society; a society worthy of and mindful of the community's war effort; and a society far removed from the inequities and inqualitites of the never-to-be forgotten interwar depression. On the other hand, however, this was (to use Beveridge's phrase) to be a 'British revolution' (above p.37): not a complete, artificial break with the past; but a conscious effort to build upon and draw together all that was best and most constructive in British social policy experience and thinking — while the time seemed ripe and while the country seemed to be calling out for comprehensive social reform. There was quite enough social policy experience, and more than sufficient ideas as a result of this experience, to furnish the wherewithal, it seemed, for a thorough-going Welfare State.[1]

To engage in simultaneous and roughly co-ordinated social policy reform across a number of (already established) social policy fronts was not quite the same thing, however, as to create a single, comprehensive Welfare State from scratch. This is not to say that the Welfare State was necessarily any the weaker for being the product of this 'British' rather than of any other sort of revolution. Indeed one might argue that its components were the more acceptable and reliable precisely because they were each the product of accumulated pre-war and/or wartime experience. Nevertheless, it would seem no accident that the corporate label 'Welfare State' should have been applied only after the event to an assortment of social policy measures that were nothing if not heterogeneous in their structures and objectives.

So far as objectives were concerned, there were two types of anomaly. To begin with, while the three so-called pillars of the Welfare State — National Insurance, National Health, and Education — were at one in their responsibility each to cater for the entire population irrespective of means or social class, this was hardly the same brand of universalism in each case. National Insurance was geared to strict equality of treatment in respect of strictly specified contingencies and strict contractual entitlements. Even safety-net National Assistance, moreover, was no less committed to the ideal of applying standard rules and offering standard rates of benefit to clients whose predicaments had, as far as possible, to be classified according to standard criteria. National Health and Education, on the other hand, were pointed in virtually an opposite direction. Their objective had to be one of varied and flexible — rather than standardized or equal — provision, if they were to cater at all apppropriately for the full variety of individual requirements.

That these two basic approaches to equality, equality of treatment (in the case of National Insurance) versus equality of effectiveness (in the case of health) or equality of opportunity (in the case of education), were in theory reconcilable, has already been acknowledged (above p.37). Nevertheless the package as a whole (and standardized National Assistance in particular) is far more readily explicable in terms of its various historical antecedents than in terms of any single, thought-out recipe for social reconstruction.

Much the same could be said, more pointedly, in respect of the second, broader anomaly: the distinction between those Welfare State social services that could seriously be described as universal in any sense, and those that could not. How else save in historical, developmental (or even accidental) terms should one try to explain what must otherwise seem an arbitrary, not to say irrational, distinction between, in effect, first and second rank social policy in the Welfare State?

Given a government commitment to full employment, for instance, it might seem odd that statutory employment services were not elevated henceforth to the status of a full comprehensive, universal service (complete with sanctions, perhaps, to encourage its general use), instead of being left to soldier on as an optional, marginal facility complete with its 1930s dole-queue image intact. Given Beveridge's inclusion of 'squalor' among his five giants on the road of social reconstruction it might seem odd, again, that housing should not have received the same headline treatment as say health or education. Shelter was supposed to be a common human need, after all, and it was common human needs that the Welfare State was supposed to be all about. A New Towns Act, a Town and Country Planning Act, and the continuance of LA responsibilities to provide rented housing for certain sections of their local populations could hardly be described, however, as a comprehensive, universalist package.

Both employment and housing could be described as relatively junior, relatively less developed, branches of statutory social policy at the time when the Welfare State was being drawn together. The same was not true, however, of that third area of 'second rank' social policy: social care or welfare services. Here the difficulty was of a rather different order. The very term welfare smacked of the Poor Law on the one hand and of charitable condescension on the other. Neither image seemed appropriate for the new-look Welfare State. Moreover, while wartime experience had demonstrated that so-called welfare needs might be no respecters of persons (and that it was necessary therefore to break away from the Poor Law/charitable image), there was genuine uncertainty over how far and in what respects social care services were going to be needed or wanted, once the Welfare State was in full swing.

A Children Act was necessary, if only to clear up a previous and glaring administrative muddle; but the new LA Children's Officers were not to be responsible for *all* children — only children in need of special local authority care. Aside from this, Poor Law welfare responsibilities in general had to be placed somewhere, of course, once the Poor Law itself had been formally abolished; but the local authorities who inherited these motley provisions were given little guidance as to the manner in which, or the scale upon which, they should be dispensed now that they were not actually to be dependent upon proof of destitution.

So much for what might be termed the inconsistencies of scope and objectives between the social services of the newly-launched Welfare State. No less evident, of course, and no less explicable in developmental terms, was the variety of administrative arrangements for such services' delivery. No single, thought-out recipe for social reconstruction would have prescribed a social security system to be run by central government, a National Health Service split three ways between two sets of ad hoc authorities and local government, an education service to be run by local government, employment services to be run mainly by central government, and housing services left mainly in the hands of local government. Nor were these merely trivial distinctions.

Differences of administrative structure, for instance, meant differences of staffing policy and characteristics. Civil servants, whether employed in National Insurance offices, National Assistance offices, or employment exchanges, were not the same sort of animal, nor expected to perform the same sort of function, as were, for instance LA career specialists in youth employment, education, or child care. LA medical officers of health, again, were expected to perform rather differently than were the paid officials of hospital management committees or executive councils. Differences of structure, in other words, meant differences of style and approach — not all of which could be justified solely by reference to the nature of the specific task in hand.

Associated with this, and of no less significance, was the effect differences of structure might be expected to exercise upon interaction between (or, in the case of the Health Service, within) existing services. Given the inevitably arbitrary nature of any dividing lines between service responsibilities, then some measure of coordination was clearly going to be required — if only because social needs were not always so neat as social service distinctions might imply. And the Welfare State, after all, was supposed to be something more than the sum of its parts. Differences of structure and style between services, however, could not but complicate coordination.

These starting characteristics of the Welfare State would seem important for several reasons. To begin with, once the breakdown of apparent public consensus had robbed the Welfare State of its halo and rendered it increasingly the subject of argument and criticism, both the criticisms voiced and the modifications eventually embarked upon could be described, more or less, as a delayed response to these same starting characteristics. However, just as the Welfare State had not begun as a single entity, so it was not to become one as a result of subsequent adjustments. In effect, services continued separately to develop and/or to expand and/or to reorganize much as they had been doing long before the 1940s. The only difference lay in the pace and scale of the changes embarked upon. The 1960s and early '70s were almost as hectic in this respect as the 1940s, albeit less dramatic.

Quite apart from any changes actually introduced, this pattern of development was to prove a significant one. In the first place, it meant that the Welfare State as a whole was never quite the same from one year to the next. So far as its protagonists were concerned, this meant of course that the Welfare State was a vital system: never standing still in the midst of changing social conditions. So far as potential users, or critics, of the system were concerned, however, it could mean simply that the Welfare State was forever a moving, shifting, even shapeless, target.

Piecemeal modification or reform, moreover, was to prove significant in three further respects. To begin with, it made it extremely unlikely that the Welfare State would ever, as a whole, break away from the inconsistencies of structure and objective characteristics of the 'system' at its inception. In the second place, of course, piecemeal alterations were liable to give rise to new dividing lines and fresh anomalies almost as fast as others were abolished.

Hence the predicament of LA social services departments, for instance, who very shortly after their own creation had to contend, not merely with NHS reorganization and the fresh boundaries this imposed between what ought properly to be regarded as social and what ought henceforth to be dismissed as health responsibilities, but with the reorganization of local government itself. Consolidation and coordination might have been the watchwords of the 1960s and early '70s, but one could not consolidate and coordinate right across the board, it seemed. Even the creation of the mammoth DHSS at central government level did not mean the coordination of *all* Welfare State social policy at the top, let alone at the bottom. And mammoth consolidation was liable, in any case, to produce its own problems. It was no short-cut to consistency, for certain.

Reorganization or reform was bound, in the third place, to absorb a certain amount of service energy and attention in itself, not merely after, but often well in advance, of its event. Hence the cumulative distraction to be expected, not merely from staggered, interrelated reorganization (as implied above), but from the literally paralysing effects within any one service of reorganization long expected but unexpectedly long in coming. At the time when I was conducting my own survey[2] into the operations of statutory social services, for instance, no less than seven of the eight types of agency approached declared themselves to be distracted, to a greater or lesser extent, by the prospect of impending reorganization. Only Supplementary Benefits, so recently re-named, seemed to feel itself temporarily immune.

No amount of rethinking or reorganization could, in any case, render the initial Welfare State ideal of equality of opportunity immediately realizable in practice. The legislators of the 1940s had been nothing if not optimistic in their apparent conviction that the mere provision of a few key universal social services would be sufficient to cancel out the effects of structural social inequalitites overnight (see above p.37). The would be reformers of the 1960s had to grapple with a circular prospect: equality of opportunity (assuming some unevenness in individual motivation and potential) could only result in an uneven social outcome (which was what society, after all, seemed to require). Such an unevenness of outcome, however, seemed bound, to judge from all the evidence available, to prejudice the next generation's chances of equality of opportunity. How far ought the state, or could the state, be expected reasonably to go in an effort to ensure that each new generation started off, in effect, on an equal footing? The chickens of the woolly 1940s were at last, it seemed, coming home to roost.

It is against this rather confused and confusing background, that we have to try to assess the impact of New Commonwealth immigration upon the workings of the Welfare State. Taking into account the discussion so far, the issues to be tackled would seem to revolve around one central theme. To what extent (if at all) has the arrival and settlement of New Commonwealth immigrants in this country presented the social services of the Welfare State, either individually or as a body, with social needs and social problems *qualitatively* different from those with which the system was bound to have to grapple in any case?

This is scarcely a simple question. On the one hand, it could be argued that the more clearly defined and categorized were service responsibilities the less likely, by definition, were such services to have to come to terms with unforeseen contingencies. Conversely, the more open-ended or comprehensive was the service responsibility, the more likely were such services to have to contend, somehow, with the unexpected or the unfamiliar, should the unexpected or the unfamiliar present itself. On the other hand however, it could be argued that, irrespective of service conventions (and a compartmentalized, pre-categorized approach to service responsibiltites was in many cases no more than a matter of convention), the Welfare State as a whole was committed, not to meeting a set list of social requirements, but to tackling social needs in general in so far as they seemed to bear upon the individual citizen's, and the general population's, quality of life in this society. Given such an ideal commitment, then it seemed likely in principle that any service might find itself having to contend with the unexpected or the unfamiliar within its general field of responsibility. Should such a situation occur, then clearly those services that were already geared to the notion of individualized, open-ended treatment were less likely to find dealing with the unexpected or the unfamiliar traumatic in the immigrant case — and less likely, indeed, to regard such events as being qualitatively different from the normal run of their experience. Such relative confidence could of course produce its own complications. The less obvious was service adaptation to meet immigrant or immigrant-associated requirements, the more difficult must it be in principle to isolate and hence assess the quality of service response in these respects.

Yet this is already, in effect, to jump the gun. We are assuming, by implication, that New Commonwealth immigrants were likely to present special social needs and special social problems, whether or not these were likely to be tackled or perceived as such by existing Welfare State social services. Yet the issue is in fact rather more complex. Given the characteristics of New Commonwealth immigration as already described and given the overall objectives of the Welfare State from its inception, the extent to which or the manner in which New Commonwealth immigration might be held to raise issues qualitatively distinct from those already bargained for can be no easy matter to resolve.

Thus, to begin with, the fact that New Commonwealth immigrants tended to be far poorer as a group than was the general population did not mean that their economic predicaments were necessarily any different in kind from those of the general population — merely more exaggerated, perhaps, and more frequent in their occurrence. (Such at least seemed to be the National Insurance and the Supplementary Benefits' view of the situation. Money was money was money, after all — see below p.195).

Yet New Commonwealth immigrants were of course not merely poor but strange: strange in the sense that they themselves were relatively unfamiliar with the ramifications of life in this country and strange also in the sense that they stood culturally and physically apart, more or less, from the rest of the population. But even such strangeness, perhaps, was no more than a matter of degree.

Given a native population which was not noted for its intimate grasp of public affairs (or of its social service facilities), and given a Welfare State which seemed to be adjusting its already complex arrangements almost week by week, New Commonwealth immigrants were not necessarily so much more ignorant as a group (and in such particular need, therefore, of advisory assistance) than were the general run of native 'needy' classes. Indeed it might be argued that, as newcomers conscious of their ignorance, immigrants were rather more likely to have done their homework in this respect than were their English counterparts (see below p.206).

Linguistic and cultural barriers would seem, nevertheless, to constitute something extra and out of the ordinary. Service accessability and appropriateness of response was bound to be affected. Even here, however, this could be interpreted as no more than a difference (albeit an extreme difference) of degree rather than one of kind, in comparison with contingencies already encountered by certain of the social services. New Commonwealth immigrants (or indeed any immigrants) were hardly the only people, for instance, to experience some measure of cultural and linguistic divide between home and school or between home and the social services department or between home and doctor. Nor could New Commonwealth linguistic and cultural characteristics, in all their variety, be described as equally and universally remote from the native continuum: West Indian linguistic and cultural 'ambivalence' being an obvious case in point.

In essence, therefore, the question of whether particular social services chose to regard New Commonwealth characteristics and requirements as different in kind or merely as different in degree from the general run of needs with which they had to contend, might seem of secondary importance. Of far more significance, in principle, was the extent of response to such needs — however they might be classified.

Such at least was to be the standard social services' view on this matter. Nevertheless, the existence of host-immigrant racial tensions seemed in effect to militate against any such altogether 'needs-centred' approach. There were two main reasons for this. To begin with, the institution of specific new social policies in aid of racial integration was bound to affect the manner in which ongoing social services went about their business. This was not simply a case of having local community relations councils or race relations conciliation committees conveniently placed in the neighbourhood to which blacks (or whites) with a race relations problem might henceforth be referred. It meant also that the social services themselves, like any other public institution or large employer, must be highly conscious of their own behaviour where immigrant staff or clients were concerned, since the services like anyone else, if not more so, could be called to account.

There was, furthermore, another side to the coin. Ongoing social services were not merely subject to the conditions of specialist integration policy measures: they themselves were expected actively to promote the integration cause in the course of their own day-to-day activities. Such services, after all were supposed to be the very stuff of the Welfare State; specialist integration policy on its own could hardly do more than patrol the marginal areas. Hence the repeated calls at national level, from the Cullingworth Committee on Council Housing,[3] for instance, and from successive Reports of the Parliamentary Select Committee on Race Relations and Immigration (1969, 1971, 1973), for existing services to take positive and deliberate action where the treatment of coloured immigrants *per se* was concerned. At the very least this seemed to mean that they should keep a separate ethnic record of clientele (just as large employers should do with their workforce) in order to monitor progress and to show, if nothing else, that justice was indeed being done.

On all these latter points there has been, as might have been expected, a somewhat adverse social services' reaction. Part of this was purely defensive. Service personnel could dislike being placed on the hook, as they saw it, and they could also resent being asked to add to their paperwork. Aside from this, however, there were more fundamental grounds for concern. The whole philosophy of the Welfare State (in so far as it possessed any whole philosophy) had hitherto seemed to centre around the idea of catering for certain categories of social need irrespective, in each case, of 'extraneous' social, cultural, or economic personal characteristics. To treat, or even to record, coloured immigrants differently, for no other reason than because they were coloured immigrants, seemed to strike at the heart of this philosophy, and to constitute a form of colour discrimination which, whether it was intended to be positive or negative in the first instance, seemed a highly dangerous and unwelcome precedent.

So strong were service sensibilities and sensitivities in this respect, that there emerged a further complication. Even where ethnic and cultural characteristics might normally be reckoned of major relevance to the case in hand (and the distinction between relevance and irrelevance need not be an easy line to draw), services could be highly self-conscious about recording such details — or at least about recording them in any form which might be construed by others as constituting systematic ethnic records. That such a line might actually militate against normal service efficiency, would seem evident enough.

All in all, it would scarcely seem a straighforward, clear-cut exercise, either to assess the impact of New Commonwealth immigration upon Welfare State social services or to assess the nature and quality of such services' response to this immigrant presence. The impact is complicated by the intervention of (in a sense) extraneous additional social policy measures and suggestions. The response cannot realistically be weighed up in isolation from service conventions and service performances in general. Once again, moreover (just as in the case of integration policy itself), there was no generally agreed 'right' balance to be struck or 'right 'solution to be pursued when it came to dealing with both host and immigrant requirements in any context, however seemingly mundane.

It is at this stage, that we must set generalities aside and concentrate upon actual service experience and response. Needless to say, this is more easily said than done — given the intricacies of the subject and given the limitations of the evidence obtainable (see above pp.118-20 and Appendix). Bearing this in mind, and bearing in mind the implications, so far, of this discussion, the simplest most direct approach seems the wisest one to adopt. We will discuss service experience and response in terms of the extent to which selected representatives of each major type of local social service considered their own agencies to have adjusted their policies and procedures (in certain specified respects) and/or to be facing particular problems as an agency, as a result of New Commonwealth settlement in their areas (see Appendix). Such material, when set against overall service objectives, scope, and structure in each case, should provide us with at least a measure of valid evidence of some relevance and usefulness to this discussion. We will deal separately with each type of social service beginning, in the present chapter, with Social Security, Health, and Education as being the so-called pillars of the Welfare State.

(ii) *Social Security*

The social security provisions embodied in the Welfare State had been designed with a lofty, blanket target in mind: the abolition of Want, no less. In practice, however, National Insurance and Supplementary Benefits administration saw itself as being responsible for meeting a strictly defined range of pecuniary social needs. National Insurance, after all, was a contractual arrangement. Even Supplementary Benefits, thanks to the drive to escape from any residual Poor Law image, were bound as far as possible to be portrayed as an impersonal form of relief: issued in standardized amounts to meet prescribed and proven contingencies.

There was virtually no room, in this context, for any specialized response to New Commonwealth immigrant financial predicaments as such. If New Commonwealth immigrant households seemed, disproportionately, to benefit from SB exceptional needs payments then this was purely incidental, since: 'In the general exercise of these powers ... no differential treatment is intended for the immigrant population as a whole' (Jones 1975 : 153. Hence forward, to the end of Chapter eight, all unattributed page references in parentheses refer to this report).

Conversely, if the levels of rent being paid by immigrant households in receipt of supplementary benefits were illegally high, then this could not generally be taken into account, since:

'In such cases the S.B. Commission normally accept for supplementary benefit purposes only the registered rent for the accommodation or an estimate of what this would be where no rent has been registered.' (p.156)

Only in certain technical respects was there what might be termed a specialized response to New Commonwealth immigration as such. Thus National Insurance might have to waive its normal record-keeping requirements in certain cases where conventional proofs of marriage, proof that the marriage was monogamous ('since a polygamous marriage is not valid for National Insurance purposes' (p.153-54)), proof of birth and proof of residence qualification were not readily available. The Supplementary Benefits Commission was prepared, for its part: 'to help with the expenses of an immigrant who wished to return to his country of origin, if certain conditions are satisfied' (p.153). Not unnaturally, however, these conditions were fairly strict:-

'The immigrant must have no prospect of settling down and making a success of life in this country; be unlikely to find work and save up the fare and the money is not available from other sources; genuinely wish to return home with his dependants, if any. Repatriation must seem to be in the immigrant's best interest and also lead to an ultimate saving in public funds.' (p.153)

Hence 'the number of cases assisted in this way is small' (p.153).

The fact of being a New Commonwealth immigrant, therefore, was for the most part not a relevant condition, so far as these cash-disbursing agencies were concerned. If the newcomers' cash requirements were in some cases less than adequately met, then this was a comment on the system as a whole, not a comment on its response to New Commonwealth immigration in particular.

So thorough was this conviction, both as regards service responsibilities and possible immigrant requirements, that there seemed no question in this case of going even so far as to furnish special (immigrant language) information leaflets for the benefit of New Commonwealth clientele, let alone of keeping systematic client records on a separate ethnic basis. National Insurance, to be sure, might require the maintenance of certain 'additional information' on persons born elsewhere than in Great Britain (p.154). In general, however,

'There's no particular reason I can think of why we should keep separate records: with regard to N.I. claims, our only interest is in proof of residence and in the contributions record; with regard to S.B. this is simply a financial calculation ... The area for discretion is in reality very small and is carefully codified in the instructions to staff.' (p.155).

The reference to staff brings us on to a further , associated, point. Since both National Insurance and Supplementary Benefits ranked as civil service-administered facilities there could be little room in practice for elaborate staff briefing or training on the subject of New Commonwealth immigration, even had the responsibilities of the service seemed to require this, which of course they did not. Moreover, any training or briefing had to come from the centre which meant inevitably that, for the majority of staff involved, New Commonwealth immigration was, to say the least, a subject of less than immediate concern. Thus:-

'A booklet has been issued to all local offices, to give information about the background and way of life of immigrants, particularly of West Indians, Indians, and Pakistanis. This has been found helpful in applying our understanding of human behaviour to actions and customs which are natural to the immigrant, but unusual to us. For the great majority of officers, of course, the booklet is seldom used, but those officers in areas ... where there are large numbers of immigrants, have found the information useful.' (p.148-49)

Actual training time, furthermore, had for practical purposes to be relatively brief. Even so, while much of the standard training might be geared to enabling officers to 'administer acts of parliament in a precise fashion' there was some time allowed for 'background instruction in mock-casework techniques to enable officers to deal effectively with the public' (p.149). It was in this 'human relations' context that 'colour problems' might frequently be touched upon in open discussion:-

'This most often arises because a white member of staff admits to some difficulty with a coloured public, but quite often also when a coloured member of staff finds antagonism in the white public ...' (p.149)

The reference to coloured staff brings us, again, to a further interesting point. National Insurance Supplementary benefits administration was seemingly conspicuous as being a large-scale employer (across the country) of New Commonwealth immigrant manpower. Yet this was in no sense, apparently, the result of any

erate policy manoeuvre. Service spokesmen indeed were insistent
'recruitment is by competition and the most suitable are selected
lless of colour or creed' (p.150).

oured staff, in other words, were not deliberately recruited as a
r of policy, either to set a good example in race relations or to be
irticular assistance in dealing with New Commonwealth
le.[4] Once appointed, they might prove helpful in this latter
t, but not necessarily so, given the cultural and linguistic divides
the immigrants community itself (p.150). But on this
, as it happened, the service view[5] was to prove entirely
ent with the views of most other social services respondents.

n all, this would seem to be a case of service responsibilities
o defined and categorized as literally to rule out the possibility
service's having to respond specifically (save in minor, mostly
al respects) to New Commonwealth needs as such. Yet this fact
___ ve interpreted in one of two ways. Either it could be taken as
proof that the social security system (and supplementary benefits
administration in particular) was indeed so comprehensive that no
further adaptation could conceivably be required to meet New
Commonwealth contingencies (which were in any case no different in
kind from those of the general population). Or it could be taken as
proof that the system was in fact too limited and too compartmentalized to be capable of any flexible response. Given the contention
surrounding New Commonwealth immigration in any case, the
former view was naturally the more reassuring to maintain.

(iii) *National Health*

Once again this was a case of machinery being established initially for
the pursuance of a very lofty, generalized objective: this time to
provide comprehensive, individualized health care services for the
whole of the population. Once again, however, the reality was to
prove rather more fragmented than the ideal. In discussing the
National Health Service prior to its eventual reorganization[6] we
shall, in effect, be discussing not one service but three. However
thorough the coordination or complex the interrelationships between
them, the organization of LA health services, ad hoc general
practitioner services and ad hoc hospital services had virtually nothing
in common so far as their respective styles and structures were
concerned. Not surprisingly, therefore, their experiences of New

Commonwealth immigration and their responses to New Commonwealth immigration seem to have had relatively few points in common either.

(a) *LA health departments*

The most striking area of interest concerns local authority health departments. These, so frequently caricatured as being the poor relations of the NHS, were far and away the most conspicious branch of the service in their efforts to come to terms with New Commonwealth immigration *per se*. The reasons for this stem, on the one hand, from the nature of health department responsibilities and, on the other, from the nature and obviousness of immigrant requirements in this sphere.

LA health departments possessed the generalized responsibility for maternity and child welfare; for preventive health measures; for health education programmes and for public health in general. As such it was they, rather than individual GPs or hospital management committees, who were most extensively involved in the implications of any change in the general balance of the local population. Where there were population changes as a result of New Commonwealth (or potentially of any foreign) immigration, this was of particular significance. Not simply might the newcomers bring special diseases, or special disease susceptibilities, with them; there might be a high proportion of young (and badly-housed) families each with family structures and customs and child-rearing practices different from the native norm; there might be language problems to contend with, quite apart from the less obvious but equally insidious effects of differing cultural attitudes to health and towards the health services themselves. All in all, therefore, local authority health departments could hardly fail to be specially aware of New Commonwealth immigration.

So far as the response to such a presence was concerned, the first major task was obvious enough: to locate and establish contact with immigrant households as soon as possible after their arrival in the area. This in itself, of course, was no simple undertaking. Only one respondent (out of thirteen) declared his department able to operate an 'automatic' visiting service of all recent immigrants (SSRC Report : 28). For the rest, it was not lack of manpower but a lack of information which seemed most decisive. They may or may not have been in receipt of port-of-entry information, warning them in advance of the numbers of immigrants ostensibly heading in their direction; but this was at best an unreliable source, and gave no indication, of course, as to the numbers of immigrants en route between centres in the UK. On the whole, therefore, departments seemed to make what use they could of whatever secondary sources of information were to hand. Immigrant grapevines could prove useful for instance (where there existed a 'good working relationship' between the health department and the immigrant community). Compulsory school medical checks for all new entrants could provide an equally promising source, as could their own health visitor reports on 'immigrant births' (p. 28).

The next hurdle consisted of persuading each newly arrived immigrant, once located, to undergo medical examination. Here again, health departments seemed nothing if not pragmatic (and necessarily so) in the methods they adopted. School medical tests,[7] for instance, could be used as an occasion for urging the rest of the family to undergo medical examination elsewhere. Health visitors, again, might be specially instructed to suggest medical examination for all members of a newly located immigrant household and to urge them, indeed, to register as soon as possible with a local GP (p. 28).

Such initial medical examinations tended to focus upon X-rays, ECG tests, and stool examinations — corresponding, it was claimed, to the observed health risks of the immigrant populations concerned (SSRC : 28). Even so, the imposition of such tests could be interpreted as a tactless, not to say discriminatory, procedure. Though health departments seemed determined to stick by their position and to declare that indeed these were purely medical procedures, medically required, this did not mean that they were unmindful of the possible constructions which could be placed upon such activities. Hence their anxiety, at least, not to seem to be discriminating between immigrants in this respect: 'European immigrants don't take very kindly to having their children vetted for worms. But we don't discriminate between immigrants' (p.28 and c.f. below p.204).

Health department responsibilities did not end, of course, with the ('voluntary') imposition of initial medical checks. Of far more significance in the long-term, it seemed, was the extent to which they managed to get on terms with and hence to educate the immigrant population on health matters in general. Thus while a few departments might have regarded this merely as a case for making 'special allowances' in a very general sense for differences of language and of culture, most seemed to feel it necessary, if not to embark on actual language classes for certain groups of immigrant mothers, then at least to utilize such clinics as were sited in immigrant areas as a general health education resource, to which health visitors already in contact with immigrant households might, for instance, be attached.

More obvious in this respect, though arguably of limited effectiveness, was the abundance of special language literature distributed through health departments and covering everything, it seemed, from baby and child care to family planning and fire prevention (p.26). LA health departments had of course long been in the business of circulating health education posters and leaflets. Few seemed very sure in this case, however, as to how valuable such literature might be. Languages could be quick to come and go (at least in a metropolitan area) and illiteracy or near-illiteracy among Asian housewives must limit leaflet usefulness in any case (p.27). Nevertheless health departments would seem conspicuous for their efforts in this field, compared to any other branch of social service.

Given the apparent marked significance of New Commonwealth immigration for this service and given its obvious efforts to respond specifically to this situation, it would have been surprising indeed had not most LA health departments been in the practice of maintaining what might roughly be termed separate, ethnic records. No less understandable, however, was the anxiety of departmental spokesmen to emphasize that, should such records be maintained in any form seeming to approximate to some sort of ethnic breakdown *per se*, then this was purely incidental. Records were maintained in such forms as medical implications would seem to necessitate. Immigrant births, for instance, were separately recorded not because they might be coloured but simply because there might be cultural, linguistic, and possibly genetic complications to be encountered in the future. Only six respondents, even so, were prepared to state initially in writing that their department maintained any separate records in this sense, although a further four suggested, when interviewed, that certain immigrant clientele were recorded as such (SSRC : 30).

It is against this background that we must review the apparent staffing policies of LA health departments — as being the means to the end in this somewhat difficult area. Two factors would seem of significance here. To begin with, while a sizeable proportion of health department staff seem to have been either exposed to, or positively encouraged to undergo, some form of special briefing or training on the subject of New Commonwealth immigration, it was mostly health visitors, district nurses, and midwives who went in for such activities. Doctors, apparently, were either too well-trained already or simply too well thought of for such special preparation. Professional status in general seemed indeed to be a frequent justification for the absence of any further special training (pp.22-3). This was, needless to say, to be an argument recurrently employed by a wide range of social service spokesmen irrespective, apparently, of the degree and length of the so-called professional training originally undertaken by their staff. It was, in a sense, one way of asserting that New Commonwealth immigrant predicaments were indeed no different in kind, however much service manoeuvres might suggest to the contrary.

Set against this, however, was the somewhat remarkable record of LA health departments not merely to have employed large numbers of New Commonwealth staff in a general, unpremeditated way (Asian doctors, for instance, being more circumscribed in their hospital prospects, were more likely on average to end up in an LA health department) (p.23), but in four cases actually to have recruited New Commonwealth staff specifically to deal with New Commonwealth clientele (p.24).

Such a policy could of course provoke its own repercussions. Asian doctors could seem at best 'more debonair' and at worst 'bloody-minded' in their treatment of fellow national clients. It was alleged that 'life is cheap' to them, and that local immigrants were 'mere peasants' to be bullied or chivvied into health (pp.24-5). In any event, Asian nurses might be quite as far removed, in social class terms, from the mass of their local Asian clientele as were any white professionals (p.25). West Indian midwives, in a more general context, might turn out to be unduly bossy and authoritarian — although different West Indian islands, according to one careful respondent, tended to produce a different quality of nurse (p. 25).

This is not to say, of course, that a multi-racial workforce might not have its incidental uses. Most departments, having once acquired a multi-racial workforce seemed inclined, formally or informally, to make use of its linguistic potential if nothing else. Thus whether staff were listed as components of a departmental language bank, or merely consulted and/or loaned out on an individual basis as and when required, the notion of using immigrants to deal with immigrants seemed acceptable in this strictly limited sense although not, it would seem, in any other.[8]

Given this background and this degree of seemingly inevitable involvement with the consequences of New Commonwealth immigration, LA health departments confessed themselves, not surprisingly, to be facing a fairly wide range of operational problems. Taken all in all, these problems seemed to fall into three component groups arising respectively from the characteristics of New Commonwealth immigrants themselves, from the intrinsic limitations of the service, and, last but not least, from the complications of a race relations policy climate.

On the first count, concern seemed to be centred both upon immigrant practices *per se* and upon immigrant reactions to the health service. Thus in its simplest form:-

'The immigrants in this area are on the whole village people from rather primitive backgrounds. Many of the women are illiterate and unused to living in an industrial urban area with an acute housing problem. There is a feeling of going backwards in time: we have to deal with problems of diet, food handling, deficiency disease etc., which have to a certain extent been overcome in the local population.' (p.32)

Given the specific departmental concern with infant and child-rearing practices, however, cultural differences in this respect could seem more than a case of mere ignorance or poor communications:-

'This is not merely a matter of language barriers, but one of getting through to people on matters they either aren't interested in or are afraid to be told about. Our staff were doing quite well, we thought, until we faced an outbreak of rickets in the Asian community. 90% of these cases happened to be girls. In other words, the health visitors *had* been getting through with their advice. It was just that these families had two standards: one for the boys and one for the girls.' (pp.32-3)

Against such a background, the alleged liability of West Indian children to end up as sexually promiscuous and/or as mentally handicapped as a result of 'frail' family structures seemed a problem almost straightforward in comparison (p.33).

West Indians, furthermore, seemed less complicated to deal with in general from the service's point of view. They might be truculent, certainly, yet 'they seem to manage their affairs alright, perhaps because they've been here longer' (p.31). Asians, in contrast, could be 'bloody minded' on the one hand, when it came to seeming health department interference, yet, on the other hand, very demanding of service attention:-

> 'They're good clinic attenders but they like too many injections — injections are like gold dust to them.'

> ' ... they don't play hard to get on this one — probably because they've been well-conditioned to this at home.' (p.31)

Faced with such complications the most obvious difficulty, from the service's point of view, was to recruit and to retain sufficient numbers of suitable staff. Only two agencies declared categorically that a New Commonwealth immigrant presence in the area made it particularly difficult for them to attract and retain professional staff, but this was not, presumably, an isolated predicament (p.35).

Far more frequently referred to, however, were the fundamental limitations of the service, with regard to housing conditions in particular. Unfit housing and overcrowded housing were both issues upon which the departments could act, indeed could feel obliged to act, yet in neither case could they do more than remove the immediate hazard: they could do nothing more constructive for the families concerned. That it went against the grain to take action in such a seemingly negative and pointless fashion seemed to go without saying:-

> 'They start off with very poor accommodation and they don't bring it up to standard, even though they spend a lot of money on these houses. The houses are palaces, of course, to what they've had before ... But they are still unfit.' (p.33)

Or, to take the overcrowding theme:-

> 'You put the overcrowding orders on and they all melt away. It's like musical chairs: when the music stops you all get off somewhere else.' (p.33)

It was against this sort of problematic background that departments were prone to feel aggrieved when confronted with an additional, race relations, complication. Yet they felt themselves bound, more or less, to encounter such complications in three particular respects.

To begin with, any medical procedures which seemed, however incidentally, to single out New Commonwealth immigrants as such could be interpreted as constituting a none too subtle form of discrimination. Departments confident in the knowledge that they were simply acting in the interests of public health could brazen this out. Immigrants who insisted upon protracted visits 'home', for instance, could meet with awkward consequences upon their return: 'They drink the local water and come back infected. Then they are annoyed when we insist on re-screening the children before we allow them back to school' (p.32) Again, where typhoid checks might seem to single out immigrants as such, departmental spokesmen might simply declare that: 'They say this is racial discrimination but we don't take any notice' (p.34). Far more common, however, was the feeling that 'we have to fall over backwards to play safe on this one' (p.34). Hence the elaborate efforts, in one case, not to give offence (at the expense, perhaps, of confusing the majority of residents):

> 'Asians use water rather than toilet paper; and they use milk bottles for the water. We thought it advisable to try to stop this. In order not to appear discriminatory we circulated *all* the houses in a given area with leaflets in English and Asian languages, stating "Please do not use milk bottles for toilet purposes".' (p.27)

Such manoeuvres might, to say the least, appear over-elaborate. Yet one careless move could perhaps bring instant embarassment. A tactless health visitor, for instance, who had demanded to know the country of origin of a father who declared that he had fought for the Empire and that 'British' should be good enough, ensured a departmental encounter with the Race Relations Board — 'that agency for trouble' (p.34).

Difficulties with the Race Relations Board, however, were also likely to arise, in the second place, from the fact of employing New Commonwealth staff. Despite such fears, only one department had actually experienced any difficulty in this respect. A newly appointed school nurse had not, after all, been guaranteed the place she evidently expected on a student nursing course.

> 'She said it was discrimination. The Board threw out the case, but I [the MOH] had to agree to give her a place since it was just conceivable that she could have misunderstood the terms of her appointment.' (p.34)

Interestingly enough, however, such staffing complications seemed to arise not as frequently as in the other — hospitals — branch of the service, also notable for its dependence upon New Commonwealth immigrant manpower (see below p.210).

The one remaining area of difficulty seemed to arise, not from immigrant, but from local host opinion. True the days of maternity bed allegations seemed thankfully to be days long past and, apart from one authority currently experiencing a sizeable Ugandan Asian influx, such 'primitive' fears were not expected to recur. Local politicians could never be relied upon, however, not to try to make some capital out of an immigrant situation — no matter how meticulous and reassuring LA health department information might set out to be. Public opinion, in such a context, was bound to be volatile, to say the least: 'Fears of TB, leprosy and smallpox are ever-present in the white population. If you combine these with fears of immigration you have an explosive mixture' (p.35).

(b) *Executive Councils*

If we compare this general picture with the impression given by executive councils, then the contrast could scarcely be more marked. Executive councils were in this case the nearest equivalent to a local agency representative of local GPs. Yet they did not employ such GPs: their role was rather one of servicing, coordinating, and (to some extent) regulating GP activities. Their functions were essentially administrative rather than medical. In this instance, therefore, we shall be considering the impact of New Commonwealth immigration not upon family doctors as such, but rather upon their supporting, administrative agencies.[9]

Given the nature of the agency, there would seem relatively little scope either for New Commonwealth immigration to make much of an impact upon its operations or vice versa. Yet the picture which emerged proves rather more interesting than might have been expected.

Naturally, the effects of New Commonwealth immigration upon executive council operations were most marked in the technical sphere. 'Inflation' (in the sense that there could be more people apparently registered with local GPs than there were members of the local population) seemed the central problem in nearly every case, and seemed a consequence, at least to a very large extent, of immigration. It was not simply that the newcomers might possess confusing names for clerks to cope with; they also tended to move around a lot, register with a succession of GPs en route and perhaps even leave the country with their registration trail still intact (p.126).

Most executive councils were making some sort of special effort to tackle this problem, usually by maintaining a temporary separate register (for the first year or eighteen months) of all newcomers to their areas, or of all immigrants coming directly from abroad. Yet this of course could look like separate ethnic records — a fact of which most respondents seemed only too aware. Hence their anxiety always to emphasize the strictly functional nature of any temporary registers and that they were in no way intended as a list of coloured immigrants as such. Since record-keeping *per se* ranked as a primary agency function, councils clearly felt themselves exposed and vulnerable on this score (p.125).

In comparison with such technical complications, there were the rather less predictable shifts in agency practice and expectations in so far as New Commonwealth immigrants seemed, if anything, to be making rather different demands upon their services than did the general population. There were several sides to this situation. To begin with, the newcomers could seem much better informed about the service than were the natives:-

'As newcomers, immigrants peruse all their documents very carefully. They are probably better-briefed than most natives as a result, and are certainly much more likely to find their way in person to the executive council.' (pp.124,127)

The last point, at least, seemed demonstrably true: the majority of executive councils seemed convinced that New Commonwealth immigrants were disproportionately represented among their personal callers (p.124). Simply by making use of the service, moreover, the newcomers seemed in effect to be prompting councils to behave — and to see themselves — in a rather different light than they might have done before. Thus: ' ... for them we function much more as a direct advice centre than we do for the general population' (p.124). There were complications of course. Immigrants might seem more demanding than the general run of personal callers (p.127). The mere fact that they made use of the service, moreover, did not necessarily mean that they did so 'appropriately'. Thus:-

'Cultural differences mean that there is a lack of understanding of the basic social structures etc. and, therefore, this makes it difficult for [immigrants] to appreciate the basic attitudes of the public to the Health Service.' (p.127)

This was perhaps more in the nature of a general comment than one specific to the work of executive councils. Of far more immediate significance was the fact that immigrant requirements for a 'suitable' GP could present executive councils with problems qualitatively different from those with which they were either accustomed or empowered to cope.

It is here, therefore, that we find five (out of ten) councils effectively skating on thin ice. They were not supposed, of course, to recommend individual doctors to individual members of the public. Nevertheless, faced with the particular cultural and linguistic requirements of immigrant clientele, they would where necessary refer patients 'informally' to doctors of the same nationality, or at least, in one case, supply them with a list of fellow-national GPs (p.125).

All in all, therefore, this could seem to be a case of an agency which had hitherto seen itself, and been seen, as primarily an impersonal administrative machine, being affected by New Commonwealth immigration not merely in a technical sense, but in the sense that it could find itself stretched to the limit (if not beyond the limit) of its formal powers — as a direct and *personal* social service. One should not of course exaggerate the change. There was no sudden burst in special training programmes, for instance, for clerical and executive staff, who were expected to be well able to handle all comers in any case (p.120). Nor was there much room for New Commonwealth staff recruitment, either as a matter of policy or otherwise. Executive councils were not large-scale employers (unlike other branches of the health service) and the jobs they could offer seemed in any case not particularly attractive to aspiring immigrants (p.121).

(c) *Hospital Management Committees*

It was unfortunate, of course, that executive councils were in no position to speak for, or on behalf of, local GPs.[10] Something of the same difficulty was to be experienced in tackling the third main branch of the Health Service. As far as the activities of hospital doctors were concerned hospital management committees, or at least their paid officials, were once again in something of a backroom position. In this case, however, the agency[11] was at least responsible for the management of the lower ranks of medical, para-medical, and ancillary staff. In this respect, hospital management committee representatives could be described as occupying a position midway between that of the all-purpose LA department, on the one hand, and the strictly servicing role of executive councils, on the other.

Much more important: hospital management committees were unique in being responsible, above all else, for the day-to-day conduct of these large and complex organizations. Consequently, this meant that respondents in this case tended to be mindful, not so much of a local hospital service, but rather of the hospital itself.[12] Hospital management, in other words, was an absorbing task and one moreover which seemed to see employees, rather than clients, as constituting its most immediate concern. Whereas staff were essential to the running of the system and, providing all went well, were destined to remain for some time within the hospital, patients were ephemeral.

In any event, when questioned about the implications of New Commonwealth immigration for their service, hospital spokesmen invariably discussed this primarily in terms of staff rather than of patients. Such a response was not merely understandable but perhaps appropriate, since the hospitals branch of the NHS was, to say the least, conspicuously reliant upon New Commonwealth immigrant manpower at all levels.

With very few exceptions (p.133), the recruitment of immigrant manpower (and not merely of New Commonwealth immigrant manpower) had been a matter not of choice but of sheer organizational necessity. Thus:-

'Recruitment has always seemed to be mostly from any oppressed areas of the world — Germany, then Czechoslovakia, Hungary, Malaysia, Jamaica, Barbados and now Mauritius and Ghana. Some genuinely want their nurses trained and want them back again (like Malaysia). Others want to ease their unemployment problems and need the currency their nurses send home. In Mauritius they have more nurses than they know what to do with ...' (p.132)

It was coping with such an intake (particularly when recruited en bloc from abroad) that, so far as most hospital management committees were concerned, seemed to spell the beginning and end of 'the impact of immigration' upon their service.

Reception and general welfare arrangements could indeed be elaborate. In one case, for instance:-

'The Rotarians show them round the town, give them tea and advise them on where to shop for food and so on. The hospital provides a central meeting place and the Rotarians show films and we arrange for special newspapers to be delivered. We have tried to operate a scheme to meet them off the plane, but this proved extremely difficult and had to be scrapped. They're not time conscious: they might easily decide to stop off in London for a few days.' (p.137)

Nor, indeed, might a lack of time-consciousness seem the only complication. Two Mauritian boys had 'misused' their flat by having girls in, and got the hospital a bad name (p.142); while, as for Moslem girls: 'It's a very difficult situation for us now that nurses homes have gone permissive. How are we to know when to tell parents or police when a Moslem girl has gone missing?' (p.134).

Not surprisingly, particular immigrant groups tended to become associated, in the eyes of other staff and administrators, with particular working characteristics. Thus Moslem nurses might be expected to make difficulties, for instance, about handling faecal discharge (p.142). Rather more worrying from the management point of view, however, was the tendency apparent for particular ethnic groups to become associated with particular types of (mostly low-grade) hospital work. Thus:-

'West Indians or Nigerians are associated with cleaning; Sikhs and Biafrans with engineering, Kenyan Asians and Sikhs with the lower clerical posts and West Indians with male porters. Nurses vary: everything from the heavy-built West Indian to the slight Asian type.' (p.142)

Such type-casting seemed worrisome as being a possible hint of racial difficulties ahead (p.142). Far more immediate, however, was the evidence of some hostility between immigrant groups themselves. Thus:-

'Ghanaians might be against Mauritians. They can operate a colour bar amongst themselves. Chinese Malaysians may be against non-Chinese Malaysians. They may even insist on separate tables in the dining room.' (p.134)

Immigrant-native tensions seemed, if anything, rather less in evidence among staff. Only in a crisis, apparently, was there likely to be a real split along host-immigrant lines and, even then, it was most likely to be manual workers who were involved (p.142). But this was not to say, of course, that the unexpected might not at any moment crop up: 'One of our clerical staff did make an accusation of witchcraft against his supervisor recently' (p.142). Rather more common, however was the feeling, on the part of hospital management, that coloured staff were frequently labouring with chips on their shoulders.

'A Jamaican nurse might come in with a complaint of being made to do all the dirty work on the ward, saying that this is because of colour. An investigation may reveal that they *all* do dirty work and she is using colour as a weapon ... Some do come over a little paranoid because of what they have been told at home.' (p.134-5)

Only two hospital management committees had actually had dealings with the Race Relations Board following allegations of discrimination. In neither case, apparently, were the allegations either justified or upheld and, all in all, this was adjudged a reasonable record for a service employing such extensive numbers of coloured immigrant personnel (p.135).

Even so, given the evident sensitivity on the race relations score, it did seem remarkable that only two hospital management committees were currently providing anything approximating to race relations briefing for their staff. In both cases these consisted of group discussions designed, in the first instance, to help certain immigrant members of staff overcome difficulties of language and, in the second instance, to help native members of staff appreciate such difficulties (p.131). Such provisions were intended merely for nurses, however, not for doctors (c.f. above p.201), and certainly not for lower ranks since, in the words of one respondent: 'there's no point in offering language training to staff whose jobs don't require a proficiency' (p.131).

Such activities, furthermore, seemed only likely to take place at all where the hospital mangagment committee deemed it necessary at least to employ a personnel officer. (Such at least was the view of our two respondents in this case — both of whom happened to be personnel officers.) That there was not more activity in this sphere, therefore, was allegedly no more than a symptom of a wider management problem:

'We are in a primitive survival situation here so far as personnel are concerned ... We need a better system of staff appraisal all round ...

But first of all we have to get the rudiments going ... In this sort of area I have a lot of battling to wage against my own management.' (p.144)

It is against this staff-orientated background that we ought perhaps to say something about patients, however briefly. As stated earlier, most respondents did not think very much in terms of patients, until specifically asked to do so in an interview situation. We depend for the most part upon interview evidence, therefore, for the points raised in this section (p.140).

Once again, the fact that hospitals were in themselves large and complex organizations very much influenced the style and extent of any specific response. Where adaptations could be deemed strictly functional to the running of the institution then there was, of course, no problem. Many hospitals, for instance, could go in for multi-lingual directional signs as well as for multi-lingual Red Cross diagnostic cards, in-patient introductory letters and visiting passes as a matter of course (p.135).

In other respects, the very comprehensiveness (allied to the specialist focus) of the hospital was supposed to be sufficient in itself to meet all relevant contingencies. Staff, for instance, could be expected as a matter of course to exercise tact and flexibility as and when required. Adjustments of visiting hours or alterations of menu to suit immigrant requirements, for instance, were invariably a matter for ward sister discretion — subject to hospital convenience. ('How flexible can you expect a hospital to be?' (p.140)) If the kitchen was not large enough, for instance, or if the hospital was not already aligned to providing special diets for its own immigrant members of staff, then special diets for immigrant patients as such, could not be guaranteed.

So far as other less specific adjustments might be concerned, then in only one case, apparently, was the need for special treatment formally spelt out to nursing staff — whose standard professionalism seemed expected otherwise to carry them through all such contingencies. In this one case, however, there was a careful attempt to spell out all the implications:-

'Diet, religious persuasion, customs, language difficulty, philosophy about the treatment they are receiving: all have to be taken into account. It is made clear to patients who to communicate to if they have any worries about their standard of care or anything pertaining to this ... Staff are asked to make sure this is clearly understood by all patients. When Nursing Officers visit wards they pay particular attention to immigrants because it has been found that some of them are reluctant to make suggestions or submit queries ... Staff show more anxiety in case their communications are misunderstood. This is healthy as it is important that the Commonwealth citizen being treated fully understands his treatment and his rights.' (p.138)

The one other possible aspect of separate treatment, namely separate (ethnic) record keeping, seemed hardly to apply in this case. Ethnic details were recorded, certainly, but only as part of a general, detailed record-keeping process. Even then: 'These facts go straight to the Regional Hospital Board's computer. They're not used for anything.' (p.141).

Attractive as this idea might have seemed to other social services respondents it did not appear, in this case, to be anything more than the automatic procedure of a large, fundamentally impersonal, machine.

Even so there were, of course, one or two problem areas, or suspected problem areas, with regard to immigrant patients. There was the odd case, for instance, of straightforward black-white hostility, operating in this case either between black staff and white patients, or simply between black and white patients. Thus on the first account:

'There is occasional evidence that white patients can feel isolated and helpless when surrounded by an all black staff. Some of them complain about the coloured staff's "take or leave it" attitude. It's difficult to say whether this arises from prejudice either way, or from a simple lack of empathy. Some coloured staff do seem to feel that, temporarily they have white people in their power.' (pp.142-43)

While on the second account:-

'Rumblings tend to come more often than not from maternity, over the 48 hour discharge policy for instance. Immigrant mothers tend to stay longer than that and whites (both mothers and staff) tend to say this is because their husbands won't take time off work to look after them.' (p.143)

Any seeming whiff of special treatment, in other words, could be open to a none-too-flattering interpretation. Against this background, one further area for staff-patient complication seems almost entertaining by comparison:-

'While the compostition of our patients is roughly parallel to that of the local community, there is a time-lag evident between the composition of patients and the composition of staff. For instance, we have mostly Polish and Russian Jews in geriatrics now, being cared for by Malaysian nurses!' (p.143)

For once, if in no other respect, there would seem to be a direct and concrete link between the second and the third case-study.

Taken as a whole, the evidence on the National Health Service would seem abundantly to illustrate the differences, not merely of structure, but of philosophy and perspective between the three sectors of the service (a factor that forthcoming reorganization was of course partly designed to overcome) (DHSS 1972 : 9-10).

(iv) *Education*

The education service seemed to offer certain obvious contrasts. Once again the 1940s had witnessed the promulgation of a lofty, idealistic target for the service as a whole: this time to provide education individually tailored to every child's age, aptitude, and ability. This time, too, the lofty target was to be cut down to rather more manageable proportions in practice; and this time, also, there was to be much variation and inconsistency within the service as to the manner in which its objectives were to be interpreted. In this case, however, there was at least to be just the one type of local organizing agency: the LEA (Local Education Authority).[13]

That this should have been a wholly local authority-administered service at ground level was only to be expected, of course, given the character of education policy development prior to the 1940s (see above Ch. 2). Nevertheless this style of administration was in itself to prove a decisive influence upon the development of education policy in general after 1944 — and upon the service's response to New Commonwealth immigration in particular. To begin with, there was the vexed question of who, central or local government, was in the last resort supposed to be in charge of *policy*, as opposed to the mere implementation of educational arrangements. The Minister of Education (subsequently the Secretary of State for Education and Science) was, according to the terms of 1944, himself to be directly responsible for 'promoting the education of the people of England and Wales', no less. Yet LEAs themselves were also responsible for making whatever educational arrangements they considered appropriate for the population in their areas. In addition, of course, parents had their own responsibility to see to it that their children were properly educated. Hence the recurrent demarcation disputes only to be expected between three such ostensibly valid partners within a policy arena far more controversial, it seemed, than had ever been anticipated in 1944. This shows itself most obviously over the question of comprehensive secondary education. But it was no less apparent and no less destructive, in its way, whenever issues relating to the education of New Commonwealth immigrants chanced to arise.

Quite apart from any such crisis points, the mere fact of entrusting the execution of a service to local authorities meant, presumably, that one believed in, or at least was prepared to accept, some measure of variety in service style and delivery. As far as the impact of and the response to New Commonwealth immigration was concerned, however, this reliance upon discretionary local government administration was to prove of double significance. First, New Commonwealth immigrants were unevenly distributed between local authority areas and, even between so-called immigrant areas, were unevenly distributed in terms of their ethnic composition. This could only add to the motivation for variation in education policy from one LA area to another. Secondly, the mere fact that LEAs were supposed to be uniquely sensitive to local needs and local wishes in education matters, propelled them into close range dealing with host-immigrant tensions and rivalries over what was universally accounted to be a vital Welfare State resource.

Why was the education service considered so vital? The answer is obvious enough: it served both to equip the individual for his eventual place in society and, apparently, to determine to a large extent what that place might be. In other words, this represented the individual's (and in a sense his parents') main, if not only, opportunity for achieving any significant change in social position.[14] Nevertheless, the objectives of a national education service, looked at from a less personal point of view, could be stated in somewhat broader terms. The ideal of individual fulfilment was ever-present, certainly; yet no less prominent were the notions of education as being, on the one hand, a vital ingredient for national prosperity — as a maximizer of skilled manpower potential among the general population — and, on the other, the principal socializing agent through which young people might not merely become attuned to society as it is, but might actively be inclined towards society as perhaps it should be.

It is against this background, of education being at once a so-called avenue to individual fulfilment and at the same time an aid to national success and/or social reconstruction, that one has to view New Commonwealth immigration as being of more drastic and immediate significance to this service than it was perhaps to any other statutory branch of the Welfare State. On the one hand there were the immediate, individual, and often very obvious needs of many immigrant children for specialist linguistic and/or cultural instruction, [15] if they were to stand any real chance of benefiting in the long term from educational provisions in general. On the other hand, however, there was also the generalized, as opposed to the individualized, responsibility: to cater for the collective social interest. In this case this meant, not merely trying to balance majority-host against minority-immigrant interests and opinion, but also trying, by implication, to reflect in the way that schooling was organized some microcosm of the sort of society that one wished to see eventually develop.[16] Education, in other words, could hardly fail to be intimately involved in any integration programme.

Having said so much we must now turn to the evidence available on actual LEA reactions and response to New Commonwealth immigration.[17] No LEA, faced with any sizeable immigrant presence in its area, could fail to be aware of the implications of such a presence — so far as its own immediate policies and room for manoeuvre was concerned. Even so, the mere fact of the problems being obvious did not of itself mean that practicable solutions could spring equally readily to mind.

The most obvious and urgent problem (from the immigrants', the general population, and the service's point of view) seemed to centre upon the needs of certain young immigrants for immediate language instruction. Clearly one could not begin to educate in any general sense without some common teaching medium. Even so, the matter was not necessarily quite so obvious as it might initially have appeared. Not all the children of immigrants (even Asian immigrants) were likely to be equally linguistically handicapped upon first entry to school. In some cases, indeed, there seemed more danger that real, but less obvious, linguistic problems might very easily be overlooked in a drive to concentrate primarily upon the most evident cases of difficulty.[18]

At all events, there could be no easy and automatic correlation to be assumed between the mere possession of immigrant nationality or immigrant parentage, and the need for particular English language instruction. The Department of Education and Science, in its efforts to provide a clarifying lead to LEAs in this situation, came up in 1966 with what was intended to be a strictly functional definition of the immigrant schoolchild for LEA purposes. An immigrant pupil was operationally to be defined as being either a child born in this country to parents of less than ten years' residence here, or else a child born abroad who had arrived in this country withing the past ten years (Townsend 1971 : 13). The ten year rule was clearly intended as some sort of rough guideline as to where linguistic (and cultural) handicaps might be most likely to occur. Nevertheless the definition was to prove impractical on two counts. It could not, on the one hand, offer any precise indication as to the location and extent of language difficulties to be tackled; nor could it, on the other hand, even furnish LEA's with a workable basis for any long-term statistical calculation: immigrants of one year, after all, were liable to become non-immigrants by definition in the next. So the DES definition was, not surprisingly, dropped, in 1974.

Definition or no definition, LEAs had, in the first instance, to grapple with the problems simply of locating and identifying newly-arrived immigrant households, much as LA health departments had to do. Once again there seemed not very much to go on. One third of all LEAs with 'substantial numbers of immigrant pupils' [19] referred in their questionnaires to the fact that immigration authorities at ports of entry might inform local health authorities about new arrivals destined for their areas — which information may or may not, it seemed, be passed on to the LEA (c.f. above p.198). Even so — unlike LA health departments — LEAs seemed bound to encounter their immigrant clientele eventually, if only at the last minute: ' ... the first information about new arrivals might come only when the child was presented at school' (Townsend 1971 : 30).

Having located their immigrant clientele, the next logical step (as in the health department case) seemed to be to ascertain what need if any there seemed to be for special treatment. Yet this in itself was of course far more easily said than done. There were two principal complications in this case. To begin with it could be far less straightforward, apparently, to set about diagnosing an individual's educational, as opposed to his health requirements. There were no thoroughly proven and acceptable culture-free tests to hand (Townsend 1971 : 38, 55). In the second place LEAs were inclined, not unnaturally, to gear any diagnostic procedures to the range of special provisions which they themselves felt able to provide.[20] So, if they felt able to respond only in terms of rudimentary compensatory instruction, then it was rudimentary shortcomings that they tended to seek out.

For the most part, therefore, LEA diagnostic arrangements seemed nothing if not pragmatic. Only two authorities, for instance, claimed to pass every known immigrant child through a reception centre for purposes of assessment, orientation, and documentation. Other authorities were inclined to be more selective: they might put every non-English speaking child through a reception centre, for instance, or every 'late-arrival' secondary age child; or even infant immigrants only (Townsend 1971 : 31). Whatever the particular recipe adopted, reception centres (where present at all) seemed very much to be regarded as an expensive resource for the identification and measurement of whatever were locally accounted to be the most urgent or intransigent problems.

What was true of diagnostic arrangements tended, naturally enough to be true of actual language teaching arrangements also. Once again this seemed, for the most part, to be a case of concentrating upon the obvious: the provision of a basic fluency in English.[21] Since candidates for such treatment, moreover, tended to be selected not on the basis of any standard 'objective' tests (Townsend 1971 : 46) but rather on the basis of teacher assessment and opinion,[22] it was not surprising to find that it was nearly always Indian and Pakistani children who were so selected; rarely West Indians.[23]

For this reason if no other, it was only to be expected that LEAs (confronted with immigrant populations of varying age and ethnic composition) would vary greatly in the extent to which and the manner in which they made any special language teaching arrangements. Hence the contrasts to be observed, for instance, between LEAs who made no special language provisions at all for infant or junior pupils, between LEAs providing full time language centres, between LEAs who merely provided one additional teacher for schools containing numbers of non-English-speaking pupils, or LEAs who went in for 'a highly organised peripatetic service of over 80 teachers' (Townsend 1971 : 37). Even within such categories of provision, there was ample variation. Full-time language centres, for instance, could range from what was effectively little more than a reception centre, keeping pupils for no more than a month (or until half-term or end of term), to 'true' language centres catering for anything from a six months' to a three-year stay, according to requirements. Again these same language centres could vary between a full-time concentration upon language instruction, and attempts to provide a wider educational experience within the centre — so as to allow for time to be taken over language training without too much cost in terms of proficiency in other school subjects (Townsend 1971 : 40-41).

This brings us to a further important issue. Quite apart from any policy decisions LEAs had to make concerning how much of their limited resources to devote to special language teaching arrangements for a given immigrant population, they were faced in addition with a more fundamental dilemma. Language instruction was not supposed to be an end in itself so much as a means towards general educational opportunity. Time spent on special language instruction, however, had to be time taken away from other school acitvities. Once again, there was no right, obvious balance to be struck between the need for specialist instruction and the need for general education in each individual case.

But this in turn brings us on to a further area of difficulty. Given the dual instructional and socializing responsibilities of the education service, it was hardly possible in practice to separate the strictly educational arguments for and against the special teaching of immigrant children from the broader social implications surrounding the issue. Thus, to those who argued that on strictly teaching grounds it was best at any rate for younger immigrant children to be pitched in at the deep end and left to pick up English as they went along (Townsend 1971 : 38), must be added those who believed that, on social grounds at least, this must be the best way to proceed.

Yet this in itself left a further question to be resolved ... If schools were supposed to be agents for socialization, then to what extent ought they to take into account immigrant, as opposed to host, cultural requirements and experience? Whose culture, or what sort of culture, was to be proclaimed? Given an integration target which included the maintenance of 'cultural diversity' among its objectives (see above p.148), then multi-racial schools might reasonably be expected to respond in this direction, in some way. Yet this, it seems was more easily said than done. True, some ten LEAs reported making special arrangements for the religious instruction of certain immigrant children (usually Sikhs or Moslems), while seven claimed to make special arrangements over school worship.[24] Ingenious compromises might indeed be arranged — as in one case where withdrawal from school premises for religious instruction was allowed on condition that the same pupils also attended morning assembly (Townsend 1971 : 62). All in all, however, this seemed a far cry from the Jewish Schools policy of the former London School Board (see above pp.106-107).

There were, of course a few gestures in other directions, mostly at head-teacher discretion. Special arrangements might be made, for instance, to offer alternative school meals to children whose religious faith precluded them from eating certain foods (Townsend 1971 : 61); and Asian girls might be permitted to wear their PE knickers over their shalwars (Townsend 1971 : 63). Rather more positive, though not specifically geared to immigrant requirements as such, were the efforts of no less than eighteen LEAs to run summer holiday projects as a means of general 'cultural enrichment' (Brittan 1971).

All in all this was hardly massive cultural adjustment. Yet massive cultural adjustment was hardly seriously to be expected, given such an unclear, intangible target (compared to that of basic language instruction for instance)[25] and given the apparent inability of schools, as institutions, to alter their procedures to any very marked extent. ('The Community Relations Officer thinks we should be teaching Gujarati but we couldn't start that caper' (Townsend 1971 : 60)). Even so there was further, greater reason for proceeding cautiously. New Commonwealth immigrants were not merely a minority population, but a minority population whose very presence and presumed requirements were liable to be interpreted by host opinion as actively prejudicial to their own children's educational interests. Inevitably, this placed LEAs in a somewhat awkward position: not only might they be unsure themselves as to how best (and how practicably) to respond, educationally and socially, to immigrant requirements; they had also to contend with majority host opinion for whose educational interests they were also responsible and whose parental views they could scarcely afford to ignore.

The answer, so far as white parents living in immigrant areas were concerned, seemed deceptively simple. Immigrant pupils (particularly non-English speaking Asian pupils) should be distributed more evenly between each authority's schools rather than allowed simply to accumulate in those schools serving immigrant districts. This way, it was argued, the teaching load would at least be spread between schools — and white children living in twilight inner-city areas would not face the additional handicap of having to attend schools overwhelmed with the problems of catering for large numbers of immigrant children. The arguments were not so very different from those employed in the East End over Jewish children at the turn of the century; but this time, interestingly enough, they were listened to (c.f. above pp.107-8).

Thus in 1963 Sir Edward Boyle (the then Minister of Education) responded to white parental protests in Southall by agreeing that the load should indeed be 'spread thinner and wider' (Patterson 1969 : 254). In 1965, furthermore, the 'benign quota' idea (that there should be no more than 33 per cent of immigrants in any one school) became enshrined in official DES policy, via the famous Circular 7/65 (Patterson 1969 : 254-57). LEAs however, did not necessarily respond to this lead. Some had already taken comparable action of course; others refused to do so; others again sought ways to bring about the same result without actually declaring a dispersal policy. Thus while some eleven LEAs informed the NFER in 1970 that they were actually operating a dispersal policy (Townsend 1971 : 33), others were not; and others again were attempting to get round the problem by adjusting catchment areas, for instance, so as to include a proportion of inner and outer-city districts,[26] or simply by having their head teachers 'persuade' Asian families to send their children to other schools.

The issues involved were clearly complex. LEAs might be convinced that, in the case of non-English-speaking children at least, dispersal was probably 'ethically wrong but educationally essential' (Townsend 1971 : 34). Nevertheless, quite apart from the organizational difficulties of arranging (and paying for) special transport, the idea of bussing groups of children elsewhere seemed socially undesirable on at least three counts: it tended to isolate such children from both neighbourhood and even school contacts (Townsend 1971 : 33-4); it visited suburban schools with problems which perhaps they, and their catchment areas, were not prepared to accept; and it put paid, of course, to the idea of neighbourhood schools precisely in those areas where (immigrant) parental contacts seemed so much in need of encouragement. Even on educational grounds, moreover, it could be argued that by spreading the load (and thereby making it easier, perhaps, to recruit teaching staff for inner-city schools) one was merely encouraging teachers to avoid coming to terms with the problems of trying to cater appropriately for the needs of immigrant children.

All in all there would seem to be three points of interest here. To begin with, the dispersal debate offers a fine example of the sort of demarcation dispute between central and local government referred to earlier. Central government declared a policy.[27] LEAs seemed to feel that they and they alone could best decide what arrangements to make in the light of local needs and their own departmental circumstances. In the second place, moreover, these events seemed to show how impossible it was for any LEA to pursue a 'purely educational' line (even had it been sure what educational line to adopt). Education was indeed as much a social as a strictly instructional resource. In the third place, despite its broad implications, the service was strictly limited in what it could effect. This was not simply a question of local budgetary and staffing limitations. However vast its social responsibilities might be adjudged, the service's powers were more or less strictly educational. Thus, asked on the one hand to promote a system of neighbourhood schools and on the other to promote a more evenly mixed school population, LEAs had effectively to chose between the one and the other in inner-city areas. They had no powers directly to influence the distribution of jobs or housing, for instance, such as might have rendered the two themes compatible.

Having discussed some of the problems and some characteristics of the response, there remains one further area for consideration: that of staffing policy. Given a service so extensively affected by the arrival of New Commonwealth immigrants then here, perhaps, one might have expected the fullest and most dramatic response in terms of additional staff training and specialist staff appointments. So far as staff training was concerned, however, there were two complications: one relating to the manner in which teacher training was organized and one relating to the status of teachers as professional workers.

Thus, to take the first point, initial teacher-training was organized, in effect, on a national basis. LEAs were of course responsible for the management of colleges of education; but they were not specifically responsible for training their own teachers. Teachers, in other words, moved around from one LEA area to another. However desirable in principle, the implications of this practice were in this case considerable. Colleges of education were catering, in effect, to meet a national teacher demand. Given the uneven distribution of New Commonwealth immigrants, the possibly temporary nature of their special needs[28] and the likelihood that no more than 15 per cent of newly qualified teachers would encounter such immigrants in their first posts, how realistic was it to expect most colleges of education to arrange special courses geared to this particular need (Townsend 1971 : 96)?

The onus, therefore, was upon those LEAs in immigrant areas to provide some form of briefing or in-service training for the teachers they actually employed. On the whole this seems to have been a challenge to which they responded. According to the NFER Report, no less than forty-one of the seventy-one LEAs making full returns were currently providing in-service training for their teachers on the subject of immigrant education (Townsend 1971 : 96-7). Few such courses, however, could be described as substantial. Of the 185 courses recorded by the NFER, 114 were of less than three days full time or fifteen hours part time duration (Townsend 1971 : 97). Yet, set against this, 108 teachers from twenty-three LEAs had attended one-term full-time courses and thirty-four teachers from fourteen LEAs had attended one-year full-time courses in the period 1967-70 (Townsend 1971 : 98).

Even so, to provide a course or even offer secondment to a full-time course elsewhere, was not the same thing as to see to it that such courses were actually attended by teaching staff. Several LEAs pointed out to the NFER that it could be very difficult to interest secondary school teachers in such courses (apart from teachers already engaged in English language or remedial work (Townsend 1971 : 94)). So far as subject specialists were concerned, in other words, there seemed no widespread recognition that the instruction of New Commonwealth immigrant children might call for any special skills or special awareness on the teacher's part.[29]

On the question of New Commonwealth staff recruitment, LEAs stood rather apart from other social services in that, in this case, the appointment of immigrant staff was usually part of a deliberate policy to secure specialist staff to cope with newly arrived or non-English-speaking immigrant clients. Twenty LEAs reported employing a total of 137 teachers from Commonwealth countries, mostly with this specialist role in mind. Even so, not all LEAs were happy with such a policy. Several spokesmen, worried at this seeming trend towards a 'separate service', justified their use of Asian teachers for Asian pupils on the grounds that Asian teachers were in fact reluctant to move into more general teaching. Other LEAs were actually unwilling to employ Asian teachers either for language instruction (where their accents might not be helpful) or for general teaching (since there was always the risk that they might slip into Asian languages when dealing with Asian pupils) (Townsend 1971 : 94)).

The picture was rather different in the case of West Indian teacher employment. Very few were employed at all. Wherever they were employed, moreover, there seemed no question in this case of employing them specifically to deal with West Indian children (Townsend 1971 : 94). Quite apart from the fact that the West Indian community seemed unable to generate large numbers of teachers, this seemed interesting if only because it suggested, once again, that West Indian children were simply not different enough to attract specialist attention from authorities which seemed geared on the whole to responding only to the obvious.

This last point could of course be phrased in another way. Given a service already equipped with blanket educational responsibilities, yet somewhat limited actual powers and resources, it was only to be expected, perhaps, that such a service should have seized upon the qualitatively different needs arising out of New Commonwealth immigration as a suitable target for specific policy measures. The line between differences of kind and mere differences of degree was not, of course, an easy line to draw. Nevertheless Asian linguistic and cultural requirements would seem to fall into the first category (so far as both immigrants and hosts were concerned) whereas West Indian linguistic and cultural requirements apparently did not. For better or for worse (and there were naturally both advantages and disadvantages to this position)[30] West Indian children would seem to have been regarded essentially as possessing no requirements different in kind from those of white children similarly housed and similarly disadvantaged. Rudimentary language instruction for Asian children was intended, presumably, to bring them also into a comparable position. If this was not, in the end, equality of opportunity then this fact in itself could hardly rank as a peculiarly immigrant predicament.

8

General policy responses (continued)

It is at this stage that we must turn from the so-called pillars of the Welfare State to what might be termed the lesser orders of statutory social policy (see above p.186). This will scarcely mean an abrupt change of direction, however: more a gradual tailing off in the scale of the evidence to be considered, since the more limited or specialized the service the more limited, by definition, must be its capacity either to be affected by or to respond to New Commonwealth immigration. Yet even this remark requires qualification. Employment services, whether geared to youth or adult requirements, were hardly less than comprehensive in their potential responsibilities: they were merely strictly limited in the extent to which they could either command or deliver the goods.

(i) *Employment*

To consider employment services en bloc, means considering together what should in many respects be defined as two fundamentally different types of social service provision. The Youth Employment Service was, strictly speaking, a branch of LEA responsibility. Adult employment services, on the other hand, were the direct responsibility of the Department of Employment. The contrasts, seemingly, could scarcely be more clear-cut. On the one hand we have a local authority administered service staffed by career professionals trained in vocational guidance. On the other hand we have a civil service facility, staffed by executive and clerical officers whose job it was primarily to assist adults to find a job.

Employment prospects in general, however, were bound to be a crucial factor where mass economic immigration was concerned; and the impact of New Commonwealth immigration would seem if anything to have drawn these two types of employment service stylistically closer together — in that both found themselves having to grapple with more or less the same range of immigrant-associated problems. On the whole, this seemed to call for an intensification — rather than for a fundamental change — of normal service activity; but the effects, understandably enough, were if anything more apparent in the adult than in the youth employment field.

To begin with, New Commonwealth immigrants seemed a particularly vulnerable, dependant group so far as these services were concerned. This might, at least in the youth employment case, mean that they were more likely to turn to the service in the first place: 'Initially at least immigrants tend to use the service more heavily than do the natives — perhaps because they read the papers less and have fewer connections' (p.47). Once there in any case, they could seem in need of specially careful treatment on four associated counts: they could be more confused and ignorant than the average native client; their parents could be more ignorant and/or more dictatorial than the average native parent; they could be both more in need of and more anxious to undergo pre-training programmes; and they could be highly sensitive, of course, to any suspicion of racial prejudice.

Thus on the first count, apparently, it seemed in essence to be a case of 'taking a lot longer to explain everything':

'The more confused a kid is, the more careful you have to be in trying to bring him to decisions. For instance, you give him all the facts on his chosen job, then try to work him around to considering alternatives or back-up lines — in order to broaden his view of the possibilities. You can't do all that in one interview.' (p.46)

This was a youth employment officer speaking. Employment exchange spokesmen were not usually inclined to go to this length, yet they seemed committed in principle to the notion of taking more time and trouble as and where necessary — so long as this did not go so far as to amount, in practice, to some form of positive discrimination at native expense (SSRC : 74). 'Lots of immigrants', after all, 'take less time to deal with than the average doss-house white' (p.74).

Parental ignorance, parental influence, and parental inaccessibility, however, could furnish both services with problems. Thus on the first count:

'If you bear in mind the different education and recruitment patterns for adolescents in this country compared to elsewhere, then its hardly surprising to find immigrant parents encouraging their children to stay on at school regardless of any apprenticeship openings or vocational courses: they don't know anything about them; "O" and "A" levels seem the best target.'[1]

Or again:-

'Many parents have a notion that *all* young people should get apprenticeships — not just one third of the age group. So they suspect discrimination if their son does not get one.' (p.78)

Or yet again:-

'Immigrant parents in general are puzzled by our reliance on IQ rather than money as the criteria for job placement.' (p.53)

Such impressions, coming from both adult and youth employment spokesmen, would seem to suggest no little lack of contact between services and parents: a fact which both services seemed anxious to draw attention to. Immigrant parents were not, it seemed, very easy to contact:

'We can't get much more thorough than writing to the parents of each child interviewed — as we do. If they don't respond then the next step would be to make a home visit. But we can't visit all the 800 or so that we should every year.' (p.48)

Three careers officer had, nevertheless, attempted to go one better — by convening a general meeting of immigrant clients and their parents. Yet this, it seemed, could be no more than a sounding board for respective grievances. Neither side, apparently, had come to listen to the other (p.48).

Given such an apparent lack of contact between either service and the parents concerned, the undoubted influence of Asian family networks (p.55) and of Asian fathers in particular upon their children's choice of career seemed doubly regretable. West Indian families, apparently, might speak against the service to their children in advance; (p.56) but, 'The Indian parent is more god-like than anyone else's' (p.48).The fact that parental influence could seem as important in the so-called adult, as in the youth employment sphere, leads us on to a further point. So far as New Commonwealth immigrants were concerned, it seemed far less practicable for these agencies to assume any inherent distinction between the sort of services young people might require and the sort of services adults might normally require in the employment field. This was not simply a case of Asian extended family networks exerting a more sustained and protracted influence over their menfolk's choice of employment. Adult immigrants, particularly those seeking employment for the first time in this country (and therefore usually young adults), seemed to require something much more akin to a youth employment than to the standard adult employment approach. They were not merely between jobs: they were in most cases in need of advice and preparation as to a choice of career.[2]

To begin with there were the obvious problems to be faced, arising out of a lack of basic education and/or a lack of fluency (or sufficient fluency) in English. Both services reported difficulties in this area — youth employment spokesmen lamenting the lack of suitable objective tests by which to ascertain such candidates' potential, (SSRC : 54) and employment exchange managers pointing out how difficult it could be either to persuade an adult immigrant he really needed additional language instruction or to bring him round to the idea of 'going back to school' at his age (p.71). Two exchanges had resolved this latter problem by arranging courses on their premises rather than at a local technical college: 'They're quite prepared to turn up here at 5 pm: it's not school and it's not too late for a family evening' (p.71). Others looked rather to employers to meet this difficulty so far as their own workforce was concerned. Yet even where employers arranged classes for their non-English speaking staff (as many large employers were prepared to do) there could be difficulties:

'Employers face a lot of trouble over this one: partly from the apathy of the immigrants and partly over the question of in *whose* time are such courses to be run? If they're in work time there are likely to be complaints from the other workers; if they're not run in work time, then there's likely to be a very low take-up.' (p.71)

Such specific difficulties apart, however, there seemed no problem, either in the adult or the youth employment case, of persuading immigrant clients to make the most of any regular pre-training courses available at local technical colleges and designed to give otherwise suitable candidates a sufficient grounding in the three Rs as to allow them to proceed onto GTC and other training opportunities. Such courses were not designed specifically to meet immigrant requirements — which partly accounted, perhaps, for their appeal. Nevertheless it was immigrants who were the most conspicuous takers, if only because: 'many English youngsters are reluctant to admit things like illiteracy' (p.46).

If matters seemed relatively straightforward in this sphere, however, there was one further area for special treatment which most respondents seemed to find far more difficult to cope with. Coloured immigrants were universally reckoned to be specially sensitive or 'touchy' whenever there was any possibility of there being a racially discriminatory element to either their treatment by the services or their treatment by employers. So far as the services themselves were concerned, this meant simply that dissatisfied clients might tend to suspect racial discrimination and would not therefore consult their officers again (p.56). At the broader level, however, there was the problem of trying to distinguish between immigrants who simply alleged discrimination every time they were disappointed: 'I have seen coloured men who complain that they can never get a job because of discrimination — but, on checking, it usually turns out that their work record is very poor' (p.78). and those who seemingly had genuine cause for complaint. Even here there could be awkward matters of principle to be resolved:

> 'Many coloured youngsters are getting on alright, in line with their qualifications. How much notice should we take if one of them doesn't? How far should we isolate his case as one of discrimination? What about the odd whites who don't get on?' (pp.78-9)

In an unfair world, in other words, how far should unfairness to coloured people be singled out as a case for special treatment? Quite how much was colour discrimination and how much was mere incidental misfortune or ineptitude was, of course, rarely an easy matter to resolve in the particular case. Even so, the scales did not seem to be evenly stacked between coloureds and whites in general: 'It takes more submissions, on average, to place an immigrant — so there must be discrimination somewhere' (p.56).

Yet this in itself brings us on to the other main side of youth employment and employment exchange business. Both sets of agencies were, in a sense, servicing two sets of clients: those in search of a career or a job, on the one hand, and those in search of employees, on the other. Neither side was compelled to make use of the statutory employment services. The independence of both sets of clients seemed to militate, in the last resort, against these agencies' capacity adequately to service either group: they could not guarantee to supply to employers the full range of workforce applicants they might require; and they could not guarantee to those in search of work or a career that the requisite openings (however carefully advised upon in principle) would actually be forthcoming. This latter limitation was, to say the least, thrown into some relief by the so-called race relations question.

Predictably enough, most respondents in both services felt a low profile, albeit a particularly careful, approach was most appropriate so far as watching over the employment, and employment opportunities, of coloured immigrants was concerned. Routine visiting of local employers was used, typically, as a means of keeping an eye on the race relations situation; while follow-up of immigrants once placed in employment was liable to be that much more painstaking than in the average white case. Any more obvious moves could only, it seemed, prove counter-productive. Thus, in the words of one (youth employment) spokesman:-

'There's no point in organising big meetings of employers — only the big companies could afford to send someone anyway, and they probably know all about it. It's much more effective to pick off individual employers and personnel chiefs one by one.' (pp.56-7)

The point was one frequently to be echoed by employment exchange managers who again stressed the preferability of dealing with any awkward customers only in the course of normal business. Sometimes, of course, this in itself could mean a trying experience:

'We had an outburst recently from one employer who declared that he didn't like unreliable workers and spongers on the Welfare State. He wasn't talking explicitly about immigrants, but he had had a couple of bad experiences with them recently ... We got the brunt of this. We were due to visit him in any case and we had actually suggested this last man for the job. This sort of experience can linger for a long time and cause an employer to draw generalisations from it.' (p.81)

Equally, however, one 'good' experience could have an opposite effect upon employers and give rise to equally embarassing complications from the services' point of view:

'One employer was so impressed with a coloured candidate that, when he was on a recruitment drive later on, he specifically asked for another half-dozen like the one coloured man we had sent him.' (p.82)

Nevertheless, there seemed little that either service could do, in the last resort, when faced with an inveterate awkard customer. Thus, to quote one youth employment spokesman:

'There's one firm in this area which is notorious on the question of race relations. Members of staff went and chatted up the management, brought it all out into the open and showed how extreme was the stance adopted not just by middle management, but right the way up. Our regional rep. came down to talk to the manager but the manager then implied that if youth employment made difficulties and insisted on sending them coloured applicants, they would cease using its services. So we then said we would look through the press advertisements and send candidates that way. All this took place some two to three years ago. There hasn't been any firm outcome on this one. We couldn't prove racial discrimination, but we have noticed that the firm has not used our services since, nor have we had an opportunity to act on press advertisements.' (p.57)

This was, of course, an isolated case. Yet employment exchange managers could also quote the isolated case:

'I know of one case where an employer has offered protracted resistance to the idea of employing immigrants. Even here it was essentially shopfloor resistance which was at the root of the problem. Now they are gradually becoming less resistant to the idea of employing immigrants — but it's useful that this firm is situated four to five miles out of town. In other words, it's not exactly a place where immigrants are queuing up at the door to get in.' (p.81)

This last report would seem to point to a broader difficulty: trades union conventions and shop floor traditions were not lightly to be set aside in response to an immigrant presence, and certainly not at the behest of youth or adult employment services. Thus, to quote one youth employment spokesman:

> 'The whole question of apprenticeships linked to fixed criteria and age of entry ought to be scrapped. A general training scheme irrespective of age of entry could obviously benefit the immigrants — but not only them.' (p.54)

All very well perhaps, yet in the words of one employment exchange manager:

> 'Where trades unions demand experience as a qualification for membership yet ensure that without membership no candidate can obtain a skilled post ... We can but try.' (p.81)

Such comments say as much about the inherent limitations of the services concerned as about the plight of coloured immigrants in particular. After all, as one exchange manager put it, 'We're here to help people get jobs. We can't alter the shape of British industry' (p.77). Even so, there were two interesting patterns to be observed within this framework; the one apparently a comment on immigrant resourcefulness and application, and the other a product apparently of careers officers' determination to be seen to be doing something.

Thus, on the first account, the (widely reported) success in immigrant candidates, whenever they were offered apprenticeship opportunities, could of course produce its own problems:

> 'One local firm was forced to take on a high percentage of Asian craft apprentices — apparently because the job had become less attractive to whites ... Now it is embarassed by the very quality of these apprentices ... Some of them will *have* to go into supervisory posts on completion ... They might very well face a backlash from the shopfloor on the grounds of favouritism to coloureds.' (pp.57-8)

Or again:

> 'Two of our six immigrant engineering apprentices are up for awards as top apprentices of the year. This has had its repercussions. It's needed a lot of forceful language towards Trades Union shop-floor convenors to get them to accept a reasonable percentage of immigrants in different parts of the firm.' (pp.72-3)

Set against this, the stated determination of at least two sets of careers officers to engineer 'breakthroughs' (as they put it) in immigrant employment, could provoke no less awkward repercussions. The idea, in principle, seemed straightforward enough:

'When we are trying for a break-through in any significant field we must adopt specific policies, then abandon them once we feel we have achieved our objectives and embark on something else.'[3]

So far so good, perhaps. Yet there could of course be complications. For instance:

'You do tend to put forward a very good candidate if it's a question of a first time break through with an awkward employer. But this is hardly fair on the best coloured candidates — they tend to get the worst employers. You can hardly blame them if they get fed up and push off after a few months, can you?' (p.50)

Even more damning, perhaps, was the view of another youth employment spokesman:

'A lot of these so-called "positive discrimination" policies are really only a response to the labour market situation. If these stores were to get off the ground at all they were *bound* to rely upon immigrant labour. So they collect the kudos for it as well *and* pick up the cream of the immigrants on offer.' (p.50)

Given such a context, the one thing neither youth employment nor adult employment agencies could profitably do was, it seemed, to wave the *Race Relations Act* in the faces of employers. They might (and normally did) inform employers, as a matter of course, of the contents of the legislation and they might, in addition, circulate them with further literature on the same theme (p.68). The idea of formally invoking legal procedures, however, struck most respondents as being totally counter-productive. Even the one (youth employment) spokesman who declared himself formally bound to support the legislation seemed to have some doubts on this latter score: ' ... I believe there is a law and it's my duty to report it, even though I may be able to see that it does more harm than good' (p.56). Employment exchange managers, indeed, could regard the mere existence of such legislation as an active impediment to their service:

'The need for us to act according to the provisions of the Race Relations Act does not help us to foster good relationships with such ["bad"] employers. It is also probable that some employers do not notify vacancies to us because they know of our obligations under the Act.' (p.80)

All in all, this scarcely seemed a straightforward situation for these services to cope with — faced as they were with their own intrinsically limited capacities, in addition to the problems of determining how best to respond to an immigrant clientele. In the words of one respondent: 'The more we go on, the less and less I feel I know about the situation' (p.58). So far these two types of statutory employment service have seemed broadly comparable, for all their differences of structure and tradition, in their stated response to New Common-wealth immigration. The question of record-keeping, as a seemingly technical issue, might have been expected to show up more extensive differences of practice. Even here, however, there seemed a surprising similarity of outlook.

The machinery actually adopted was of course quite different in each case. Employment exchanges were required to furnish the Department of Employment with quarterly unemployment returns detailing the numbers of New Commonwealth immigrants so listed; but they were neither required nor empowered to compile separate records in any other sense. Nor, apparently, were they anxious to have to do so. To compile such additional records would be even more discriminatory than were the present quarterly unemployment returns (about which many staff were unhappy) (p.75). Nor could such a practice be necessary, since 'we rely on memory'; since individual case notes usually contained such details where they were relevant; and since, should there be any obvious case of discrimination, a local enquiry would invariably be carried out (pp.75-6). Nor, of course, was there any enthusiasm for adding to the paperwork: 'Our job is to find people work not assemble statistics' (p.76). Not that such a delving operation could seem helpful in any case: 'You don't plant an apple tree and then keep digging it up to look at the roots' (p.76). Nor did there seem much point to keeping elaborate records unless it was felt that the service was in some way going to be able to respond to whatever they revealed: 'If you *were* to keep elaborate records, you would then have to try to interpret them and decide what — if anything — you could to about your finding.' (p.76).

Leaving the quarterly unemployment returns apart, every one of these points was repeated by youth employment spokesmen. They too

seemed to feel that the compilation of such records must be
fundamentally discriminatory and therefore disparaging; they too
seemed to feel it must be fundamentally unnecessary (given the
detailed personal record-keeping traditions of the service in any case)
(p.52); they too resented the idea of additional paperwork on
principle (p.52); and they too felt there could be no point to keeping
records more elaborate than service resources could hope to cope with
or respond to (p.52).

There were merely two particular features in the youth employment
case: careers offices, to begin with, were already involved in recording
client country of origin (or ethnic background) on their standard
record cards; yet all careers offices, in the second place, were staffed by
people who saw themselves as professional workers and who could be
relied upon, therefore, to react with particular vehemence and
principle to this same separate record-keeping system: 'Inevitably it
provokes their liberal unease, since it means asking a lot of
impertinent questions which are not asked of whites' (p.52). Nor need
this be simply a concern about good manners: 'The careers officer's
job is to establish rapport at the first interview and to get people work.
What if these special questions interfere with this?' (p.52)

The fact that most respondents here were fully conversant with the
arguments put forward by the Parliamentary Select Committee in
favour of separate record keeping (1969 : Ch. IX), moreover, did not
mean that most were at all convinced that the end might justify the
means in this case. Indeed: 'I mind because I can no longer say I have
no statistics. It was very helpful not to have them in the early days.
They can be put to twisted use' (p.53). Or, as another spokesman put
it, even more pointedly:

> 'Statistics like this can be used as a means of cooking the books. If
> you count all the coloured together it can mask the fact that the
> West Indian unemployment rate is twice anyone else's whereas the
> Indian rate is very low: so the two together equate with the national
> average.' (p.53)

On the question of staff training and staff appointments, however,
the differences between the two services were inevitably to appear at
their most marked. Employment exchanges, as a civil-service-staffed
system, could obviously go in for special staff training on the subject of
New Commonwealth immigration only to a strictly limited extent.
Even so they had at least a fairly elaborate internal briefing system to

draw upon, under the auspices of their regional race relations employment advisers (p.63). Set against this picture, the situation with regard to careers officers was at once more ambitious and, in a sense, less complete. Careers officers might pursue a variety of courses ranging from day-long or half-day sessions with the local community relations council to week-long courses arranged by the Central Youth Employment Executive (p.39). In the last resort, however, it was very much up to the individual officer as to which (if any) courses he pursued — 'there are so many blasted courses when you think of it' (p.39). The mere fact that these were professional officers professionally trained, (or at least awaiting professional training) could in itself make any additional training seem something of an optional extra — and certainly no substitute for experience (p.39). Special courses, indeed, could even seem a barrier to efficiency:

'At the time in the mid 1950s we regretted the lack of facilities for staff training and the near absence of any printed information on immigrant backgrounds. With hindsight, however, we have come to see that we were privileged to have had the opportunity to meet young immigrants face to face and to get to know them as individuals, before we became involved in all the jargon, the stereotypes and the generalised opinions, which have characterised some courses and conferences on the subject of race relations.' (pp.39-40)

With regard to New Commonwealth staff appointments, the differences between the two services were even more marked. Employment exchanges could see it as their responsibility to set an example in this sphere by recruiting without reference to race or creed. As a result, it seemed, they employed large numbers of immigrant staff up and down the country although not, save in the most incidental (linguistic) sense, to deal specifically with immigrant clientele (pp.65-7). Careers offices, in contrast, were in a much more delicate position. They too felt the need to be setting a good example but, as agencies employing relatively small numbers of professional — or potentially professional — staff, they hardly seemed to be in so strong a market position.

To all intents and purposes, there seemed no ready supply of immigrant manpower to draw upon: 'they are just not available' (p.41). The reasons for this could seem obvious enough:

'You have to bear in mind the differences of background — not just in cultural matters but also in the sorts of training offered and the sorts of courses and qualifications available in the home country. There are no equivalent qualifications for people to acquire in the West Indies, India or Pakistan.' (p.41)

For the odd candidate who might be suitably qualified, moreover: 'The pay and prestige of this job simply aren't good enough. They will be looking for something much better' (p.41). The consequences could of course be embarassing:

'I find myself constantly having to account, if not exactly to apologise, for the fact that my office happens to have nobody from a New Commonwealth country on its careers office staff. The Select Committee [1969 : paras. 235-6] which some four years ago recommended the employment of coloured careers officers, and all my interrogators since that time, seem to have assumed that well-educated coloured men and women were eager to train for, and to work in, the Youth Employment Service. This has not been my experience.' (p.42)

Hence the efforts reported by so many youth employment spokesmen, of recruitment drives specifically geared to attracting New Commonwealth recruits (p.41) or of (in one case) an appointment committee falling over backwards to give full consideration to a candidate with bad references but who was at least coloured (p.43). None of these stratagems, however, seemed to have produced the desired result.

Even so, there were of course some New Commonwealth immigrants in the careers service employ — although once again, as in the adult employment case, there was no marked evidence of any tendency to expect such officers to deal particularly with immigrant clientele. Indeed the reverse was, if anything, the case:

'We do occasionally use our West Indian careers officer to cope with any obstreperous West Indian youth who might have a chip on his shoulder. But it doesn't seem very satisfactory. The officer is all too likely to seem some sort of an Uncle Tom to the discontented client.' (p.43)

All in all, this seemed to be a case of two very different but associated services making no inconsiderable efforts to come to terms with the implications of New Commonwealth immigration: yet highly conscious, at the same time, of their own intrinsic limitations. The latter consciousness was not helped in either case by the sense of unease which the prospect of jobshops (p.83), on the one hand, and of impending local government reorganization (p.40), on the other, seemed to generate. If both services were in the last resort optimistic with regard to the long-term employment prospects of New Commonwealth immigrants, this was not so much a comment on their faith in the efficacy of their own efforts, as a comment upon their expectations of a sustained buoyancy in the labour market (p.59, pp.83-4). This was, to say the least, a less than perfect basis for optimism.

(ii) *Housing*

If employment and youth employment services had broad responsibilities but few powers, the LA housing departments were in a sense more consistent: having few powers, they saw themselves for the most part as having only strictly limited responsibilities also. This is not to say that local authorities as a whole did not possess varied and extensive powers and responsibilities in the housing field. Houses could be declared unfit or overcrowded; houses could be compulsorily purchased; houses could be demolished; housing areas could be developed or redeveloped; home loans and improvement grants could be administered; and housing owned and managed by the local authority could be rented out to selected local families. All in all it was a not inconsiderable package, albeit dependent extensively on central government approval and support.

This was one area, however, in which local authorities were neither obliged nor accustomed to place all their eggs in one basket by concentrating all these powers and responsibilities into one department. Most housing departments, so-called, were responsible for little (if anything) more than the management and letting of existing council housing.[4] For the rest it was public health, town planning, highways, or even clerks departments which were responsible. Even the new housing advice centres, established under the Urban Aid programme in no less than five out of the thirteen areas we contacted (see Appendix), were not usually formally a part of the housing departments themselves.

This situation was significant on three counts. To begin with it seemed hardly conducive to the pursuance, by any one local authority, of a comprehensive integrated housing policy, even though the requisite powers for such a policy might already, separately, exist. In the second place, it meant that housing departments as they were stood every chance, not merely of being in a highly dependent position *vis à vis* other local authority departments (whose decisions might so very much impinge upon their own field of action), but of actually feeling themselves to be the poor relations of the local authority network. In the third place, the fact that they were operating within a strictly limited section of the housing field inclined housing departments, not unnaturally, to interpret their responsibilities in strictly limited terms: they were not there to solve the housing problem; they were there to select tenants according to certain established criteria and to manage council housing estates.

Against this background, the fact that housing constituted a major area of grievance and concern so far as New Commonwealth immigration was concerned, did not mean that there was likely to be any conspicuous drive on the part of housing departments to combat these problems *per se*. Given the position of the housing departments themselves, there was of course some justification for making no elaborate response.

To begin with: New Commonwealth housing difficulties, though possibly more pronounced than the native average, were no different in kind from native experience. It just happened that the newcomers happened to settle in areas already chock-a-block with housing problems. Thus in the words of one manager:

'Housing problems in this area stem mainly from an overall shortage of reasonably rented accommodation, coupled with a high percentage of houses in multi-occupation which are frequently let on furnished tenancies. The resultant problems of overcrowding and bad living conditions may well have been exacerbated by the presence of New Commonwealth immigrants ... Their needs are, however, the same as those of any families living under such conditions, namely adequate accommodation with security of tenure at a rent they can afford.' (p.97)

In such circumstances housing managers, who saw their prime responsibility as being to deal with individual housing needs on a strictly individual basis, could see no justification whatsoever for treating New Commonwealth clientele in any way differently from other clientele. If they were disproportionately disadvantaged and hence disproportionately likely to benefit from any departmental initiative, then this did not in itself constitute 'special treatment for immigrants' (p.92).

This did not mean, of course, that departments might not make special allowances, in an incidental sense, for differences of language or culture — so far as they felt this necessary. They might distribute Department of Environment leaflets in immigrant languages (p.90), for instance, or might instruct that all interviews with immigrants be conducted with due regard for differences of language and custom (p.91). Most dramatic, of course, were the housing advice centre developments, although here housing spokesmen were anxious always to emphasize that, however much these might look like special aids for immigrants, such an impression was no more than coincidence. Just as it was logical for most HACs to be sited in areas of current housing stress, so it was only to be expected that a sizeable proportion of their current clientele would tend to be immigrant (p.94).

The idea that they were, fundamentally, treating immigrants no differently from anyone else was of course a vital principle for housing departments to proclaim — for reasons of politics as well as of principle. Housing was after all both an expensive and a much competed-for commodity. Nevertheless, in at least two respects, New Commonwealth immigrants did seem to be presenting the service with particular problems calling for some sort of specialized response — a fact which, understandably, caused the services some concern.

To begin with, immigrants were not merely more than averagely likely to be resident in areas scheduled for clearance (and therefore eligible usually for rehousing by the council), they seemed more likely, on average, to want to stick together and not to have to move very far. Thus:

'For every coloured family wanting to move there must be 50 wanting to stay. They often buy large old houses which will be demolished and sublet them to 15 or 16 families. The problem is that it takes longer to rehouse people who do not want to move far.' (p.98)

Moreover: 'You need larger houses if you are going to rehouse them and we haven't enough of these at present. So what can we do?' (p.97). One authority at least had attempted to meet this difficulty simply by purchasing 'a lot more larger houses, lately, for conversion' (p.97). Even so, the fact that immigrant households tended to be larger than the average and that they tended to want to stick together might make things awkward, from a housing management point of view, yet it would not, strictly speaking, be regarded as a characteristic peculiar to immigrants: 'Whites in the inner city are just as keen not to have to move out … and equally prone to want to stick together' (p.99). The real difficulty, it seemed, lay in the effects such immigrant 'conglomerations' were expected to exercise upon host-immigrant relationships.

Here housing departments seemed to feel themselves caught in a dilemma. To treat all clients on an equal basis meant offering all of them the same range of choice as to where, out of all the council property available, they might wish to reside. Yet to do so could have seemingly disastrous consequences from a race relations point of view. Hence the dilemma:

> 'Whilst we recognise that in theory it is wise from the housing management's point of view to help disperse concentrations of coloured people, we realise that in rehousing people from clearance areas, it is important to give people the optimum choice in deciding which estate they would like to be rehoused in. This generally means enabling coloured families to be rehoused in the inner-city areas which are close to their work, night bus routes, near to the Pentecostal Churches, the Mosque Temple etc., and also near to their specialist shops.' (p.93)

Even so, according to the same respondent:

> 'Dispersal is probably desirable — if one is to avoid a concentration of slum-clearance coloured and "bad" waiting list whites in an area of unpopular medium-rise development in the inner-city.' (pp.93-4)

The 'syndrome of unpopular properties, coloureds and "bad" waiting list whites' (p.99) seemed one that several departments were highly conscious of and anxious somehow to avoid. Even so, there seemed not very much that they could do, other than try, informally, to persuade immigrant families to scatter. Thus:

> 'We don't formally influence people either way, since we feel it is important to emphasise the individual's right to choose. But where we know immigrants are already accumulated (in tower blocks, for instance, in an area of already dense immigrant settlement) then we do our best to steer other immigrants away from this property.' (p.93)

Even so, according to the same respondent: 'We can't really affect the total situation since we can't interfere in exchanges between corporation tenants. So we can't stop more immigrants coming in' (p.93). In effect, housing departments seemed to be trying to treat immigrants differently (and, as they saw it, with good reason) without, however, being seen to be doing so.

Much the same seemed eminently true in the case of record-keeping. While departments might, in theory, recognize the arguments in favour of openly maintaining separate records relating either to waiting list applicants or to current council house tenants ('There *could* be a case for separate records. I can't say there isn't since the government says there is' (p.96)), to do so in practice seemed quite out of the question to all except three of our respondents. This did not mean that the others were not in effect keeping separate records. It merely meant that they were not doing so openly. Waiting list records, for instance, usually contained a list of the applicant's previous addresses and so could 'give us a fair enough idea' so far as the numbers of immigrants were concerned. Or it might simply by 'generally well known who gets on the waiting list' or who gets a council house (p.96).

Most revealing of all, perhaps, was the written questionnaire response of one department where, having described separate records as a useful tool whereby a check could be kept, over time, on the standard of treatment afforded to immigrant clients, this answer was then erased; to be replaced by the simple statement that no records were in fact being kept (p.96).

With housing departments apparently trying their utmost to maintain the appearance of treating New Commonwealth immigrants in no way differently from other clientele, there was, in consequence, little evidence of staff training or staff briefing programmes geared towards an appreciation of New Commonwealth needs as such. Housing departments were not, of course, large-scale employers of skilled manpower. Housing visitors, nevertheless, were normally reckoned to have received sufficient professional training as to equip them to cope with allcomers — although in one case, at least, these same housing visitors had asked for and received a series of special lectures from the local community relations council (p.87). There was only one case reported of an immigrant housing visitor being appointed — but not specifically to deal with immigrants of course, any more than were immigrant clerks or manual personnel appointed with any specific function or policy in mind (p.89). All in all, for a local authority service, housing departments seemed to correspond, even in their own eyes, more to a bureaucratic than to a personalized service image. Thus, in the words of one housing manager:

'One must expect a certain inflexibility to develop in staff mentality. Once on the job for a long time you tend to get ideas and to get into a routine and tend to have a fairly inflexible way of assessing people and going about your business. But this is not particularly a matter of race relations — just an instance of how jobs tend to fossilize on individuals.' (pp.100-101)

(iii) *Social Care*

LA social services departments would seem to differ sharply from housing departments on at least three associated counts. To begin with, unlike housing departments with their strictly focussed responsibilities, social services departments were themselves the product of a recent reorganization designed to draw together existing local authority responsibilities in the field of personal social care into one, comprehensive department: precisely the sort of reorganization, in other words, which might seem to be required, but which had not so far generally taken place, where LA housing responsibilities were concerned (above p.237). In consequence, social services departments were equipped, not with strictly limited, but with definitionally open-ended responsibilities. In the third place, moreover, they were committed to an ideal, not of treating every client on precisely the same, albeit 'individual', basis, but of treating each case as unique and of reacting to it, therefore, on a strictly personal, non-standard basis. The contrasts between these two departments could scarcely have been more profound.

Social services departments, nevertheless, had their own problems to contend with. As recent creations, cobbled together, some might say, out of an assortment of parts, they were still in the throes of trying to draw together a collection of social workers, for instance, whose training and/or experience was disparate to say the least, into an integrated, comprehensive team. The mere fact of reorganization, moreover, did not of itself increase the supply of trained social worker manpower, any more than it guaranteed to such departments sufficient resources (what could be sufficient resources?) to meet their potentially limitless responsibilities. The fact that most such departments were (at the time of this enquiry) awaiting further reorganization as a bye-product of local government reform, could only have added to their difficulties. In such circumstances it was scarcely surprising to find them attempting to operate, not so much an open-ended personal service on demand, as a strictly crisis-oriented operation.

This being so, the significance of New Commonwealth immigration for this service was less than clear. True such immigrants might be expected to display unusual linguistic and cultural characteristics; to face special problems of adjustment (not to say discrimination); and to fall disproportionately within the categories of families deemed particularly at risk. Nevertheless, to a service geared ostensibly to meeting personal problems in general, these were by definition problems different neither in kind nor in degree from the general run — since there was supposed to be no general run.

There was little evidence, therefore, of any tendency to treat immigrants in any particular fashion simply because they were immigrants. Superficially, of course, special allowances might be made:

'All staff in contact with New Commonwealth immigrant clients are made aware of the need to be sensitive and to seek to understand the problems as perceived by the client, which in some circumstances may originate from ethnic differences.' (p.111)

Nevertheless, in the words of another respondent:

'It is the Department's responsibility to provide an individualised service for everyone. This includes immigrants on the same basis as everyone else, even though they might call for *more* individualised or more exceptional treatment.' (p.112)

Even so, there were doubts occasionally expressed as to the sufficiency of departmental response in this case: 'There is gradually a growing awareness of the need for *some sort* of differential approach with regard to immigrant families' (p.112). Immigrant working parents and therefore immigrant child-minders, for instance, could seem to constitute a rather special problem while, at a more fundamental level:

'We are concerned that Asian families attempt to absorb more problems than they can bear. They won't come to us soon enough

... It's partly because immigrants are not used to there being our sort of agency around.' (p.115)

The differences, in other words, might be more than simple differences of degree. Nevertheless there could, it seemed, be a relatively easy way round such problems for hard-pressed social workers to adopt: 'If it's specifically an immigration problem we would refer them to the CRC' (p.110). Not that such a policy was universally favoured of course:

> 'The CRC tends to do a lot of the jobs around here that social workers in other places might feel bound to do for themselves. They have developed an awful habit of referring any Blacks to the CRC.' (p.111)

So the mere existence of a community relations council, in other words, might actively impede adaptation on the part of ongoing personal social services.

.   Social services departments were of course unique as a statutory service in the extent to which their output consisted, largely, of the quality and the skills of their staff. A good deal of their service amounted simply to providing a social worker. Not surprisingly, in consequence, there was great sensitivity apparent over the question of the training and capacities of these workers. As was the case with other professional workers there were those, of course, who insisted that the social worker's basic training was more than sufficient to equip him or her to meet all contingencies competently. Nevertheless there were those who had their doubts:

> 'We do really need specialists to cope, on occasion, with cultural and religious differences — especially with regard to initial visits and assessment, since these can effectively decide the course of what happens to the client thereafter. There have been several gaffs in this respect by social workers, unfamiliar with the background, leaping to conclusions by comparing them with native families.' (p.108)

No less than nine out of the thirteen departments participating in this enquiry claimed, in fact, that some or all of their social worker staff had received a measure of specific training or briefing on the subject of New Commonwealth immigration. Equally significant, however, was the fact that such training had often only been provided, upon social worker request, once actual 'trouble' had been experienced. Thus, to quote one example:

> 'Briefing has been going on ever since the difficulties. Social workers themselves realised the problems and sought assistance. We always say we will provide a course (on anything) if there is a demand for it ...' (p.104)

Rather more spectacular, on the whole, were the efforts made by social services departments to recruit and deploy New Commonwealth immigrant manpower. Eleven of the thirteen departments contacted claimed currently to be employing one or more New Commonwealth immigrants among their social work staff although most, just as in the Youth employment case (see above pp.235-36), reported some difficulties of recruitment. Once again, it seemed, there were not sufficient suitably qualified candidates available. Yet, given an overall dependence upon unqualified social worker staff, this rationale could strike some respondents at least as unrealistic:-

> 'I regret very much that we have never had immigrants among the general run of our social workers. Since we employ about 30-40 social workers altogether I think we should have had 3-4 coloureds, since this would have been a fair reflection of the local population make-up. But it's been the usual reason given — "there haven't been any qualified applicants" — although we do employ many unqualified white people.' (pp.105-6)

At least one department, however, had made special efforts to overcome this problem:

> 'There's been a lot of campaigning locally on the lines that one should not merely treat immigrants *the same* as everyone else, but should offer them additional facilities and make special allowances over qualifications etc. Partly because of voluntary pressure and partly because of councillor interest, the Department has been very much involved in this. The policy seems to be to appoint people *if* they are coloured — but this is an exaggeration: we only appoint people with potential — where it would seem that their lack of qualifications was the result simply of a disadvantaged background.' (p.106)

Yet such a policy could hardly fail, of course, to provoke repercussions among existing staff who could feel that they were being discriminated against since they at least had had to face standard entrance procedures (p.106).

Of no less significance than any specific New Commonwealth recruitment drives was the fact that, in two cases at least, such staff were expected to act not merely as incidental 'consultants', so far as other immigrants were concerned, but were deputed specifically to operate in an immigrant context. Thus, in the first case, a West Indian area officer had deliberately been placed in charge of an area of high immigrant concentration and had also been deputed to liaise, on behalf of the Department, with the local community relations council. Neither move, however, seemed to have turned out well since 'He seems to be regarded by the immigrant community as something of an Uncle Tom' (p.107 and c.f. above p.167).

The second case concerned the appointment of a West Indian social worker, paid for out of Urban Aid, to work jointly for the Department and the local community relations council. Once again, this did not seem too promising an arrangement: 'He's there to work with these mythical alienated West Indians — but so far he doesn't seem to have been able to find many of them. I'm dubious about this sort of appointment altogether' (p.107). Such an opinion was no different, in essence, from those expressed by so many other social service representatives — against the very idea of using immigrants to deal with immigrants and of risking thereby the creation of a separate (possibly second-rate) service for Blacks. Thus:

> 'I can't believe this sort of separation is good. It's probably bad for our own social workers: it encourages them to keep on thinking that you don't have things like coloured social workers actually among them; and that blacks or coloured immigrant cases are something normally seen to by someone else.' (p.107)

Much the same had of course been said in respect of community relations councils and their possible impact upon social services departments. The strength of feeling against any suspicion of a separate service, however, was to prove of particular significance in one very specialized respect: that of record-keeping. In this case, the objection was not so much against the principle of recording ethnic details *per se* (the filing system of any social services department, after all, was overflowing with personal details of no less import to the persons concerned, than mere 'ethnic details' might be to immigrant clients), but against the idea of assembling these together as the basis for any overall client statistics. Departmental statistics were designed primarily to give some indication of the balance of case-types or of problems presented. The mere fact of being an immigrant should not, it was argued, be regarded in itself as either a case-type or a presenting problem.

Such at least was the principle upheld. There were, nevertheless, two predictable complications. To begin with, the fact that most social services did not maintain separate ethnic records, within the commonly accepted meaning of the term, made it difficult either for them to demonstrate or for others to estimate just how adequate, individualized, comprehensive, and flexible was the service in the immigrant case. The very open-endedness and individualistic philosophy of social services departments, in other words, rendered their activities, at least in this respect, more or less invisible to scrutiny.

The second complication was perhaps more open to correction. Just as other professionals in the social services field could become not a little fraught over the very principle of recording ethnic details (cf. above p.234 for instance), so social workers could, notwithstanding their general obligation to record all relevant details in the individual's case file and notwithstanding the fact that such files were normally to be regarded as highly confidential, feel so strongly on the 'ethnic details' issue as to refrain from placing such details on record even where they might seem of direct relevance to the case in hand. Thus, in the words of one spokesman:-

'All the sensitivity about separate record-keeping can be quite dangerous. I attended an assessment conference recently where they were dealing with a delinquent boy, where there was no mention on his record of the fact that his parents came from two different countries. People were so sensitive on this matter that it had been left off the record even though, in this case, it was highly relevant to the problem. People have been over-sensitised on this issue. We are trying now to get a more realistic approach put into practice — where ethnic background *is* relevant to the case.' (p.113)

However this may be, the outstanding impression left by departments of social service was not one relating to the quality or otherwise of their performance under difficult conditions, but simply to their inaccessibility, as a group, to outside enquiry. They may well have been busy and crisis-ridden. But then so were many other branches of statutory social service, in their own estimation at least. It seemed significant that, in this case, it was not possible to interview a single director of social services; only, in four cases out of the thirteen initially replying to the questionnaire, a delegated member of his staff (p.102). This fact, added to the intrinsic invisibility of much of the work being carried out, made it impossible, in the last resort, to make any overall assessment of social services department efforts in this context. Given the instances already referred to, suggestive of so much adaptation in response to a New Commonwealth immigrant presence, this lack of more substantial evidence was unfortunate.

(iv) *Conclusions*

We have looked, in some detail, at the evidence relating to the social services' response to New Commonwealth immigration. We may now sum up in terms of our three starting propositions: namely that the experience of such immigration tends to show up the scope and ethos of prevailing social policy; that such social policy may, in the second place, function as a problem-solving device within the host-immigrant context; but that, third, it may also serve to create or exacerbate problems in this situation.

The relationship of specialist integration policy to the established social services would seem, in a curious way, to illustrate all three of these propositions — just as does statutory social policy as a whole in relation to New Commonwealth immigration. Thus, to begin with, one might argue that the very creation of specialist integration policies amounted to an implicit comment on the capacity and ability of existing social services to cope adequately with the consequences of New Commonwealth immigration on their own. In the second place, specialist integration machinery, whether in the form of the Race Relations Board and its conciliation committees or in the form of the Community Relations Commission and its local community relations councils, clearly constituted an additional problem-solving device for established services to call upon in this situtation. In the third place, however, the presence of such machinery and such policies could also create problems for the existing social services: it could place additional constraints on their room for manouevre, on the one hand, and, on the other, could encourage an unhealthy side-stepping of responsibilities so far as immigrant clients were concerned.

As far as the conventional social services themselves were concerned, the burden of the present and the previous chapter shows that the presence and the needs of New Commonwealth immigrants did serve to highlight many aspects of the services' scope and ethos. However, the impression thus conveyed is not necessarily either a complete of balanced one: for the characteristics of the New Commonwealth population, as (a) an unusually disadvantaged, (b) strange, and (c) controversial section of society, were such as to expose the limitations and the limits rather than the middle ground, of statutory social policy.

First, in so far as the newcomers were an unusually disadvantaged group: their requirements showed up how far exising social services, in this respect, were able or inclined to cope fully with all predicaments falling nominally within their respective areas of responsibility. LA health departments, and for that matter executive councils and hospital management committees, felt themselves similarly bound to respond, somehow, to apparent health needs. But universal National Insurance in conjunction with Supplementary Benefits, felt bound to respond only in so far as immigrant requirements fell within the (theoretically comprehensive) guidelines of these services. Hence the inability of National Insurance, on the one hand, to take account of more than one wife, for instance, and the inability of Supplementary Benefits, on the other hand, to take account of anything over and above a 'reasonable' rent. This from services which had been intended, in conjunction, to constitute a comprehensive social security system.

Housing and employment services were never intended, of course, to be anything like 'comprehensive' in their powers. In this case, the fact that New Commonwealth (and clearly not only New Commonwealth) disadvantage seemed so much the product of housing and employment conditions seemed to call in question the validity of a non-universalist and non-comprehensive statutory approach in both these fields. However much careers officers or employment officers might attempt to overcome the limitations of their services' position when dealing with New Commonwealth, and other client, requirements, they were hardly better-placed than any LA housing manager to influence, let alone control, the total situation.

All this being so, one might have expected LA departments of social service, as the welfare catch-alls of the Welfare State, to have been unusually busy; coping with the consequent personal problems of New Commonwealth (along with native) families trapped in poor employment and/or poor housing situations. Yet, if the potential responsibilities of social service departments were limitless, their resources were of course those of a 'second-rank', non-universal service. If, as a result, this crisis-oriented service became overstretched the very nature of its social work operations, however, seemed to make it peculiarly opaque to outside scrutiny. Its general significance in the face of New Commonwealth immigrant predicaments remains therefore, a matter for conjecture.

Second, to the extent that the newcomers were strange: in this respect their special needs could test out the flexibility and capacity for innovation of the various social services affected. One might have supposed that the more comprehensive and universal the service, the greater its capacity for an individually tailored response. Yet this, as we have seen, was not altogether the case. LEAs seem to have been inventive to an extent which National Insurance and Supplementary Benefits could not attempt to emulate. LA health departments, and even executive councils, seem to have been more prone to innovation than were hospital management committees. Youth and adult employment services seem to have been no less inventive than LEAs in general, notwithstanding the employment services' relatively marginal position. LA housing departments seem to have been the more consistent in this respect — since their limited innovation record was more or less of a piece with their perceived limited room for manoeuvre. LA social service departments varied between what could be termed drastic innovation and inveterate conventionality according to the apparent circumstances of each department and each case. In all these instances, needless to say, service traditions could be quite as decisive as formal service powers and responsibilities; and the reliance ostensibly placed upon staff judgement in an awkward situation need not necessarily be related to the extent to which such members of staff had professionally been trained for such responsibilities.

Finally: in so far as New Commonwealth immigrants were controversial — in this respect their apparent sectional demands could place any implicated social service agency in an awkward position from a general public point of view. This was most notable with regard to LA-administered services, these being, on the face of things, the services most directly answerable to local consumer and local political opinion. Hence the tendency of most LA health departments always to be conscious, not merely of immigrant, but of native ratepayer and possible councillor reaction on matters of local, seemingly challenged public health. Hence, even more dramatically, the efforts of both LEAs and local authority housing departments to secure, in many cases, the effective dispersal of immigrant clientele without, however, having formally to acknowledge that any deliberate dispersal of either immigrant schoolchildren or immigrant council tenants had ever in principle been decided upon. For all this, however, the readiness of central government, at least, to espouse immigrant pupil dispersal as official policy in response to certain local, white, parental pressure, would seem in stark contrast to the activities of the London School Board at the time of the new Jewish invasion. Local, native sentiment would seem to have been much the same where the new Jews, as where the New Commonwealth, were concerned. The London School Board, however, had seemingly been better placed to set aside such local demands.

To talk of the social services' response to strange and controversial immigrant requirements is, however, to imply something of the services' problem-solving capacities, on the one hand, and of their problem-exacerbating potential, on the other.

So far as problem-solving is concerned, we have seen just how resourceful and elaborate could be the response of individual social service agencies to the presence of New Commonwealth immigrants in their areas. They might, for instance, have had their staff specially briefed on the subject of New Commonwealth immigration; they might have made special arrangements for interpretation or for the distribution of information leaflets in immigrant languages; they might have instituted special advisory procedures; they might even on occasion have felt obliged to provide certain forms of special treatment — where linguistic, educational, or cultural requirements might have seemed so different from the general run as to constitute, from the service's point of view, a special case (even though this might not formally be described as being a response specific to immigrants as such). Also we have the example of most local social services being fairly deliberate, so far as their efforts to recruit New Commonwealth staff were concerned, even though they would not usually depart from their standard criteria in order to effect such appointments; nor would they normally appoint New Commonwealth staff specifically to deal with New Commonwealth problems. No one was keen to encourage any 'separate service' developments in this respect. 'Separate records' again, proved a similar case where service spokesmen might well be familiar with the arguments in favour of separately accounting for their New Commonwealth clientele (if only to monitor their progress) but none were anxious to be seen to discriminate in this way between clients.

Taking all this evidence together, one could argue that the services were doing the best they could — given their position, their role, their various structures, and their separate traditions — to cope with the New Commonwealth presence. However this is not to say that they were intrinsically well placed to respond specifically to host-immigrant tensions. Therefore, while it might seem self-evident that the statutory social services, must, broadly speaking, have been helpful devices in a general sense — by virtue of the fact that they existed 'for the general good'; to go further than this and assert that the social services might in any more specific sense have been problem-solving in this context, is really to make two major assumptions.

To begin with, one has to assume that racial tension was and is essentially the product of adverse, or extremely adverse, social conditions. There is indeed circumstantial evidence to support this view. Racial tensions do tend to be at their most obvious in conditions of social hardship, affecting both immigrants and local natives alike. Nevertheless this is only circumstantial evidence. It does not of itself prove a causal relationship between adverse social conditions and the existence of racial tensions. It does not follow, therefore, that a marked amelioration of such social conditions would of itself produce a lessening or an elimination of racial tension. The nature of racial prejudice, and the precise relationship between prejudicial attitudes and prejudicial actions is still, to say the least, unproven territory.

In the second place, even if one accepts that racial tensions may, to a very large extent, be the product of adverse social conditions, one has also to assume that the statutory social services as they currently exist are capable of mounting a systematic attack, if indeed they are not already doing so, upon these same adverse social conditions. Yet all the evidence we have discussed so far concerning the nature of the Welfare State would seem to suggest that this is not so. Quite apart from the inconsistencies of scope and objectives between services, for instance, it could be argued that the Welfare State as such was never really geared to the notion of an immediate levelling up in material social conditions, but rather to the notion of long-term social reconstruction via individual equality of opportunity as this gradually worked its way through the system. The fact that this had not, apparently, worked its way through the system by the 1960s was in itself a matter of much concern and disappointment. Hence, for instance, the resort to additional, positive discrimination programmes, geared specifically to the amelioration of at least the very worst pockets of social deprivation, on top of the existing statutory structure. Yet such temporary, crash programmes could not of course resolve the basic dilemma.

For the statutory social services to try to tackle current inequalities head-on, as it were, cut right across ideals variously held of treating all people on essentially the same basis, of disregarding social backgrounds and of according the same dignity and the same rights to every client. These problems were inevitably highlighted, however, once there was an association between colour and the extremes of deprivation. How far in this case could any service move in the direction of policies designed specifically to help those currently living in deprived circumstances, when a large proportion of these people were going to be coloured? In these circumstances, issues which were bound to trouble the social services in any case, such as their fears of ever seeming to provide some sort of separate, second-rate or even preferential service for a particular social category of client, must obviously be highlighted in a colour context where, as already suggested, the social services would in any case be feeling somewhat exposed.

In other words, the social services themselves were placed in a difficult position as a result of the association between pockets of racial tensions and pockets of extreme social deprivation.

Closely associated with this is the third point: the fact that the social services themselves could create or exacerbate problems, albeit unintentionally, in a host-immigrant situation. The reasons for this were as follows. Given the fact that social services are not as full and as perfect and as complete or as systematic as perhaps might be wished then, in effect, they function as scarce resources, as valued resources, and as resources which are indeed much publicized as being vital to individual life-chances. The consequences here are much as might be expected. The services themselves and the facilities they provide become potential bones of contention between immigrants and hosts, precisely in those areas where the services themselves are likely to be most stretched or thinnest on the ground in relation to the social needs to be met. In such a situation, furthermore, the social services are if anything less in a position to act than normally, because of what might be termed the 'race relations paralysis effect': they could feel it difficult to move in any direction for fear of alienating someone or seeming to favour someone else. Once again the colour factor would seem to have highlighted an otherwise far less prominent social services' dilemma.

All in all, therefore, our threefold hypotheses: that New Commonwealth immigration would tend to expose the state of current statutory social policy, reveal its problem-solving capabilities, and show up its problem-exacerbating potential in this context, would seem very much to fit the facts.

9

Immigration and social policy – general conclusions

Early Irish, East European Jewish, and New Commonwealth immigration are broadly comparable in having made an impact upon contemporary statutory social policy. I have shown something of how, and how far, the presence of such immigrants served on each occasion to make manifest the scope and ethos of prevailing social policy, to stretch its problem-solving capabilities and, also, to reveal its problem-exacerbating potential. Nevertheless, from the first case to the last, the immigration-social policy encounter has clearly been one of mounting complexity and intensity. Having examined the cases individually, we may now review the grounds for this apparent escalation. I shall do this by looking once more at some of the characteristics of each wave of immigrants, and of the social policy these different waves encountered.

'Mass economic immigration', in the broad sense in which I have used the term, can be used to describe the Irish, Jewish, and New Commonwealth influxes respectively — but this does not necessarily mean that these three sets of newcomers possessed anything more in common than that they were all predominantly poor, numerous, and strange.

To take the last point first: these newcomers were not all equally 'strange', or strange in the same respects. Thus the Irish, as 'less civilized' outsider citizens, dressing oddly and speaking oddly upon first arrival, and associated, moreover, with a somewhat suspect Christian church, were arguably not so strange by British reckoning as was the later, wholly alien Jew. Yet the Jew, in turn, was if anything less strange than the eventual varieties of New Commonwealth immigrant. There may or may not have been marked differences of language and religion in the latter case (depending on the groups of immigrants in question), but a coloured appearance was both more obvious and more permanent than any mere peculiarities of dress, or even of facial characteristics.

Second, the mere fact that the immigrants were 'numerous' does not mean that each wave made the same sort of mass impression. The Jews were both fewer in number and geographically more confined than the Irish had been before them. Nevertheless, the fact that the new Jews happened to be concentrated within the capital city of all places, ensured their presence being noticed out of all proportion to their numbers over the country as a whole. New Commonwealth immigrants being the most numerous of all were also the most conspicuous in national terms: coloured settlement areas becoming a feature, not merely of the capital city, but of most large scale centres of employment in England.

Even to be poor, finally, was not necessarily to be poor in the same way — or with the same reputation. The early Irish were liable to be dismissed by British spokesmen as being a low-class, unskilled, and unambitious population. The Jews, though equally poor and industrially unskilled upon arrival, were nevertheless liable to be reckoned both able and ambitious; a rather more disturbing proposition. New Commonwealth immigrants, in all their variety, seemed to include both the clever and the not so clever, the ambitious and the unambitious, within their ranks — albeit in an unclear and unpredictable fashion. Such at least would appear to be a prevailing host society impression. On this account again, therefore, New Commonwealth immigrants represented the most awkward (or at least the most complicated) group of newcomers for the host society to come to terms with.

Native sentiment and reaction was also the product in part, however, of one further related factor: namely the reasons, as publicly perceived, for Britain becoming host to such immigrants in the first place. The less immediate or the less incontrovertible the newcomers' links with and/or claims upon the host society, the more was such immigration liable to be challenged in itself.

Thus the Irish, as near neighbours and actual citizens, were fundamentally less controversial as immigrants (there seemed little question, after all, of their basic right to come, however much their coming might be resented) than were the new Jews. The latter were open to challenge (and eventually to immigration controls legislation) since, despite the convenience of Britain as a stopping-off point for uncertain venturers to the United States and despite these apparent refugees' moral claims upon a self-styled moral pace-setter among nations, they were neither geographical neighbours, nor citizens. Most controversial of all, however, were New Commonwealth immigrants, these being the farthest removed geographically yet (thanks to the British Empire) with concrete rights of citizenship for all that.

Even so, the more controversial the connection between each group of immigrants and the host society, the more conspicuous was the type of support (if any) such immigrants could expect from within the ranks of the host society. The local, lesser-citizen-Irish had no British backers worth the name. Migrant Jews, however, had the Anglo-Jewish establishment to look towards, which for all its ambivalence in this respect served not merely to encourage new Jewish settlement and aspirations by its mere existence, but actively to promote the immigrants' cause and social well-being. New Commonwealth immigrants, in contrast again, had the services not of fellow-kinsmen or co-religionists to look towards upon first arrival, but those of a far less equivocal, far more openly partisan assortment of self-selected, self-declared supporters committed variously to the principles of New Commonwealth entry to, and integration within, British society.

Bearing all these considerations in mind, I suggest that the new Jews posed a greater social policy challenge than the Irish had done before them; and that the New Commonwealth immigrants were intrinsically the most challenging of all the three. In so far as one can reasonably weigh up the implications of immigration in isolation from the social policy it encountered, therefore, this explains one side of the immigration-social policy 'escalation' referred to above.

We have now to turn to the other side of the coin: namely the style and scope of prevailing statutory social policy in each case. Two factors seem relevant here: the range of social policy objectives and machinery on the one hand, and the nature of its accountability on the other. Both factors, needless to say, are intimately related the one with the other yet, for the sake of clarity, we will deal with them each in turn.

Clearly, the broader, the more complex, and the more ambitious social policy objectives, the greater was the scope for issues to be raised or highlighted by the presence of poor, numerous, and strange outsiders. An Irish presence served effectively to expose the limited capabilities of the Poor Laws (old and new) for controlling the poor; and to indicate (at least to later commentators) just how marginal could be the impact of early public health and education manoeuvres upon the condition of the labouring classes. Jewish immigration, however, could highlight the range, capabilities, and dilemmas of a much wider, and growing, assortment of social services, designed ostensibly to boost the well-being of the working classes. Witness the ambivalence of Poor Law policies in this period, the cautiousness of the first attempts to provide cash services outside the Poor Law, the slow build-up of effective public health machinery, but the surprising potential of the 1870 *Education Act*. New Commonwealth immigrants, finally, arrived as citizens in a supposedly comprehensive Welfare State, with social services impinging upon virtually every aspect of life-chances within the society — and all shot through, of course, with the notion of equality of opportunity, whatever that was taken to imply. There was ample scope here for issues to be raised or highlighted by the presence of such immigrants. Equality of opportunity, for instance, ensured that, for the first time, anti-immigrant discrimination could feature as a social policy issue in itself.

This last was only to be expected, of course, given the position of New Commonwealth immigrants as citizens in a democratic Welfare State. Yet this brings us to our second consideration: namely the accountability of social policy. The broader the accountability, I would suggest, the more intense, immediate, and potentially explosive must be the immigration-social policy debate.

Mid-nineteenth century social policy was, as we have seen, enacted by and mainly in the interests of the voting, ratepaying classes. Not only did this give a particular style and flavour to the social policy thus enacted, it meant that those in charge of and those represented in social policy deliberations were (except for interested employers) not those sections of society most immediately affected or conceivably threatened by an Irish (competitor) presence. Those who felt themselves immediately threatened by the Jewish presence were of course in a much stronger position to voice their opinions and to expect to be listened to; yet their demands were not invariably met — as the example of the London School Board and its Jewish schools policy shows very well. New Commonwealth immigrants, finally, arrived in an age of universal citizen rights and responsibilities. As a result, not only might their nearest British competitors be well placed to voice their demands; but the immigrants themselves were entitled also to be heard. Hence the increasingly vociferous and polarized social policy debate on this occasion.

In summary therefore: not only might the nature of the immigration be deemed more challenging from one case to the next, but the nature of the social policy encountered was such as to ensure a progressively more extensive and intensive immigration-social policy debate.

There remains one final consideration to take into account which, this time, is of relevance to the subject as a whole, namely the extent (if at all) to which international considerations played a part in these debates. We have noted, in the course of the case-studies, how anti-semitism in the Jewish case was seemingly quite different from the sort of dislike or distaste the Irish had encountered, and how colour-prejudice in the New Commonwealth case was apparently quite different again from anything hitherto experienced in Britain. Both forms of racial prejudice, however, were of more than domestic implication. Here, once again, there is an escalating sequence to be traced.

Thus Irish immigration was both technically and effectively an internal, domestic issue. Jewish immigration was a much more sensitive issue in international terms, owing to the status of these newcomers as victims of religious persecution (a factor of some significance in tempering political reactions to their arrival). Yet anti-semitism during this period was nothing like the international issue it was later to become in the 1930s — and certainly nothing like the international issue that colour prejudice was eventually to show itself to be. The international factor, in this latter case, clearly influenced both host and newcomer attitudes and expectations. Blacks in a white-dominated society were liable to be compared, and to compare themselves, with Blacks in other white-dominated societies. On this account again, therefore, one could expect a more polarized and volatile public debate to ensue — along with a more selfconscious, not to say wary, social policy response.

All in all, therefore, an escalating immigration-social policy encounter from the first to the third of our case-studies does not seem difficult to justify. Nevertheless, this finding does raise two important questions. To begin with, we are bound to ask to what extent has this been a chance escalation? In the second place, equally, we are bound to wonder what comes next. The answer to the first question seems, in my opinion, to point the answer to the second.

All the evidence we have considered and referred to in this study suggests that this escalation in the immigration-social policy encounter was not wholly chance. On the contrary, both the waves of immigration I have reviewed and the stages of social policy development they encountered, can be interpreted as being each related to the same underlying national situation. This is not to say, therefore, either that immigration primarily influenced social policy development or that, conversely, social policy development served consistently to attract particular groups of immigrants at particular times — even though both these propositions must contain an element of truth. More fundamental and more to the point in this context, is the evidence that mass economic immigration, on the one hand, and statutory social policy, on the other, are both closely related to Britain's industrial revolution and post industrial development.

Economic growth engendered not simply general employment prospects for potential migrants; it guaranteed a Britain which was continuously striving to reach or maintain an international position and reputation such as could only serve to encourage certain forms of mass immigration. One could not lay claim to be the workshop of the world, or to a moral pre-eminence born of apparent material success, or even to an empire whose members should be thankful, without the risk, after all, of having some of the chickens respectively coming home to roost.

Precisely the same economic growth and developement, however, engendered those political upheavals and social discontents within British society, such as sparked off, and thereafter served to fuel, statutory social policy expansion. Such statutory social policy was indicative, on the one hand, of some national official unease about the state of the society and, on the other, of some heightening national self-consciousness if not professed solidarity. Either way it seems scarcely remarkable that none of the groups of immigrants under review should have chanced, apparently, upon a good time for their arrival. The more Britain possessed in the way of statutory social policy, in other words, the more anxious and self-conscious (by implication) was the society and the less inclined was it towards any bulk acceptance of outsiders — however understandable their claims or however convenient their manpower.

It is at this point that we may profitably ask — what next? Given the escalating immigration-social policy sequence already remarked upon, is it logical to expect, perhaps, that some further even more challenging wave of mass immigration must eventually materialize — only to meet with an even more pretentious and provocative set of social policy institutions? After coloured immigration, what then? Or after the Welfare State, what then? Both these latter questions, however, seem otiose and for the same reason.

If Britain's economic growth and development, from the industrial revolution onwards, was at the root, as I have suggested, of both her mass immigration experiences and her social policy expansion, then the current prospect of nil, if not negative, economic growth makes the likelihood of any further mass immigration, or any medium-term social policy expansion, seem unlikely to say the least. New Commonwealth immigration, after all, was arguably a response to a past rather than a present international situation, to an economy which was already fundamentally on the decline and to a Welfare State which was beginning to count its costs almost before the social services concerned had had a chance to make their mark.

In this context, when social service executives have, for the first time, to assume that they will be called upon to cut down rather than to expand upon their activities, one may indeed question what the prospects for current, second-generation New Commonwealth immigrants, or their third generation offspring, may be. The original early Irish (though not their latter-day followers) have in effect disappeared. So have the onetime new Jews — into at least the Anglo-Jewish community. New Commonwealth immigrants, however, have not merely the badge of colour to contend with, with all its seeming permanence as a proof of separateness, but a contracting jobs situation together with an increasingly 'scarce resources' social policy front. However vociferous or otherwise the immigration-social policy debate may turn out to be in this unprecedented situation, New Commonwealth immigrants would seem, ironically, to be far more trapped in their position of being poor, strange outsiders than their less outspoken, and less dramatically championed, predecessors. This may turn out, *par excellence* perhaps, to be a case of mistimed, belated arrival.

Appendix

The SSRC Survey: The response of the statutory social services to New Commonwealth immigration

My enquiry was designed to explore the extent to which local statutory social services had:

(a) made specific adjustments to their practices and procedures, and

(b) felt themselves, as agencies, to be experiencing particular problems

as a result of the presence within their areas of a New Commonwealth immigrant population.[1]

This was, therefore, an agency-centred approach and one which was intended to cover a wide cross-section of statutory social services, with the exception of education.[2] Some services were of course more suited to this type of approach than others. Within the National Health Service, for instance. LA health departments seemed better placed to act as local spokesmen for their branch of the Service than were either hospital management committes or executive councils. The other types of agency approached were as follows: LA Careers offices, housing departments, and social services departments; local employment exchanges and SB/social security offices.[3]

These agencies were approached in respect of some sixteen selected LA areas of New Commonwealth immigrant settlement. Since we did not wish the enquiry to be concentrated exclusively upon parts of Greater London and the West Midlands (where the largest concentrations of New Commonwealth immigrants were to be found), the areas were selected by reference first to the overall distribution of the New Commonwealth population between the Regions (1966 Sample Census figures). Within each of those Regions accounting for at least 5 per cent of the overall New Commonwealth population, we selected the areas of greatest New Commonwealth concentration, relative to their total populations. However the number of such areas selected within any one Region was in rough relationship to the overall proportion of the New Commonwealth population present in that region. Thus the South East, accounting for roughly 60 per cent of the total New Commonwealth population was represented by six (Greater London Borough) areas; whereas the South-West, accounting for a mere 5 per cent, was represented by one county borough area.

The initial approach was by means of a postal questionnaire (addressed to the manager/director etc. of the local agency in question). The questionnaire invited respondents to comment on whether, for instance, any members of their staff had been specially briefed or trained on the subject of New Commonwealth immigration; on whether they employed any New Commonwealth members of staff (and if so in what capacities); on whether they produced or distributed any information literature designed specifically to meet the needs of New Commonwealth clientele; on whether their agency operated any other forms of what might be termed special treatment in relation to such clientele; and on whether or not the agency kept separate records or statistics relating to some or all New Commonwealth immigrant groups. In addition respondents were asked whether, in their opinion, their agency had faced or was facing particular problems arising out of the presence locally of a New Commonwealth population.

The rate of response to this stage of the enquiry was impressive: 113 (89 per cent) completed questionnaires being returned out of a total of 127 distributed. Needless to say, this overall rate was only achieved after some months of waiting and follow-up correspondence. It was boosted, moreover, but the fact that employment exchange and SB response rates were in each case 100 per cent — thanks to central government support and direction in both these areas.

Following this, we attempted to interview every questionnaire respondent who was willing to be interviewed, on an informal basis, in order to clarify and add depth to the information presented in the questionnaire. There were three complications, however, to this manoeuvre. To begin with, while the Department of Employment was willing to have its local employment exchange managers interviewed, should they themselves be inclined to participate. The DHSS did not consider it appropriate or practicable to have its local social security administrators questioned in person. It seemed more appropriate to offer a central, group interview in this case — which is what in fact occurrred. Second, so far as other social service agencies were concerned, respondents' willingness, in principle, to be interviewed did not always mean that an interview could be arranged — given the limited time and resources available to the survey. Thus eleven respondents who had expressed a willingness to be interviewed were subjected, instead, to further correspondence — to which ten had the forebearance to respond. Third and last, the interviewee was not necessarily the same person as the questionnnaire respondent (if indeed there had been any single questionnaire respondent) in each case. Nor, indeed, were they necessarily persons in charge of their particular agency. Thus, while most LA health department interviewees were medical officers of health and all employment exchange spokesmen were themselves exchange managers, half of those interviewed in the hospital management case were personnel administrators; while so far as social services departments were concerned, it was in no case possible to interview a director of social services. Bearing such limitations in mind (and leaving SB respondents out of the reckoning) then fifty-six (61 per cent) our of ninety questiionnaire respondents expressed a willingness to be interviewed, of whom forty-five were actually interviewed and eleven subjected to further correspondence.

There remains one further point. I have made no attempt, either in this book or in the original SSRC Report, to distinguish systematically between quotations taken from questionnaire and quotations taken from interview material. To do so would have been both cumbersome and, I believe, unnecessary. The interviews were informal. Nevertheless the exchanges which took place were taken down fully in shorthand and transcribed on the same day either onto tape or into typescript. The fact that this enquiry was conducted on the principle of respondent anonymity made it possible, of course, to utilize such material with a freedom which might not otherwise have been either fair or practicable.

The overall returns can be summarized as follows:

type of service	questionnaire response	interview	further correspondence answered (*instead of interview*)	total first approached (a)
LA :				
Health	13	8	1	16
Yth. Empl.	12	6	4	13
Housing	13	5	3	16
Soc. Serv.	13	4	-	16
Other:				
Empl. Exch.	16	11	1	16
Exec. Councils	10	5	1	12
HMCs	13	6	-	15
SB	23	1(b)	-	23
total	113	46	10	127

Notes:

a. Many of the services did not relate strictly to borough boundaries: hence the totals do not always correspond to the number of areas first selected.

b. One interview with central government spokesmen being carried out in this case.

References

Abbott, S. (ed.) (1971) *The Prevention of Racial Discrimination in Britain*. London: Institute of Race Relations/Oxford University Press.

Ashton, T.S. (1949) The Standard of Life of the Workers in England 1790-1830. *Journal of Economic History*. Supplement IX : 19-38.

Bagley, J.J. and Bagley, A.J. (1969) *The State and Education in England and Wales 1833-1968*. London: Macmillan.

Baksi, J. (1970) Race Relations: The Case for Community Development. *Race Today* 2 (11). November.

Barnard, H.C. (1947) *A History of English Education*. London: University of London Press.

Barnes, H. (1934) *The Slum: Its Story and Solution*. Hempstead: The Mill Press.

Blondel, J. (1963) *Voters, Parties and Leaders*. Harmondsworth: Penguin.

Booth, C. (1889-1903) *Life and Labour of the People of London*. London

Bottoms, A.E. (1967) Delinquency among Immigrants. *Race* VIII (4). April.

Briggs, A. (1959) National Bearings. In Briggs (ed.) *Chartist Studies*. London: Macmillan.

——— (1959) *The Age of Improvement*. London: Longmans Green & Co.

British Medical Association (1965) *Medical Examination of Immigrants: report of the working party*. London: BMA.

Brittan, E.M. (1971) Summer Holiday Projects. In Townsend (1971).

Brown, M. (1969) *Introduction to Social Administration in Britain*. London: Hutchinson.

Burney, E. (1967) *Housing on Trial: A Study of Immigrants and Local Government*. London: Institute of Race Relations/Oxford University Press.

Butterworth, E. (1972a) Dilemmas of Community Relations — I. *New Community* I (3). Spring.

——— (1972b) Dilemmas of Community Relations — II. *New Community* 1 (5). Autumn.

Carley, M.M. (1963) *Jamaica: the Old and the New*. London: George Allen & Unwin.

Chadwick, E. (1842) *The Sanitary Condition of the Labouring Population of Great Britain*. Section V, Pecuniary Burdens Created by Neglect of Sanitary Measures. Edinburgh: Edinburgh University Press.

Chopre, Subbash (1970) Immigrants and the Police. *Race Today* 2 (8). August.

Collins, W. (1957) *Coloured Minorities in Britain*. London: Butterworth Press.

Committee on Old Age Pensions (1903) *Old Age Pensions: The Case Against Old Age Pensions Schemes*. London.

Community Development Project (1974) *Inter-Project Report*. London: CDP Information and Intelligence Unit.

―――― (1975) *Forward Plan 1975-6*. London: CDP Information and Intelligence Unit.

Cook, G. (1974) The Development of the Four Principle Charitable Housing Trusts of London. Unpublished MA thesis, University of Manchester.

Crawford, J. (1972) Integration or Independence: A Strategy for Black Groups. *Race Today* 5 (I). January.

Cullingworth, J.B. (1966) *Housing and Local Government*. London: George Allen & Unwin.

Cunningham, W. (1969) *Alien Immigration to England* (2nd. edition). London: Frank Cars & Co (first published 1897).

Curtis, E. (1957) Ireland. In *Encyclopaedia Britannica*.

Curtis, S.J. (1963) *History of Education in Great Britain* (5th edition). London: University Tutorial Press.

Davison, R.B. (1966) *Black British*. London: Institute of Race Relations/Oxford University Press.

Department of Education and Science (1971) *The Education of Immigrants*. Education Survey No. 13. London: HMSO.

Department of Health and Social Security (1972) *Management Arrangements for the Reorganized National Health Service*. London: HMSO.

Desai, R. (1963) *Indian Immigrants in Britain*. London: Institute of Race Relations/Oxford University Press.

Dicey, A.W. (1905) *Law and Public Opinion in England During the Nineteenth Century*. London: Macmillan.

Dodge, J.S. and Myers, F.H. (1969) The Immigrant and the Public Health Law. In J.S. Dodge (ed.), *The Field Worker in Immigrant Health*. London: Staples Press.

Employment Service Agency/Manpower Services Commission (1974) *The Employment Service: Plans and Programmes*. London : HMSO.

Engels, F. (1969) *The Condition of the Working Class in England*. London: Panther (first published in Leipzig in 1845).

Eversley, D. and Sukedo, P. (1969) *The Dependants of the Coloured Commonwealth Population of England and Wales*. London: Institute of Race Relations.

Finer, S.E. (1952) *The Life and Times of Sir Edwin Chadwick*. London: Methuen.

Finestein, I. (1971) Jewish Immigration in British Party Politics in the 1890s. In A. Newman (ed.), *Migration and Settlement*. London: Jewish Historical Society.

Fishman, W. (1975) *East End Jewish Radicals 1875-1914*. London: Duckworth.

Foot, P. (1965) *Immigration and Race in British Politics*. Harmondsworth: Penguin.

Fraser, D. (1973) *The Evolution of the British Welfare State*. London: Macmillan.

Garner, B. (1972) *The Alien Invasion*. London: Heinemann Educational.

Garrard, J.A. (1971) *The English and Immigration*. London: Oxford University Press.

Gartner, L.P. (1960) *The Jewish Immigrant in England, 1870-1914*. London: George Allen & Unwin.

George, V. (1968) *Social Security: Beveridge and After*. London: Routledge & Kegan Paul.

Gilbert, B.B. (1966) *The Evolution of National Insurance in Great Britain: The Origins of the Welfare State*. London: Michael Joseph.

―――― (1970) *British Social Policy 1914-39*. London: B.T. Batsford.

Glass, R. (1960) *Newcomers*. London: Centre for Urban Studies and George Allen & Unwin.

Glean, M. (1973) Review of *The Politics of the Powerless* by B.W. Heinemann Jnr. *Race Today* 5 (1). January.

Gosden, M. (1974) *Self Help: Voluntary Associations in Nineteenth Century Britain.* New York: Barnes & Noble.

HM Government (1835) *Poor Law Enquiry (Ireland).* Appendix G: Report on the State of the Irish Poor in Great Britain. London.

―――― (1858-61) *Report of the Royal Commission on 'The Present State of Popular Education in England'* (Newcastle Commission). Cd.2794. London.

―――― (1885) *Royal Commission on the Housing of the Working Classes: Report.* Cd. 4402. London.

―――― (1902-3) *Royal Commission on Alien Immigration.* Cd. 1742. London.

―――― (1904) *Report of the Interdepartment Committee on Physical Deterioration.* Cd. 2175. London.

―――― (1909) *Royal Commission on the Poor Laws and the Relief of Distress.* Reports (Majority and Minority). Cd. 4499. London.

―――― (1920) *Consultative Council on Medical and Allied Services. Report.* Cd. 693. London.

―――― (1926) *The Education of the Adolescent* (Hadow Report). London.

―――― (1931) *The Primary School* (Hadow Report). London.

―――― (1942) *Social Insurance and Allied Services* (Beveridge Report). Cmnd. 6404. London.

―――― (1967) *Children and their Primary Schools: A Report of the Central Advisory Council for Education* (Plowden Report). London.

Halsey, A.J. (ed.) (1972, 74, 75) *Educational Priority.* Report of a Research Project Sponsored by the DES and the SSRC. Vols 1, 2, 3, 4. London.

―――― (1975) *Race Relations Board Report for 1974.* London.

Hartford, I. (1972) Defining Problems and Objectives in Community Relations Forum. *New Community* 1 (13). Spring.

Hartwell, R.M. (1961) The Rising Standard of Living in England 1800-1850. *Economic History Review* XIII (3): 397.

Heinemann, B.W. Jnr. (1972) *The Politics of the Powerless: A Study of the Campaign Against Racial Discrimination.* London: Institute of Race Relations/Oxford University Press.

Henriques, L.F.M. (1953) *Family and Colour in Jamaica.* London: Eyre and Spottiswoode.

Hepple, B. (1970) *Race, Jobs and the Law in Britain.* Harmondsworth: Penguin.

Herberg, W. (1956) *Protestant-Catholic-Jew.* New York: Doubleday.

Herskovitz, M.J. and Herskovitz, F.S. (1947) *Trinidad Village.* New York: Alfred Knopf.

Heywood, J. (1965) *Children in Care* (2nd edition). London: Routledge & Kegan Paul.

Hill, M.J. and Issacharoff, R.M. (1971) *Community Action and Race Relations.* London: Institute of Race Relations/Oxford University Press.

Hiro, D. (1972) *Black British White British.* London: Eyre and Spottiswoode.

Hobsbawn, E.J. (1957) The British Standard of Living 1790-1850. *Economic History Review.* 2nd series, X (1): 46.

―――― (1964) *Labouring Men.* London: Weidenfeld & Nicolson.

Hobson, J.A. (1892) *The Problems of Poverty.* London.

Jackson, J. (1963) *The Irish in Britian.* London: Routledge & Kegan Paul.

Jeyes, S.H. (1892) Foreign Pauper Immigration. In White (1892).

John, D. (1969) *Indian Workers' Associations in Britian.* London: Institute of Race Relations/Oxford University Press.

Johnson, H. (Chief Superintendent) (1970) The Police and the Community. *Race Today* 2 (11). November.

Jones, C.J. (1971) Immigration and Social Adjustment: A Case Study in West Indian Food Habits in London. Unpublished Ph.D. thesis, University of London.

—— (1975) The response of the Statutory Social Services in New Commonwealth Immigration. Report in the SSRC.

Jones, K. and Smith, A.D. (1970) *The Economic Impact of Commonwealth Immigration*. Cambridge: Cambridge University Press.

Katznelson, I. (1973) *Black Men White Cities: Race Politics and Migration in the United States 1900-30 and Britain 1948-68*. London: Oxford University Press.

Kerr, M. (1952) *Personality and Conflict in Jamaica*. Liverpool: Liverpool University Press.

Kushnick, L. (1971) British Anti-Discrimination Legislation. In S. Abbot (ed.) *The Prevention of Racial Discrimination*. London: Institute of Race Relations/Oxford University Press.

Lambert, J.R. (1970a) *Crime, Police and Race Relations*. London: Institute of Race Relations/Oxford University Press.

—— (1970b) The Police and the Community. *Race Today* 2 (11). November.

Levy, S. (1943-4) Problems of Anglicisation. *Jewish Annual 1943-44*.

Lipman, V.D. (1959) *A Century of Social Service 1859-1959. The Jewish Board of Guardians*. London: Routledge & Kegan Paul.

Little, K. (1947) *Negroes in Britain*. London: Routledge & Kegan Paul.

Lowe, R. (1867) *Primary and Classical Education* (pamphlet).

Lowndes, G.A.N. (1937) *The Silent Social Revolution*. London: Oxford University Press.

Madoe, P. (1965) The Transition from Light-Skinned to 'Coloured'. In J. Tajfel and J.L. Dawson (eds), *Disappointed Guests*. London: Institute of Race Relations/Oxford University Press.

Mathias, P. (1969) *The First Industrial Nation*. London: Methuen.

McKenzie, R. and Silver, A. (1968) *Angels in Marble*. London: Heinemann.

McMillan, M. (1911) *The Child and the State*. Manchester: National Labour Press.

McNeal, J. (1971) Education. In Abbot (1971).

Nandy, D. (1967) An Illusion of Competence. In A. Lester and N. Deakin (eds.), *Policies for Racial Equality*. Fabian Research Series No. 262. London.

National Committee for Commonwealth Immigrants (1967) *Racial Equality in Employment*. Report of Conference held in London, February 1967.

National Foundation for Educational Research (1971) *Immigrant Pupils in England: The LEA response*. Slough: NFER.

Parliamentary Select Committee on Race Relations and Immigration (1969) *The Problems of Coloured School Leavers*. London: HMSO.

Parry, J.H. and Sherlock, P.M. (1968) *A Short History of the West Indies*. London: Macmillan.

Patterson, S. (1963) *Dark Strangers*. London: Tavistock.

—— (1968) *Immigrants in Industry*. London: Institute of Race Relations/Oxford University Press.

—— (1969) *Immigration and Race Relations in Britain, 1960-67*. London: Institute of Race Relations/Oxford University Press.

Peach, G.C.K. (1966) Under Enumeration of West Indians in the 1961 Census. *Sociological Review* 14 (1). March.

—— (1968) *West Indian Migration to Britain: A Social Geography*. London: Institute of Race Relations/Oxford University Press.

Peacock, A.T. and Wiseman, J. (1961) *The Growth of Public Expenditure in the United Kingdom*. Princeton, N.J.: Princeton University Press.

Perry, J. (1973) *The Fair Housing Experiment: Community Relations Councils and the Housing of Minority Groups.* London: PEP.

Pickett, K. (1975) Housing. In J. Mays, A. Forder and O. Keidan (eds.), *Penelope Hall's Social Services of England and Wales* (9th edition). New York: Routledge & Kegan Paul.

Political and Economic Planning and Research Services Ltd (1967) *Racial Discrimination.* London: PEP.

———— (1974a) *Racial Disadvantage in Employment.* London: PEP.

———— (1974b) *The Extent of Racial Discrimination.* London: PEP.

Race Today (1973) Black People and the Police: Special Report. Vol 5 (II). December.

Ratcliffe, J. (1974) *An Introduction to Town and Country Planning.* London: Hutchinson.

Redlich, J. and Hirst, F.W. (1958) *The History of Local Government in England.* London: Macmillan.

Rees, A.M. (1972-3) Thoughts on a Local Community Relations Structure. *New Community* 2 (1). Winter.

Richmond, A.H. (1969) Migration in Industrial Societies. In J.A. Jackson (ed.), *Migration.* Cambridge: Cambridge University Press.

Roberts, G.W. and Mills, D.O. (1958) Study of External Migration Affecting Jamaica 1953-55. *Social and Economic Studies* VII (2): Supplement.

Rodgers, B.R. (1969) *The Battle Against Poverty.* London: Routledge & Kegan Paul.

Rose, E.J.B. (1969) *Colour and Citizenship: A Report on British Race Relations.* London: Institute of Race Relations/Oxford University Press.

Rose, M. (1971) *The English Poor Law 1780-1930.* Newton Abbott: David & Charles.

Rose, M.E. (1972) *The Relief of Poverty 1834-1914.* London: Macmillan.

Rowntree, B.S. (1902) *Poverty: A Study of Town Life.* London: Macmillan.

Ruck, S.K. (ed.) (1960) *The West Indian comes to England: A Report prepared for the Trustees of the London Parochial Charities by the Family Welfare Association.* London: Routledge & Kegan Paul.

Runnymede Trust (1974/75) Trade Unions and Immigrant Workers. *New Community* IV (1). Winter/Spring.

Russell, C. (1900) The Jewish Question in the East End. In C. Russell and H.S. Lewis (eds.), *The Jew in London.* London (Edinburgh PR).

Select Committee on Race Relations and Immigration (1969) *The Problems of Coloured School Leavers.* London: HMSO.

———— (1971) *Housing.* London: HMSO.

———— (1973) *Education.* London: HMSO.

Silberner, E. (1952) British Socialism and the Jews. *Historica Judica* XIV (1): 4. April.

Simey, M.B. (1951) *Charitable Effort in Liverpool in the Nineteenth Century.* Liverpool: Liverpool University Press.

Skone, J.F. (1968) *Public Health Aspects of Immigration.* London: Community Relations Commission.

Smellie, J.B. (1968) *The History of Local Government* (4th edition). London: George Allen & Unwin.

Stacey, T. (1970) *Immigration and Enoch Powell.* London: Tom Stacey Ltd.

Street, H., Howe, G., and Bindman, G. (1967) *Report on Anti-Discrimination Legislation.* London: PEP.

Tannahill, J.A. (1958) *Volunteer Workers in Great Britain.* Manchester: Manchester University Press.

Taylor, W.E.K. (1972) The Community Relations Office — Aims, Roles and Training. *New Community* I (2). January.

Temple, W. (1941) *Citizen and Churchman.* London: Eyre & Spottiswoode.

Tennent, Sir J.E. (1860) *Proceedings of the National Association for the Promotion of Social Sciences:* 142.

Thomas, J.A. (1939) *The House of Commons 1832-1901.* Cardiff: University of Wales Press Board.

Titmuss, R. (1950) *Problems of Social Policy.* (History of the Second World War). London: HMSO and Longmans.

—— (1958) *Essays on the Welfare State.* London: George Allen & Unwin.

—— (1962) *Income Distribution and Social Change.* London: George Allen & Unwin.

Townsend, H.E.R. (1971) *Immigrant Pupils in England: the LEA Response.* Slough: NFER.

Ward, R. (1971) *Coloured Families in Council Houses.* Manchester: Manchester Community Relations Council.

Webb, B. and Webb, S. (1929) *English Local Government. English Poor Law History.* Part II, Vol I, Vol II. Private Subscription Edition.

—— (1963) *English Local Government, Vol I: The Parish and the County.* London: Frank Cass & Co. Ltd. (First published 1906. London: Longmans, Green & Co.)

Weightmen, G. (1976) The CDP File, *New Society* 35 (702). March 18.

Wells, H.G. (1934) An Act to Educate the Lower Classes for Employment on Lower Class Lines and with Specially Trained Inferior Teachers. In *Experiment in Autobiography.* London: Gollancz.

White, A. (1892) *The Destitute Alien in Great Britain.* London: Swan Sonnenschein & Co.

Wilkins, W.H. (1892) *The Alien Invasion.* London.

Wilson, C., Hutt, W.H., Collard, D., Misham, E.J., and Hallett, G. (1970) *Economic Issues in Immigration.* London: Institute of Economic Affairs.

Wilson, F.L. (1946) The Irish in Great Britain during the First Half of the Nineteenth Century. Unpublished M.A. thesis, University of Manchester.

Wright, P.L. (1968) *The Coloured Worker in British Industry.* London: Institute of Race Relations/Oxford University Press.

Yudkin, S. (1965) *Health and Welfare of the Immigrant Child.* London: Community Relations Commission.

Notes

Chapter One

1. These are arbitrary dates of course. The starting date is in each case deliberately approximate, while the closing date was selected in each to coincide with the time of a Census enquiry.

2. I had at one stage, for instance, planned to include a study of Euro-pean Volunteer Workers in this review. (See J.A. Tannahill 1958.) But the evidence readily available proved insufficient for comparative purposes.

3. Jones (1975). Also see Appendix.

4. A term specifically applied to the early Irish. See below, p.48.

Chapter Two

1. This is, of course, no more than my personal view. It is, moreover, a view which accords — some may think too conveniently — with the overall design of this work and the spacing of the case-studies. Yet this in itself was one reason for my choice of these particular case-studies. The reader must judge for himself as to the validity of the approach.

2. Hence the so-called Standard of Living Debate: e.g. Hobsbawn (1957 : 46), Hartwell (1961 : 397), and Ashton (1949).

3. Wage Fund Theory and Malthus' ominous population predictions were at one, for instance, in their condem-nation of excessive poor relief expen-diture as an active threat to the nation's economic well-being. See Webb and Webb 1929 : 21-2.

4. It was, in fact, left to the Central Poor Law Commission to take the initiative so far as the formation of unions and the setting up of qualifi-cations for would be guardians of the poor, were concerned. — Poor Law Amendment Act 1834, (4 and 5 William c.76) Sections 26-29 and 38-41.

5. The process did not stop here of course. To some extent one can observe a repeat experience taking place in the present century — with 'new' local government becoming progressively more obsolete and ineffective in the face of ongoing social, economic, and political

developments: until the pressures, first to get round it and then to reform it, became irresistible.

6. Only 178 municipalities were immediately affected (Smellie 1968 : 31).

7. Some 62 new boroughs had been incorporated by 1876 (Smellie, 1968 : 33).

8. Dicey was quite clear on this point of course. Individualism (or 'Benthamism') gives way to collectivism (or 'socialism') because circumstances are such as to incline public opinion towards acceptance of collectivist ideas and because social legislation is itself parent to the collectivist thought. Which seems a little too clear and a little too circular to take us very far (Dicey 1905).

9. These being the 'National Society for Promoting the Education of the Poor in the Principles of the Established Church' and the 'British and Foreign Schools Society' respectively. See for instance Curtis (1963 : 223-4).

10. In other words 'Payment by Results' — see Curtis (1963 : 257-69).

11. See Forster's speech introducing the 1870 Elementary Education Bill — (1st Reading) Parliamentary Debates, 3rd Series; Vol. CCXIX, col. 444, 17 Feb. 1870.

12. *Transactions of the NAPSS* for 1858, pp.56-68.

13. See Curtis (1963) or Barnard: *A History of English Education* (1947), for a discussion of 'the religious difficulty'.

14. The immediate political consequences of so extending the franchise, of course, turned out to be far less dramatic and far less destructive than had generally been forecast. See R. McKenzie and A. Silver (1968).

15. See for instance Gladstone's famous speech to the House of Commons (1864) and Briggs (1959 : 491-492, 493).

16. This is not of course to deny the role played by individual reformers — such as J.S. Mill — committed on principle to the cause of electoral reform.

17. Secret Ballot Act 1872.

18. 'In the year 1868, out of a total of 944 economic interests returned to the House of Commons, 416, or 44 per cent represented Land, while 528, or 56 per cent represented Commerce and Industry. By the year 1900 ... out of a total of 894 combined landholding and 'newer' interests returned to Parliament, Land accounted for 205, or only 23 per cent, while Commerce and Industry had a total of 689, or 77 per cent.' Of the latter, in 1900, only 10 of those returned (6 Liberal, 1 Radical, and 3 'Socialist') could be described as representatives of working men (Thomas 1939 : 18-19, 14-17).

19. As early as 1874, the first two Liberal Labour candidates had been returned to the House of Commons. The Liberals were seemingly better-placed than were the 'landed' Conservatives to draw upon such support after 1867. Yet they failed, of course, to hold on to it (see McKenzie and Silver 1968 : 40).

20. See for instance, Committee on Old Age Pensions (1903).

21. See B.B. Gilbert (1966) for a thorough discussion.

22. NB The example of Bismarck's Germany — so impressive, apparently, to Lloyd George — was nothing if not patriarchal in its social policy implications.

23. In fact, of course, friendly societies were destined to come off badly after all. See Gilbert (1966); Chapter 6.

24. See for instance Webb and Webb (1929) Vol. II : Ch. 5.

25. *Primary poverty*: 'families whose total earnings are insufficient to obtain the minimum necessaries for the maintenance of merely physical efficiency.'

Secondary poverty: 'families whose total earnings would be sufficient for the maintenance of merely physical efficiency were it not that some portion of it is absorbed by other expenditure, either useful or wasteful' (Rowntree 1903).

26. In 1939 the powers of the UAB were enlarged to assist 'those persons in distress from the war'. In 1940 it became the Assistance Board.

27. See for instance Asquith's speech to the House of Commons March 28, 1917. — Parliamentary Debates, 5th Series, Vol. 92, col. 469.

28. The term was reportedly first used by Archbishop Temple in 1941 — in contrast to the 'power state' of Nazi Germany (Temple 1941 : ch. 2). It was only applied after the event to the social legislation of the 1940s; i.e. this legislation was not proclaimed, in advance, as being the makings of a welfare state.

Chapter Three

Chapter Three

1. Poor Law Enquiry (Ireland): Appendix G: Report on the State of the Irish poor in Great Britain, 1835. (NB Subsequent page references to this Report refer to the Report itself — in the case of Roman numerals — and to the evidence submitted to the Commissioners — in the case of Arabic numerals).

2. Census Reports — 1841, 1851, 1861. 1851 was in fact the high watermark of the first wave of Irish immigrants to Britain.

3. Poor Law Enquiry, p. 18. Also echoed in M.B. Simey (1951 : 9-10).

4. This was, after all, the age of Chartism.

5. Poor Law Enquiry p. xiii. But c.f. the earlier comments on Irish 'improveability' — above pp. 50.

6. The extent of this coincidence has almost certainly been exaggerated by this study's extensive reliance upon the evidence of a *Poor Law* Report for much of its evidence.

7. Until the Unions became the units responsible: temporarily from 1847 and permanently from 1865.

8. See the Reports of the 1905-09 Royal Commission on the Poor Laws and the Relief of Distress.

Chapter Four

Chapter Four

1. It was only from 1858, for instance, that Jewish candidates were enabled to stand for parliamentary election.

2. Garrard 1971 : 214. Also see above, p.44, for comparison.

3. Garrard 1971 : 214-215 and Gainer 1972 : 6. Also see below, p.122 for comparison.

4. See above, p.47, for comparison re. the Irish-Catholic dimension.

5. Board of Trade Annual Returns on Immigration and Emigration.

6. Census 1871, 1881, 1891, 1901, 1911.

7. Gartner 1960 : 36. (1902-4: approximate rate of exchange = 20.5 marks to £1. The National Westminster Bank Foreign Research Department.)

8. Census 1901.

9. Such a concentration of immigrant manpower within a relatively few 'immigrant trades' seems, if anything, to have become increasingly pronounced — despite the active efforts of the Jewish Board of Guardians to encourage a wider dispersal (Lipman 1959 : 119).

10. *Hansard* 48 H(8) 1205, 11.2.1893.

11. Parl. Deb. 3rd Series 1890, Vol. 346, col. 635.

12. Lord Dudley, Parl. Deb. 4th Series 1898, Vol. 58, col. 274.

13. The fact that from the 1880s peak periods of East European immigration happened to coincide with periods of trade depression and higher than average local unemployment rates, only emphasized such an impression. See Lipman (1959).

14. It was the Liberal Party which had campaigned for and engineered the 1858 Act.

15. Parl. Deb. 4th Series 1898, Vol. 59, Col. 728-35.

16. House of Commons Select Committee on Alien Immigration. Report and minutes of evidence 1888 (Vol. 1), pp.456-72. Vol. III, 1889, App. 9.

17. Although cf. the reference to immigrant landlords; above p.76.

18. A 'Conjoint Committee' (representing the Mansion House Fund and the Jewish Board of Guardians from 1882, and the Russo-Jewish Committee together with the Jewish Board of Guardians from 1891) was established, nevertheless, to handle immediate claims from genuine victims of persecution (Lipman 1959 : 78-9).

19. 5 Ed VII Cap 13: An Act to amend the law with regard to aliens (*Aliens Act* 1905).

20. Subsumed under the Local Government Board, from 1871.

21. Lipman (1959 : 51) — notwithstanding this community's long tradition of expecting to care for its own.

22. The Jewish Board of Guardians supported these arrangements to the extent that they undertook to supplement any Union payments made, and to guarantee the provision of apprenticeships, for the children concerned. Anxious as they were, however, to see Jewish children removed from the workhouse environment, the Jewish Board was equally concerned not to seem to encourage 'neglect or depravity' on the part of parents by supporting the removal of all such children to Jewish voluntary homes. Except in cases of double orphans, therefore, the Board's attitude and advice was both cautious and selective (Lipman 1959 : 50).

23. Even sweating was not exclusively a Jewish occupation — see for instance, Gartner 1960 : 93.

24. The fact that any aliens insured would be eligible for no more than seven-ninths of normal sick benefit (or three-quarters if they were women), made the irrelevance indeed seem more than accidental. See for instance, Lipman 1959 : 87-8.

25. See for instance, Royal Commission on Alien Immigration, p. 286, par. 8559, for remarks about the emptying of local churches, along with the immigrant concentration in local schools.

26. The democratic constitution of school boards and even of Boards of Guardians in this period, would not seem seriously to have challenged this picture. Without means, after all, it was difficult to serve.

27. For a comment, both on the 'interested MPs' and on the (new) Liberal government's rather less than wholehearted implementation of the 1905 Act, see Gainer 1972, Chapters 8-9 especially.

Chapter Five

Chapter Five

1. Jones (1975). Also see Appendix.

2. 1971 being an arbitrary cut-off point for the purposes of this study. See above, Chapter One, note 1.

3. Sample Census 1966. Commonwealth Immigrant Tables, p. vii.

4. The 1962 Act also resulted in an increased proportion of dependants being brought to this country and, therefore, in a consolidation of existing immigrant settlements.

5. The Home Office had kept figures before 1955; but these had been estimates of total arrivals rather than of net immigration — e.g. Peach, 1966: 11-12.

6. Home Office estimates (summarized in Rose 1969 : 83).

7. Census 1961. Birthplace and Nationality Tables. 'New Commonwealth' totals arrived at by subtracting the figures of those born in Canada, Australia, New Zealand, and the Union of South Africa from the totals given for the population born in Commonwealth countries, Colonies, and Protectorates. Estimated 'white Asian' figures taken from Rose 1969 : 97.

8. Home Office estimates.

9. *Commonwealth Immigrants Act 1962: Control of Immigration; Statistics 1963.* Total numbers fluctuated considerably, however, from one year to the next in the 1960s.

10. See for instance the 1965 White Paper: 'Immigration from the Commonwealth' Cmnd. 2739 — an early example.

11. This was an attempt to enumerate children born in this country to immigrant parents. It was also intended as a check on the numbers of children born abroad to British nationals. However it had the effect also of rendering the children (born here) of children born abroad to British nationals, second-generation immigrants. The writer, for instance, stands as 50 per cent second-generation Chinese on this showing, since her mother was born in Hong Kong.

12. Commonwealth Immigrants Acts 1962 and 1968; Control of Immigration: Statistics 1962-71.

13. Sample Census 1966, Commonwealth Immigrant Tables. Estimated 'white Asian' figures taken from Rose 1969 : 97.

14. Census 1971, Commonwealth Immigrant Tables.

15. As also were Indian seamen (Rose 1969 : 68 and Desai 1963 : 3).

16. New Town employment arrangements, of course, were usually such as effectively to rule out early immigrant (unskilled) penetration in any case. Picket (1975).

17. Cf. the earlier tendency of West Indians to settle in the coloured quarters of ports such as Liverpool and Cardiff. NB also the improved internal transport arrangements within the Britain of the 1950s, compared to those available for early Irish or Jewish migrants.

18. Village-kin networks, once established at all, provided a considerable spur and support to such mobility (Desai 1963 : 17-18).

19. See for instance Patterson (1969 : 12-13) for a resume of Institute of Race Relations' findings 1966-67 on immigrant distribution; also pp. 134-141 for discussion of the different types of industry and jobs that attracted West Indians and Asians.

20. Sample Census 1966. Commonwealth Immigrant Tables.

21. See for instance Dilip Hiro (1972) for a general discussion.

22. The term originally applied to the Irish — see above, p.48.

23. E.g. Foot (1965 : 12) for a comment on Sir Cyril Osborne's determination 'to keep blacks out, regardless of race, colour or creed'. Also see Stacey (1970).

24. Birmingham Immigration Control Association: Smethwick Branch meeting 25.4.61; — quoted from Foot (1965 : 36).

25. See for instance Glass (1960 : 265-6). NB unlike the Irish, the Jews were not by this time associated with residence in well-known 'immigrant areas'.

26. Speaker at Smethwick Branch of Birmingham Immigration Control Association; — quoted from Foot (1965).

27. The Milner Holland Report (Cmnd 2605) on 'Housing in Greater London', 1965, being a much publicized early example.

28. Re-named Supplementary Benefits from 1966.

29. Lawrence Rieper: Letter to the *Smethwick Telephone*, 22.7.60. (Quoted from Foot (1965 : 33).

30. See for instance Wright (1968) for a detailed discussion of employer attitudes, and inter-group relations at shop-floor level. See also Patterson (1968).

31. See for instance Patterson (1969 : 180-81). Yet attitudes were clearly far less uniform and extreme than in the Jewish case.

32. There has been no development of 'coloured only' unions, however, comparable to the growth of Jewish trades unions at the turn of the century (Hepple 1970 : 107).

33. See for instance Patterson (1966 : 175-77). Also, for a more up to date review of the situation, The Runnymede Trust (1974-5).

34. See for instance Patterson (1969 : 381-66) and NB the Asian reputation for fraudulent entry to this country.

35. See Lambert's illuminating study (1970): also Bottoms 1967.

36. See for instance Chopre (1970) arguing the need for a much more determined effort by the police, if further polarization, and even further immigrant alienation is to be prevented. See also *Race Today* (1973).

37. Although the process was not necessarily as straightforward as this implies — see for instance John (1969).

38. For general illustration of these positions, at a political level, see Foot (1965 : 153-58 and 189-90).

39. And could sometimes feel bruised as a result — see for instance the paper Madoe (1965).

40. *Address given by the Home Secretary ... On the 23rd May 1966 ... to a meeting of Voluntary Liaison Committees*. National Committee for Commonwealth Immigrants 1966.

41. At one level, of course, this could be described as no more than a response to an increasingly intransigent host society (witness the destructive impact of the 1968 *Commonwealth Immigrants Act* — Rose 1969 : 614-21); yet this in itself does not explain the fact of the immigrants' involvement; it merely justifies their discontent.

42. See Collins (1957 : 30-32) for discussion of role and status of immigrant persons.

43. SSRC survey report (p.56).

44. Or not at all. See for instance Crawford (1972).

45. This was true at least of the most publicized and publicity-conscious sections of West Indian community leadership.

46. See the two crisis-focussed editions of the 'old style' *Race Today* — Vol. 4 Nos 4 and 5 April and May 1972.

47. They suggested, at least, that the 'classic' models of initial immigrant disadvantage, followed by eventual upward mobility could not apply in the Black case — See for instance Richmond (1969).

Chapter Six

Chapter Six

1. Large-scale coloured immigration had not, of course, figured among the contingencies foreseen in the 1940s.

2. Witness the recent White Paper 'Equality for Women', Cmnd. 5734.

3. Even though it might popularly have been interpreted as such (Rose 1969 : 621-23. Also below p.181).

4. See for instance the 1965 White Paper 'Immigration from the Commonwealth', Cmnd. 2379 para. 53.

5. For a fuller account of this sequence (prior to 1968), see for instance Patterson (1969 : 114-28).

6. *Race Relations Act* 1968. Part III ('Miscellaneous and General') Section 25, subsection (3).

7 . Given the polarization of immigrant versus native opinion in the meantime (see above p.149).

8. 1965 *Race Relations Act*, Sections 1-5. (Section 6 covered incitement to racial hatred and Section 7 extended the *Public Order Act* of 1936 to include written material).

9. Both this and the above quoted PEP Report were sponsored by the Race Relations Board itself, in collaboration with the NCCI.

10. Report of the Race Relations Board, 1966-7.

11. 1968 *Race Relations Act*. Part I. Sections 2-6.

12. *Race Relations Act* 1968. Part II, Section 17.

13. Part II, Section 19.

14. See above, p.148. Not that this was, as a package, very clearly spelt out to the public in 1968.

15. The Conservative election landslide of 1959 returning many 'right-wing', inner-city MPs in this respect (see Foot 1965 : 133).

16. E.g. Parliamentary Debates (Commons); 5th Series; Vol. 649, col. 694 (Butler in 2nd Reading Debate on Commonwealth Immigrants Bill, 16.11.61); and Vol. 721, cols. 358-59 (Roy Hattersley on Committee Stage of Expiring Laws Continuance Bill, 23.11.65).

17. NB the opposition of Hugh Gaitskell among others, to 'this miserable, shameful, shabby Bill' (the Commonwealth Immigrants Bill of 1961) —

Parl. Debates (Commons) 5th Series, Col. 649, col. 803 (2nd Reading Debate), 16.11.61.

18. Labour Party Manifesto (1964) 'The New Britain'. See section 'A New Role for Britain' — subsection on Commonwealth immigration.

19. Cmnd. 2379 (above, note 4).

20. *Commonwealth Immigrants Act* 1968; Section 1, (the idea was to be taken somewhat further in the 1971 *Immigration Act* — see Section 2 of the same).

21. The White Paper 'Immigration from the Commonwealth' being published in August 1965 and the first *Race Relations Act* receiving Royal Assent in November 1965.

22. This factor was at its most evident of course in middle years of the nineteenth century — but it has hardly disappeared since, Welfare State or no Welfare State. See Chapter 2.

23. Much the same could be said also of when governments had roughly comparable or usable statutory precedents to draw upon. See Chapter 2.

24. Integration had, in a manner of speaking, been practised before — in connection with the settlement of Polish ex-servicemen and European volunteer workers in Britain. But the meaning and context of 'integration' was in this case rather different (see Tannahill 1958).

25. See for instance Enoch Powell's speech at Birmingham on April 20, 1968 (Stacey 1970 : 87-8).

26. On the part of immigrant and pro-immigrant opinion.

27. At worst, of course, it could be dismissed as a publicity stunt designed to lure immigrant opinion away from more radical action. See for instance Hill and Issacharoff (1971 : 31).

28. And it, too, could be criticized for its heavy handedness as a result. See for instance Hill & Issacharoff (1971 : 264-5).

29. As it happens, CRC Annual Reports seem to be more concerned with explaining the Commission's intent and operations rather than with accounting in detail for their past year's activity. See for instance the CRC Report for 1974-5; although this does provide a useful source of reference relating to the numbers and work of community relations councils, etc.

30. For a comment on minority group 'leader' characteristics and opinions see R. Manderson-Jones and Jyothi Kamath in Abbott (1971 : Ch. 8).

31. The outcry in question centred around a proposal that the CRC should donate some £2,000 towards the stocking of a library for the Black House Commune, Holloway Road, Islington. The proposal was eventually vetoed by Frank Cousins as the then Chairman of the CRC — but not before considerable opposition and disquiet had been expressed both within and without the Commission itself (*Daily Telegraph*, 14.10.70).

32. See above, p.151 on the difficulties in general of 'middle-men' in this context.

33. More than two stools of course, since one can hardly equate government versus voluntary; with immigrant (and pro-immigrant) versus anti-immigrant opinion.

34. The 1965 White Paper *op. cit.* par. 66 marked the effective beginning of this policy.

35. By definition, however, this meant that immigrant organizations could only participate indirectly, by means of representation — a point of no small grievance.

36. See for instance Hill and Issacharoff (1971 : Chs. 4-6) for a general discussion of Community Relations Council structure and composition. Also Butterworth (1972a).

37. Witness, for instance, Manchester Community Relations Council's anxiety to disassociate itself, as a body, from the findings of its own Fair Housing Group's report *Coloured Families in Council Houses* (Ward 1971), even though the report in question could hardly be described as critical of the local authority in this case. But see also Perry (1973).

38. Coming this time from the host community, rather than from immigrant or pro-immigrant groups (as in the Community Relations case). See above pp.164-65 for comparison. This, after all, was a case of allegedly too definite action — not too *in*definite action, as in the Community Relations case.

39. See for instance the Race Relations Board Report for 1974 on the anomalies of 'private' clubs, paras. 16-18.

40. As it happens, the latest governmental response ('*Racial Discrimination*' Cmnd. 6234, 1975 and the Race Relations Bill, 1976) would seem, for all its apparent daring, to be geared essentially towards the immediate rather than any longer-term objective. True the Race Relations Board is to be replaced by a new body with wider powers: a proposed Race Relations Commission is to take over (it is hoped) from both the Board and the Community Relations Commission. This new Commission is no longer to be concerned (save in an incidental, helping sense) with individual complaints: it will be empowered to conduct broad investigations into areas of possible discrimination and it will, for these purposes, be able to demand written information and documents and to summon witnesses to give evidence. Sporting and social clubs are no longer to enjoy immunity and the 'racial balance' clause for employers is to be dropped. Nevertheless the proposed Race Relations Commission, for all its streamlined powers, is still to be effectively an immigrant-specific organization. There is to be

no merger, in the short term at least, between the treatment of sex and of race — although the proposed Race Relations Commission 'will have similar functions and powers to those conferred upon the Equal Opportunities Commission' (White Paper, par. 49). Community relations, moreover, remains an unclear field: decisions in this respect have been deferred pending further consultation (White Paper, par. 52); the tradition of liaison between government and voluntary effort is however to be perpetuated via a proposed new Standing Advisory Council, under the chairmanship of the Home Secretary, to co-ordinate and advise on all aspects of race policy. All in all, therefore, this would seem to represent a strengthening of existing trends, rather than a departure from them. As such it scarcely promises to resolve the fundamental problems noted already. The fact that both immigrant spokesmen and 'right-wing' native spokesmen have come out already in opposition to these latest proposals seems scarcely surprising — but scarcely an augur of good things to come.

41. Or, at the very least, a system of CROs wholly financed from central funds. See Rees (1972-3).

42. As Lambeth, for instance, had been among the first to do. See Foot (1965 : 166).

43. It is significant, in this context, that Urban Programme funds should also have been used to finance the Home Office's Community Development Project — which began operations from 1970 (Home Office Notes *op. cit*. p.5).

44. The mere fact that it was the Home Office, rather than a Secretary of State for Social Affairs, which was in charge of the Programme, seemed significant (Rose 1969 : 684-85).

45. Home Office Press Notice on Urban Aid Programme, Jan. 21, 1969 : 1.

46. The National Community Development Project, launched by the Home Office in 1969, has been left out of this account despite its relevance to the theme of positive (area) discrimination, since in only three of the twelve 'disadvantaged' areas selected for this 'neighbourhood-based experiment', was the presence of New Commonwealth immigrants a factor apparently contributing to their selection. The Project itself, however, clearly owed much to the example of Urban Aid and earlier positive discrimination manoeuvres, themselves partly inspired by the effects of New Commonwealth immigration. For further discussion of the twelve projects and their development, see Community Development Project (1974, 1975) and Weightman (1971).

Chapter Seven

1. See above, Ch. 2, for recurrent discussion of the effects of social policy experience and pp.31-3 in particular.

2. The survey itself was carried out more or less in the midst of this organizational upheaval: after the creation of LA social services departments, but before the reorganization of local government itself and of the National Health Service had taken effect.

Job shops were still no more than a gleam (or glare) in the eye of employment exchange managers; and comprehensive LA housing departments were only an occasional reality.

3. Housing Management Sub Committee of the Central Housing Advisory Committee: *Council Housing: Purposes, Procedures and Priorities,* HMSO, 1969.

4. These being the two main reasons given for specific efforts to recruit New Commonwealth staff in any other service context.

5. NB it was only possible to obtain an interview at central level in this case — see Appendix.

6. The author's enquiry being conducted on the eve of 1974 reorganization's coming into effect. See below, Appendix, and above, note 2.

7. Not directly the responsibility of the health departments themselves, but of the education service at that time.

8. Jones 1975 : 25-6. To most respondents, indeed, the idea that one might use immigrants in general particularly to deal with immigrants in general, seemed wild dangerous nonsense. 'Black to yellow' after all 'could be worse than white to yellow'.

9. This was, of course, the nearest we could get to an agency GP reaction. See Appendix.

10. Had they been in a position to do so, then of course the evidence on both 'staff training' and New Commonwealth immigrant employment might have been more illuminating.

11. Once again, as in the case of executive councils, this was a case of approaching the agency which seemed the most approximately representative of the local service in question.

12. This factor was exaggerated, undoubtedly, by the fact that our enquiries were always referred to administrative or personnel officers. Medical social workers, interestingly enough, were never deputed to respond — which was perhaps as much a comment on their status within the hospital as on the perceived focus of this enquiry (Jones 1975 : 130).

13. At least so far as the mass of the school-age population was concerned.

14. Equal educational opportunity could be held, in a sense, to be no more than a fresh, more effective, means of freezing the social structure: Education qualifications, if any, being far more absolute a criteria for social position than mere social class; the more so since the two tended in any case to go together.

15. Although not necessarily so obvious, of course, in the West Indian case.

16. Witness the arguments advanced in support of comprehensive secondary education: these being as much social as strictly educational in their content.

17. We shall in this case be relying, not upon the evidence of our own survey operation, but upon the fruits of a much larger and more exhaustive enquiry recently undertaken by the National Foundation for Educational Research in England and Wales into the LEA response to immigration. This was a three-stage enquiry: concentrating in the first instance upon LEA questionnaire and selective interview response; in the second instance upon primary and secondary school response; and in the third stage upon an in-depth exploration of the workings of some ten 'sets' of multi-racial primary and secondary schools (Townsend 1971 : Ch. 1). For the sake of comparability with the evidence presented elsewhere in this chapter, we will concentrate upon the results of the first stage of this enquiry; as outlined in Townsend above.

18. West Indian linguistic difficulties being an obvious case in point.

19. Townsend 1971 : 30. 'Substantial numbers of immigrant pupils', incidentally, was never defined in this case — although this was the basis upon which 51 LEAs were interviewed, after the initial return of 71/146 'fully completed' questionnaires (pp. 16-17).

20 . This being a further consequence, of course, of having LEAs, so unequal in their individual scope and resources, as the first line of adminis-

tration in the education case. EPAs (see above, p.179) were an attempt merely to alleviate the worst extremes of this situation.

21. The lack of provision for 'second-stage' English or West Indian English instruction was repeatedly referred to in the NFER Report. See for instance pp. 47-51.

22. Townsend 1971 : 25. Although there were some notable attempts to improve upon this (Townsend 1971 : 39).

23. Half of those LEAs with 50 plus immigrant children did not include any West Indian children from the English-speaking Caribbean in their language provisions (Townsend 1971 : 49).

24. Townsend 1971 : 61. This was one area, however, where parents might insist but the LEA need not necessarily respond.

25. Cf. the earlier remarks concerning intangibility of community relations objectives — above, p.163.

26. Townsend 1971 : 34. This was of course a way round actually suggested in Circular 7/65.

27. Which it subsequently abandoned, formally, in 1971. See Department of Education (1971 : 16-21).

28. This was a point of some relevance to the whole question of special education facilities and equipment: how economic was it likely to be, given Commonwealth immigration control?

29. Any differences, in other words, were not reckoned to be differences of kind in this respect.

30. West Indian children were less likely to be bussed, for instance (Townsend : 35), but they were more likely, of course, to end up in remedial education streams, if not actually to be classified as ESN.

Chapter Eight

1. Jones 1975 : 48. Although head-masters, it seemed, could very much encourage this belief: 'It's alright if they *get* their qualifications after-wards — but what if they don't?' (p.47).

2. That presumed 'adult' and 'youth' needs should not so arbitrarily be divided was of course generally implied in the service's own forth-coming plans and programmes; see The Employment Service Agency/ Manpower Services Commission

(1974).

3. Jones 1975 : 50. In such a cause, for instance, normal entrance require-ments might have to be waived, temporarily.

4. Several authorities had in fact taken steps to remedy this situation by creating multi-purpose housing departments under Directors of Housing rather than (mere) Housing Managers. None of the departments participating in this enquiry, how-ever, enjoyed this status at the time.

Appendix

1. For a fuller account of survey methods see Jones 1975, *op. cit.* pp. 1-14.

2. For reasons already stated: see above, Chapter 5, p.119.

3. Some NI and Supplementary Benefits Offices had recently been combined; but others, at that time, had not.

Index

Trades Union Congress, and Race
  Relations Act, 143
trades unions
  and Irish immigrants, 54-5
  and Jewish immigrants, 82-3
  and New Commonwealth immigrants,
    143-4, 231
training or briefing of staff for work with
    immigrants
  in education, 221-2
  in employment services, 204-5
  in health departments, 201
  in housing departments, 241-2
  in social care departments, 244-5
  in social security services, 196
tuberculosis among immigrants
  Asian, 138
  Jewish, 76, 99-101

Uganda, Asians from, 205
unemployment, among New
  Commonwealth immigrants, 234
unemployment insurance, 27, 30, 32, 34
  applicable at first only to six branches of
    industry, 102, 117
United States of America
  Irish migration to, 44, 45
  Jewish migration to, 68, 69, 86, 87, 257
  reception of successive waves of
    immigrants in, 152
  War on Poverty programme in, 179
Urban Aid
  housing advice centres under, 237
  social workers paid by, 246
Urban Programme (1968), 157, 162,
  180-3

venereal disease, 138

wages
  Irish immigration and, 50-2
  Jewish immigration and, 78-81

wages *cont.*
  New Commonwealth immigration and,
    141
war-time experience, and social policy,
  33-6
Welfare State, 31, 33, 37, 38, 118
  anomalies between branches of, 185-8
  effects of reorganizations in, 188-9
  New Commonwealth immigrants and,
    149, 154, 189-94, 258
  original characteristics of, 184-5
  question of its ability to cope with New
    Commonwealth immigrants, 155,
    182-3
  regarded as an attraction to
    immigrants, 140-1
  shortcomings of, exposed by
    immigration, 178, 182
West Indian immigrants, 121, 122, 123-4
  health departments and, 202-3
  information to social security staffs
    about, 196
  preponderant up to 1962, 124-6
  types of hospital work taken up by, 209
  unemployment among, 234
women
  employment of, among New
    Commonwealth immigrants, 130,
    131
  enfranchisement of, 34
  in New Commonwealth immigration,
    126
Working Men's Club and Institute
  Union: clubs of, excluded from Race
    Relations Act, 174
workshops
  employment of Jewish immigrants in,
    71
  inspected by Jewish Board of
    Guardians, 98-9

Youth Employment Service (under local
  authorities), and immigrants, 224,
  225-7, 233-4, 235